He Kissed Him and They Wept

'This book represents a real breakthrough. It contains structured theological dialogue with no no-go areas. It takes us well down its intended path to a relationship of mutual respect and acceptance and the formation of a partnership in God's name for the repair and well being of humanity and the globe.'

Rabbi Dow Marmur, Executive Director, World Union for Progressive Judaism

'This text is a signpost indicating that the relationship between Catholics and Jews has reached a depth which permits, in a spirit of mutual respect of our differences, an exploration of religious issues which previously have been the cause of division and opposition. Today we are invited to engage in a common search for a faithful understanding of our bond as brothers and sisters.

As this book bears witness, the deep dialogue between Jews and Catholics does not damage in the slightest the identity of either. The Jewish voices heard here are rooted in the deepest of religious traditions of the Jewish people, ignoring neither history nor philosophy. Thus, solidly founded in the believing memory, their perspective opens a space for future relations with Christians, on paths which are faithful and sure. Likewise, by drawing on biblical and conciliar sources, but attentive to the words and initiatives of John Paul II, the Catholic authors herein express a fraternal attitude towards Judaism without wavering in their faith in Jesus Christ.

I welcome this work, not only for its insights but above all because it offers theological and halachic foundations for a dialogue between Jews and Christians which is at once anchored in our deepest roots and leading towards the mystery of our future.'

Cardinal Kasper, President, Vatican Commission for Religious Relations with the Jews

He Kissed Him and They Wept

*Towards a Theology of
Jewish–Catholic Partnership*

Edited by

Rabbi Tony Bayfield,
Rabbi Dr Sidney Brichto
and Dr Eugene J. Fisher

scm press

©The Editors and Contributors 2001

British Library Cataloguing in Publication data

A catalogue record of this book is available
from the British Library

0 334 02826 4

First published in 2001 by SCM Press
9–17 St Albans Place, London N1 0NX

SCM Press is a division of
SCM-Canterbury Press Ltd

Typeset by Regent Typesetting, London
and printed in Great Britain by
Biddles Ltd, Guildford and King's Lynn

Contents

Acknowledgements   ix

Preface – Eugene J. Fisher   xi

1. Introduction – Tony Bayfield   1

2. Opening the encounter   9
   Edward Idris Cassidy   9
   Sigmund Sternberg   17
   Richard Block   20

3. The Theology of Partnership   25
A. Partnership in Covenant – Tony Bayfield   25
   Discussant – Joann Spillman   41
B. Partnership in Covenant – Clemens Thoma   45
   Discussant – Tovia Ben-Chorin   55
   Discussion recorder – Andrew Goldstein   57
C. Understanding Election – Elliot Dorff   60
   Discussant – Margaret Shepherd   80
D. Understanding Election – Edward Ondrako   84
   Discussant – David Goldberg   105
   Discussion recorder – Peter Keenan   107

4. The Context of Partnership   110

A. Reading Our Sacred Texts Today – Jonathan Magonet   110

   Discussant – Robert Murray   120

B. Reading Our Sacred Texts Today – John Pawlikowski   123

   Discussant – Alexandra Wright   137
   Discussion recorder – Elizabeth Tikvah Sarah   141

C. The Challenge of Modernity and Postmodernity –
   Susannah Heschel   144

   Discussant – Michael McGarry   159

D. The Challenge of Modernity and Postmodernity – Janet
   Martin Soskice   162

   Discussant – Guy Stroumsa   176
   Discussion recorder – Clare Jardine   177

5. A Partnership for the Glory of God, the Good of
   Humanity and the Future of the Planet   180

A. Religion, Government and Society – David Rosen   180

   Discussant – Mary Boys   189

B. Religion, Government and Society – Adrian van Luyn 192

   Discussant – Richard Block   209
   Discussion recorder – Michael Hilton   213

C. The Values We Bring to the Partnership – Sidney
   Brichto   218

   Discussant – John D'Arcy May   228

D. The Values We Bring to the Partnership – Eugene
   Fisher   233

   Discussant – Ron Kronish   247
   Discussion recorder – Mary Kelly   249

6. Clarifying the Partnership and Setting Its Agenda   252

    Sybil Sheridan   252

    Kieran Heskin   257

    Mark Winer   259

7. Concluding the Encounter – Sidney Brichto   264

The Contributors and Participants   268

Dedication

This book is dedicated to Edward Idris Cardinal Cassidy and Sir Sigmund Sternberg KCSG, giants and heroes of Catholic–Jewish reconciliation and dialogue.

Acknowledgements

The editors would like to thank Edward Idris Cardinal Cassidy and Sir Sigmund Sternberg without whose inspiration and patronage the conference which gave birth to this book could never have taken place.

They would also like to thank Mgr Remi Hoeckman, secretary to the Commission for Religious Relations with the Jews.

Deep thanks are also due to the Millennium Conference organizing group, Rabbi Dr David Goldberg, Rabbi Sybil Sheridan, Rabbi Jacqueline Tabick and Rabbi Dr Mark Winer, and to their Catholic counterparts in London led by Bishop Charles Henderson and Sister Clare Jardine; to Sister Margaret Shepherd who coordinated both groups and to the conference organizers, Ruth Silver and Cathryn Brichto.

The names of the contributors and participants appear at the end of this book and to them, of course, deep thanks are due.

We would also like to thank Pam Lewis for her help with the manuscript of the book.

Last, but by no means least, special thanks are due to the sponsors of the conference who heeded Sir Sigmund's call for support: Isaac Kaye, Kennedy Leigh Foundation, Clive Marks, Sir Evelyn de Rothschild and R. Stephen Rubin.

Preface

– Eugene J. Fisher

Secretariat for Ecumenical and Inter-religious Affairs
United States Conference of Catholic Bishops
July 20, 2001

While credit for the unusually high quality of this volume needs be shared with other organizers and with the participants themselves, Rabbis Bayfield and Brichto should feel great satisfaction at having preserved for the historical record, and for the enrichment of both Jewish and Christian theological studies, what can only be described as an immensely significant exchange of the highest order between our two ancient religious communities.

The text more than validates the judgment of those in both communities who have long argued that, despite the troubled, too often tragic history of disputations and forced conversions that sets the context for our present, theological dialogue between Catholics and Jews is ripe with promise for the future.

The dialogue itself took place in the Millennial Year and does, I believe, represent a 'crossing of the threshold', to use Pope John Paul II's phrase, in the relationship between the Catholic Church and the Jewish People. It was of course set in the midst of other events marking milestones in the relationship: the formal liturgy of repentance (*teshuvah*) lead by the Pope in St Peter's Basilica itself, in which the sins of Christians of all levels and times against Jews, many of them of a theological order (as in Jules Isaac's telling phrase, 'the teaching of contempt'), were acknowledged before God and all humanity; the pilgrimage of the Pope to Israel, and in Jerusalem to Yad VaShem and to the Kotel, the Western Wall, where the Pope asked forgiveness of God at Judaism's most sacred site; and the issuance of *Dabru Emet* ('To Speak Truth') by a large group of Jewish scholars and rabbis framing for the first time a consensus statement of religious Jews in response to the profound changes in Christian theology that have taken place over the last two generations since World War II.

One cannot overstate the importance of the great gestures, both Catholic and Jewish, which took place in the Millennial Year, or the decades of effort by thousands of persons of good will, courage and dedication in both communities around the world which made such startling gestures conceivable in our time. No one would have thought, say, in 1960, that such dramatic moments of healing and mutual affirmation would have been possible.

Many of us who have long been involved in the dialogue, quite frankly, simply broke down and cried tears of joy when we saw the Bishop of Rome place his humble petition in the Western Wall as generation after generation of pious Jews had done before him. Peter had come home to pray. Seeing such moments, and knowing that we in our generation have it in our hands to shift the very course of Christian–Jewish relations from its millennial malaise to one of joint witness to the sacred meaning of human history and joint efforts to ameliorate the suffering of humanity, thereby working together for *Tikkun olam* (the mending of the world), many ask today, 'What is the next step? After accomplishing so much in so short a span of time, where do we go from here?' This volume attempts to answer that question, and to a remarkable degree succeeds. It is a well-organized collection of formal essays and responses by many of the world's leading scholars in the field, with remarkable distillations of the very fruitful dialogues that ensued after each. It brings to life the dialogue as it took place in London and captures something of its hope-filled spirit and wonderfully nuanced exchange.

Readers, of course, will not agree with every sentiment articulated here. Some will surprise them with their audacity and vision. But even where readers may disagree, they will leave the engagement with this volume vastly more informed and more challenged, theologically more sensitive and spiritually enriched. Anyone interested in the future of Catholicism or Judaism, or how the two may work to form their future together, should read this book.

20 July 2001

1

Introduction

– Tony Bayfield

This book is called *He Kissed Him and They Wept*. The title is an example of my occasional obstinacy since by no means all of the contributors were convinced about the choice. The reference is, of course, to the famous story in the book of Genesis in which Jacob and his twin brother Esau meet again after many years apart. Jacob has behaved badly towards his older twin, tricked him out of both birthright and blessing, fled the family home and spent two decades in exile. After wrestling with the mysterious being at the ford Jabbok, he and Esau finally meet again. The meeting is described in verse 4 of chapter 33 as follows: Esau ran to meet him and embraced him and fell on his neck and he kissed him and they wept.

In using a key phrase from this scene to refer to the Catholic–Jewish encounter in our times, I lay myself open to some very profound objections. First, Jacob and Esau are both men whereas Catholics and Jews are women as well as men. No charge or challenge against Judaism and Christianity is more profound than that of patriarchy and male abuse of power, of being 'half empty bookcases'. Furthermore, Catholics and Jews both view this story as part of their heritage and it is then not clear who is Jacob and who is Esau. Hence, the objections to the title.

But there is reason for my obstinacy. Jews have always seen themselves as the descendents of Jacob, and Esau as the hostile non-Jew. We have defended Jacob and vilified Esau even though this often does violence to the plain meaning of the text. More than a thousand years ago a group of Jewish scholars called the Masoretes worked on the various manuscripts of the Hebrew text. They were clearly so bothered by 'he kissed him' that they placed dots over the Hebrew word, alluding to the fact that the word could easily be read not as 'he kissed him' but as 'he bit him'. Reconciliation is not as easy as an embrace and a kiss. Suspicion and misunderstanding linger on. If you read on in the book of Genesis, it quickly becomes apparent that Jacob and Esau went their separate ways, leaving an impression of truce, of worst fears allayed, of separate existence rather than of lasting reconciliation and of sibling rediscovery.

Catholics and Jews are by no means fully reconciled and living together as only loving siblings can. We are embarked upon an arduous journey and have a long way to go. We are, both of us, both Esau and Jacob (and Rachel and Leah), and all the resonances of 'he kissed him and they wept' are very much with us. Hence my obstinacy over the title. It actually claims less than at first appears and therefore alludes to how much there is still to do. But let me now move from the title to the origins of the book itself.

Sir Sigmund Sternberg is a truly remarkable man. A Hungarian-born refugee from the Nazis, he pursued a successful commercial career in Britain before devoting his life to bridge-building and reconciliation, seeking understanding and harmony between religious and ethnic groups. Nearing his eightieth birthday and honoured the world over – a British Knight, a papal Knight, a Templeton prize winner, President of the Reform Synagogues of Great Britain – an astonishing array of political and religious doors are open to him. He decided to take a small group of British Reform and Liberal rabbis to Rome.

We were privileged to have an audience with the Pope, take tea with the Italian President in the Quirinale Palace, receive hospitality from numerous ambassadors to the Holy See – and spend an extremely fruitful morning with Cardinal Cassidy and Mgr Remi Hoeckman who constituted the Vatican's Commission for Religious Relations with the Jews.

We were, of course, wisely briefed by Sir Sigmund, an old friend of Cardinal Cassidy. Over recent years giant strides have, without doubt, been taken in repairing the relationship between the Catholic Church and the Jews. From the tireless work of the Sisters of Sion to some remarkable statements and actions by the Pope himself, signs of goodwill are readily apparent and many successes can be pointed to. Yet a relatively narrow range of 'political issues' keeps surfacing and disturbing the positive atmosphere. Convents and crosses at Auschwitz, recognition of Israel and attitudes to Israel and the Palestinians, the record of Pope Pius XII, the beatification of Edith Stein are all examples. All are issues of enormous emotional significance to a Jewish community which is still profoundly affected by the *Shoah* (Holocaust).

We suggested to Cardinal Cassidy that it would be good to mark the beginning of the third Christian millennium by looking forward rather than back and by beginning to talk about a theology of partnership – how Jews and Catholics can create the theological space necessary for mutuality and respect and how we can then take forward a common agenda of concern for humanity and the globe – peace between our faiths contributing to peace in the world. The response was overwhelmingly positive and the London-based Millennium Conference sponsored by the Vatican and the World Union for Progressive Judaism was born. Its title quickly became 'The Theology of Partnership'.

We were clear almost from the outset about what we wanted to do. First, we wanted to see whether theological reflection and interchange had reached the point where Catholics and Jews are able to grant each other respectful and full theological space. Had we moved beyond or could we move beyond supercessionism, triumphalism, claiming that each was anonymously the other to the point where each could accept the other as a true vehicle for revelation and source of salvation in its own right? To put it in more graphic language, could Catholics move beyond saying that Judaism was a wonderful tradition which shed light on the origins of Christianity but what a pity Jews were missing out on the best and only truth of all? Could Jews move beyond praising Christianity for its architecture, music and self-sacrificing love yet silently qualifying that endorsement with a throwaway line about having based their faith on a complete misunderstanding of a rather ordinary Jew? Secondly, we wanted to look at the context in which we both do theology today, what Rabbi Norman Solomon has called 'the third dialogue partner' – modernity and postmodernity. Thirdly and finally, we were determined to look at what a partnership could achieve in terms of pooling shared insights for the common good of humanity, sharing global responsibility, working together for the repair of the world. With the help of my friend and mentor, Revd Dr John Bowden, the Anglican theologian, the programme quickly came together.

What evolved fifteen months later in May 2000 was a three-day gathering at the Sternberg Centre in North West London. Some forty-four Catholic and Jewish scholars took part, the Jewish scholars nominated by the Jews and the Catholics by the Vatican and their local organizing committee led by Bishop Charles Henderson. Only the opening session, addressed by Cardinal Cassidy, Sir Sigmund and Rabbi Richard Block (and graced by a brief selection of songs from a choir composed of children from a Jewish and a Catholic Primary School who work together) was public. The rest of the time was for the forty-four scholars to talk to each other.

There were six pairs of papers, all pre-circulated and pre-digested, to give the maximum time for discussion. There were discussants, discussions and a significant agenda-defining session.

We began with the Theology of Partnership itself. I opened with a paper on covenant, arguing that siblings provide the best metaphor for understanding the nature of the relationship between Jews and Catholics and affirming covenant as the most appropriate theological concept for granting mutuality, respect and independent space. Professor Dr Clemens Thoma from Switzerland responded on the covenant theme and concurred that issues surrounding covenant lie at the very heart of the relationship, both its past difficulties and its future potentialities. These two papers come very close to meeting. Although subsequent discussion threw up, on the Jewish side, a question about the place of covenant in the history of Jewish theology, there was a broad measure of consensus that this is the way forward and offers every possibility for a partnership based upon mutual respect and independent theological space. The metaphor of siblings was also found helpful though it is particularly challenging for Jews and, like all metaphors, can be pushed too far. Later on in the dialogue Edward Ondrako would advance the alternative metaphor of mother and nursing child.

Rabbi Professor Elliot Dorff from the United States explored the concept of chosenness, providing a historical background and his own interpretation that allowed for mutuality and respect. His paper was paralleled by that of his compatriot Revd Dr Edward Ondrako. Dr Ondrako, quoting extensively from Catholic sources, tackled election and the church, the doctrine of *nulla salus* (outside the church there is no salvation), and the sinfulness of some Christians in contradistinction to the infallibility of the church. He notes considerable progress over recent years, though some participants were impatient for further progress, expressing the view that full independence of space and mutuality of respect were not yet apparent.

We then moved on to the context of the partnership, with Rabbi Professor Jonathan Magonet, the Principal of Leo Baeck College in London, looking at the way Jews have read and read our sacred texts and challenging Catholics to learn from this particular Jewish *specialité de la maison*. Magonet asserted the relative aridity of Catholic biblical exegesis compared with the dynamism and variety of Jewish commentary. Professor Magonet stressed his personal experience of the joy of sharing this rich Jewish resource. He then pointed to the danger inherent in the way the text of the Hebrew Bible may be read in the context of the shift from powerlessness to power in contemporary Jewish life in Israel. He asked for Catholic help as a model of self-criticism in the new situation. His fellow-speaker Professor John Pawlikowski from Chicago concentrated on the text as an obstacle to a respectful and fruitful relationship between Catholics and Jews. He focused on the First (or Old) Testament, and on texts which have historically provided a supposed biblical basis for a theology of Jewish covenantal displacement. He underlined the positive value of Jewish interpretation of these texts. He went on to grapple with the problems raised by certain New Testament texts for a theology of respect and for Catholic liturgy.

Professor Susannah Heschel, daughter of one of this century's most famous rabbis and a brilliant scholar in her own right, contributed what was undoubtedly the most challenging lecture to both Catholics and Jews. She suggested that the very questions being posed are dated and not those of postmodernism. She subjected both religious traditions to a postmodernist critique based upon feminist theory and postcolonial theory. This analysis underscored profound shared challenges which Catholicism and Judaism, except in certain rarefied academic circles, have scarcely begun to pose let alone respond to. Dr Janet Martin Soskice from Cambridge approached the challenge of postmodernity from a different perspective and emphasized the way in which binarism – the logic that suggests that 'I am good because you are bad' and 'I am right because you are wrong' – has deeply affected the Catholic approach to Judaism, and the need to move beyond such unhelpful logic.

We then moved on to the third and final theme, grandiosely entitled 'A partnership for the glory of God, the good of humanity and the future of the planet – the values we bring to the partnership'. Rabbi David Rosen from Israel addressed issues of power and powerlessness. He argued that consultation with the people is deeply rooted in Jewish tradition. Basing himself on, amongst others, the medieval philosopher Rabbi Nissim of Gerondi he argued for a broad civil moral structure and a non-coercive religious framework and the separation of religion and state. He concluded that we should not ask whether God is on our side but whether we are on God's side, and further argued that we are on God's side when we are on the side of the needy and vulnerable.

Bishop Adrian van Luyn from Rotterdam presented a paper that both complemented that of Rabbi Rosen and identified a significant volume of shared work to be undertaken in the context of rich and developed Western countries. He emphasized both the impact of the 'First Modernization' and that of the Second, the information technology revolution now globalizing society. He invited Jews to join Catholics in work with the European community.

Tackling the values we bring to partnership, Rabbi Dr Sidney Brichto brought a special warmth, openness and enthusiasm to the agenda and urged Jews to be much more open to and understanding of the Christian covenant. He began the enumeration of the 'values' agenda, though he recognized that Catholics and Jews sometimes come to different conclusions about values and ethical issues. In a responsive paper, Dr Eugene Fisher spelled out how much Catholics and Jews have had in common in the United States where both have been outsiders. This has given a unique impetus to partnership, and Dr Fisher described just how much has been achieved in the United States. Methodology for dealing with different conclusions over issues such as abortion have been evolved and are particularly helpful. It was sobering to realize how ignorant many Catholics and Jews are of the work already accomplished in the United States. We must be aware of the need to build upon this rather than to seek to reinvent the wheel.

Since the authors of the papers only spoke very briefly, the discussants – each paper was followed by a person from the other faith tradition bringing out the salient points and questions – proved very important. Amongst them were Professor Joann Spillman (USA), Rabbi Tovia Ben-Chorin (Switzerland), Sr Margaret Shepherd (UK), Rabbi Dr David Goldberg (UK), Revd Dr Robert Murray (UK), Rabbi Alexandra Wright (UK), Revd Michael McGarry (Israel), Professor Guy Stroumsa (Israel), Professor Mary Boys (USA), Rabbi Richard Block (Israel), Dr John D'Arcy May (Ireland) and Rabbi Ron Kronish (Israel).

The discussion, like the papers, was uncompromisingly theological. For some present, this was new. Although Jews were often forced into theological dialogue and debate in the Middle Ages, recent trends in Orthodox Judaism have resolutely set their face against any such enterprise. One of the key figures of modern orthodoxy, Rabbi J. B. Soloveitchik rules explicitly against theological discussion and this is reinforced by the views of orthodoxy's leading Holocaust theologian, Eliezer Berkovits. My impression is that all participants found the venture into theology stimulating, refreshing and exciting.

Each day mass was celebrated in the Interfaith Centre of what is the largest Jewish religious, educational and cultural centre in Europe. So too were Jewish daily services. Jews witnessed mass and Catholics, Jewish prayers. In some ways that was the most moving aspect of the whole project, deepening understanding without in any way compromising anyone's religious integrity.

During the three days there were occasional moments of tension but almost every one of them was either internal to the Catholics or internal to the Jews, almost never between us. The exception was the response to Susannah Heschel's feminist and postcolonial critique. Here there were ruffled feathers across both faith groups. The charge of failing fully to address questions of patriarchy and the male abuse of power is a shared challenge and the issues lie close to the surface of many of the essays. One only has to look at the language, some gender inclusive much not, to realize the tensions raised by this particular aspect of any discussion of or between religions today.

There was one moment that I will never forget because it touched upon my own particular preoccupations. I had been arguing with all the force that I could muster for the importance of Catholics declaring the covenant with the Jews unbroken and Jews confirming that, by virtue of the New Testament and the events that it describes, Christians stand in covenantal relationship with God as well. I asked for help in clarifying whether there were two independent covenants or both were strands of the covenant with Abraham or indeed of the covenant with Noah. One of my colleagues responded by suggesting that for most of the last 2000 years the concept of covenant had not played a terribly important part in Jewish theology. I heard a leading Catholic present mutter in exasperation 'no sooner do we start to shift in their direction on covenant than they tell us it isn't important anyway'. I suggested to him that we aren't known as 'a peculiar people' for nothing!

Re-reading the papers and listening again to the dialogue in order to co-edit this book, a number of things struck me very forcibly. They are, in no particular order:

- How close we came to a key objective of establishing independent theological space for each other and agreeing a theological relationship of mutual respect. Covenant, *pace* one critical colleague, clearly seems to be a really fruitful vehicle for this.
- That we can retain our respective particularity without inference of superiority and that chosenness and election need not be stumbling blocks.
- That we are both aware of the richness of both of our scriptures, of the potential that they offer and of the challenge that they present if we are to avoid perpetuating the mistakes of the past.

- That there is a stupendous task of education and dissemination ahead of us.
- That so much has already been written and tried of which few of us are aware.
- That the postmodern agenda, particularly the feminist critique, is profound and yet all too inadequately responded to.
- That issues of power and its misuse are very high, or should be very high, on the agenda of both faiths.
- That there is a vast potential for us to face the challenges of the contemporary world together and, even when we differ, shared values are seldom far away.
- That talk must lead to action.
- That more progress has been made in the past decades than in the preceding millennia. *Nostra Aetate* is more quoted in this book than almost any other source and the present Pope has contributed more to progress in Catholic–Jewish relations than perhaps any other human being in the last 100 years.
- The realization that we are, truly, siblings with all the baggage, tension and loving potential that implies and that it is not enough simply to embrace briefly, nor even to weep over past misunderstandings. Meaningful coexistence, true partnership, demands on-going humility and continuing effort.

But all of that is my narrow and particular perspective. Sidney Brichto, Eugene Fisher and I hope that you will read the essays, responses, discussions and conclusions, come to your own view and join us all on an ultimately exhilarating journey.

2

Opening the encounter

The opening session was the only public session. The West London Synagogue of British Jews, the oldest Reform Synagogue in Britain (founded in 1840) was packed. The evening began with a short concert given by a combined children's choir of the Akiva School (North West London) and the St Francis of Assisi Catholic School (West London). Led by their respective head teachers, the two schools have been working together for some years on building understanding and friendship between Jewish and Catholic children of primary school age. Their singing together was a moving prelude to the address given by Edward Cardinal Cassidy.

Edward Idris Cassidy

This evening represents a very important stage in the on-going process of reconciliation between Jews and Christians. As President of the Vatican Commission for Religious Relations with the Jews, I feel a deep sense of satisfaction at being able to participate in a conference organized by the Reform and Liberal Jewish Movements of Great Britain that challenges us to look to the future, a future of Catholics and Jews in partnership. My special thanks go to Rabbi Tony Bayfield, who conceived the idea of this conference and together with Sir Sigmund Sternberg and others has brought us here together in West London Synagogue this evening.

I come to you just one month after having taken part in the historic visit to Israel of Pope John Paul II, a visit which made manifest to the whole world the new relationship that characterizes Jewish–Catholic relations at the beginning of this century and third Christian millennium. The presence of the Bishop of Rome at Yad Vashem paying homage to the victims of the *Shoah* and at the Western Wall of the Temple in Jerusalem leaving there a message of *teshuvah* (repentance) for the anti-Judaism of the sons and daughters of the church in the past, gave more eloquent witness to this relationship than any words of mine can describe.

This new relationship is the fruit of the rich Jewish/Catholic dialogue of recent years, based on the decisions of the Second Vatican Council set out in the document *Nostra Aetate*, No. 4. We have travelled quite a long way together since *Nostra Aetate* was promulgated in 1965. We have built a solid relationship between our communities that will last, no matter what storms may come to try us or new obstacles delay our progress. Credit for this is due to members of both our communities: to the Catholic Church which in *Nostra Aetate* offered the hand of friendship and the Jewish community which, despite its memory of past experiences, took that hand and began our common journey of reconciliation

Our success has been due to a large extent to sincere dialogue. We have come to know one another, appreciate one another and accept one another. As was to be expected after such a long period of distrust, discrimination and unjust accusation, dialogue has not been easy and many were the hurdles to be overcome. As we leave behind a century which saw an attempt to eliminate the Jewish people from the soil of Europe, we give thanks for and rejoice in the new relationship that has been established, 'a relationship that emphasises co-operation, mutual understanding and reconciliation; goodwill and common goals'.[1]

What of this relationship in this conference? In order that our dialogue takes us forward, it must, in my opinion, be characterized above all by mutual esteem and have common goals.

Mutual esteem or respect is a basic element of true dialogue. It is something that we have been seeking to build over the past thirty-five years through a deeper understanding one of the other and through a common approach to the questions that were troubling our communities. The commitment to understanding and mutual respect is a process that begins in our own individual hearts and spreads throughout our own community and into the world in which we live. To a large extent we have succeeded. But more has to be done. Not all those who are involved in our dialogue have shown the respect and esteem for the other that is essential for fruitful dialogue. Pope Paul VI, in his Encyclical *Ecclesiam Siam*, has described dialogue as 'the simple exchange of gifts'. There is no place in such dialogue for judgments, unfounded accusations, negative actions or attitudes that are unworthy of the new relationship we are seeking to build.

Of course, Jews and Catholics will not agree on all things. We are two distinct faith communities. We have inherited a long history, in which the Jewish people 'while bearing their unique witness to the Holy One of Israel and to the *Torah* have suffered much at different times and in many places'.[2] The *Shoah*, which was certainly the worst suffering of all, is still very much part of the memory of the Jewish people. We Catholics do not wish to put this aside or forget the past. We are well aware of the fact that the attitudes and actions of Christians down through the centuries were often responsible for the suffering of the Jewish people.

On 12 March 2000, Pope John Paul II, in a special penitential service in St Peter's Basilica, asked pardon of God, on behalf of the whole Church, for the sins committed by Christians against the people of Israel throughout history with these words:

God of our fathers, you chose Abraham and his descendants
to bring your Name to the Nations:
We are deeply saddened by the behaviour of those
who in the course of history have caused
these children of yours to suffer
and, asking your forgiveness,
we wish to commit ourselves to genuine brotherhood
with the people of the Covenant.

To which the many thousands gathered in the basilica and in the square outside replied: '*Kyrie, eleison* – Lord, have mercy!'

This solemn act recalled at once the statement made in the document of the Holy See *We Remember* of 16 March 1998.

At the end of this Millennium the Catholic Church desires to express her deep sorrow for the failures of her sons and daughters in every age. This is an act of repentance (*teshuvah*), since, as members of the Church, we are linked to the sins as well as to the merits of all her children.[3]

We cannot, and must not forget the past. In the Mausoleum at Yad Vashem, Pope John Paul declared: 'We wish to remember. But we wish to remember for a purpose, namely, to ensure that evil will never again prevail, as it did for the millions of innocent victims of Nazism.' We remember, but we look to the future and seek to build a new partnership between Jews and Catholics. For this we must learn to trust one another.

In Jewish–Catholic dialogue, we are concerned with mutual respect and esteem of communities who share a unique spiritual heritage.

Cardinal Carlo Maria Martini, Archbishop of Milan, speaking to young members of the Catholic community of his diocese, described the kind of respect and esteem that Catholics should have for their Jewish 'elder brothers':

> It is necessary therefore to be for the Jewish people, for their culture, for their values, for their human and spiritual riches, for their history, for their extraordinary religious witness. It is necessary to be for those values that enrich all humanity.[4]

If we would have this kind of mutual respect, one for the other, what a splendid dialogue we would have! In Prague, September 1990, we stated:

> After two millennia of estrangement and hostility, we have a sacred duty as Catholics and Jews to strive to create a genuine culture of mutual esteem and reciprocal caring.[5]

Already in Prague, we pledged ourselves to seek *Common Goals*. It is not always clear what a particular person or organization has in mind when deciding to be part of our dialogue. It is good for each and every one of us, I think, to reflect from time to time on the question that Rabbi Siegman asked already twenty years ago: 'What impels us to dialogue, and what does each of us seek to get out of it?' The goal has gradually been changing as our relationship has developed and difficult problems have been resolved. Of course, unless we are in agreement on where we wish to go, our dialogue will not be a very happy experience, nor will it produce noteworthy results. I can only place before you this evening, very briefly, some of the goals that we in the Commission for Religious Relations with the Jews seek to keep before our eyes.

Our first aim is to consolidate the gains that we have made over the past forty years, and above all to avoid any going back in this relationship to the 'past spirit of suspicion, resentment and distrust'.[6] On many occasions I have stressed the importance in this connection of education and information. The late Geoffrey Wigoder reminded the International Catholic–Jewish Liaison Committee, at its meeting in Jerusalem in 1994, 'of the abyss of ignorance in both our communities concerning the other, which includes dangerous myths and prejudices'.[7] And quite recently, Rabbi Eric H.Yoffie, the President of the Union of American Hebrew Congregations, which unites more than one million Reform Jews in over 900 synagogues in North

America, urged the Catholic Church and his organization to undertake a joint campaign about the two religions. 'This means', he said, 'that the Catholics need to educate Catholics about Jews, and the Jews to educate Jews about Catholics.'[8] Here I wish to pay tribute to all those who have seen the need of ridding our relationship of 'dangerous myths and prejudices' through education and information. Still, it is in this field particularly that much remains to be done.

Speaking of the recent visit of Pope John Paul II to the holy places of Israel, Rabbi David Rosen of the Anti-Defamation League stated:

> I think that the visit just concluded will provide among other things a new opportunity for the Jews to be informed, educated and brought up to date with regard to the many steps that the Catholic Church has taken, especially under the direction of John XXIII and the present Pontiff.[9]

We must – both Jews and Christians – bring the great news of Jewish–Christian reconciliation to the members of our communities if we wish to ensure that the edifice we are building is constructed on a solid foundation.

Secondly, while preserving past gains, I would hope that we, Catholics and Jews, might move towards a closer partnership, and here we enter into the subject of this conference. I would wish to see our dialogue as the work of two equal partners seeking together to build a better world. We began our discussion in order to solve our problems and promote a new relationship. It seems to me that we need now to go further and move our gaze from the bilateral relations of Jews and Christians to a wider world.

As our relationship has matured, we have become more and more aware of how much we Jews and Christians have in common. When we open the books most sacred to us, the sacred scriptures, we often open them at the same page. We look to those same pages for many of the prayers we address daily to God. We have but one God and we each understand ourselves as being in a special, covenantal relationship with that God. Our understanding of the fundamental questions of life is the same, based on that revelation; our moral code rests on the same basic commandments. We Christians 'draw sustenance daily from the root of the good olive tree of the Hebrew Scriptures onto which the Church has been grafted'.[10]

All this has not been given to us for ourselves or for our own personal sanctification. We are called to be a light to the nations or, in the words of Pope John Paul II,

As Christians and Jews, following the example of the faith of Abraham, we are called to be a blessing to the world. This is a common task awaiting us. It is therefore necessary for us, Christians and Jews, to be first a blessing to one another.[11]

Our role is to project to the world a deeper vision of life, revealing its meaning, direction and ultimate goal, being bearers of hope.

Our agenda should then be one that keeps this calling of ours in mind. We should be busy about giving the world a common witness to the values that make us what we are: Christians and Jews. I believe we have much to say together on questions of vital interest to our society of today. Already within our International Catholic–Jewish Liaison Committee, we have spoken out together on the family[12] and on preserving the environment.[13] We had a document on violence that unfortunately we have not yet been able to discuss. Human rights, justice and peace, and questions concerning life itself are other obvious fields of common witness.

At the conclusion of his meeting with the two Chief Rabbis of Israel, at the Hechal Shlomo in Jerusalem, on 23 March last [1999], Pope John Paul II did not hesitate to affirm:

> There is much that we have in common. There is so much that we can do together for peace, for justice, for a more human and fraternal world. May the Lord of heaven and earth lead us to a new and fruitful era of mutual respect and co-operation, for the benefit of all.[14]

For quite some time now, I have been asking our Jewish partners in dialogue to consider seriously the possibility of moving ahead into a serious theological dialogue. To my delight, recently I am hearing more and more Jewish voices making the same request. Rabbi Eric Yoffie, in the lecture already mentioned, calls for a broadening of the agenda in our dialogue. While the Holocaust remains for him, as for Catholics, a deep concern, he believes that 'a dialogue of grievance can no longer dominate our relations'. Let me quote his words in this connection:

> Not everyone in the Jewish community is prepared to engage in theological exchange, but the largest religious movements are, and it is not essential that everyone be around the table. I am interested in discussing ethics and redemption and sin. I would like to read the Hebrew Bible with you (Catholics). And I want to do this not

because I expect to win your agreement or elicit your approval, but because I want you to understand Judaism as a living and dynamic religion. Through these discussions I expect to stimulate your thinking and anticipate that you will stimulate mine.[15]

Rabbi Leon Klenicki, of the Anti-Defamation League, has also suggested a dialogue of this nature. In a dialogue with Revd James Loughran on *The Thought and Life of Elijah Benamozegh*, Rabbi Klenicki stated: 'we have the need, I would even say obligation, to consider theological matters'. He would prefer that we speak of 'discussions', rather than 'dialogue' – and this perhaps would be a wise approach to a rather delicate subject. As the Rabbi points out, 'considering and discussing theology evokes for Jews the memory of the reality of medieval European confrontations'.[16]

The Center for Christian–Jewish Understanding of the Sacred Heart University, Fairfield, Connecticut, in cooperation with the Elijah School for the Study of Wisdom in World Religions (Jerusalem) held an international conference in Jerusalem in February of this year [2000]. The theme was: 'What do we want the other to teach about us?' The present leadership of our long-time Jewish partner International Jewish Christian Liaison Committee is also discussing with us a future agenda more orientated to matters of concern to us as faith communities.

This Millennium Conference then is the beginning of this discussion and a response to a growing desire for such dialogue or discussions. Our Commission for Religious Relations with the Jews strongly supports this undertaking and in this we are greatly encouraged by the words addressed by Pope John Paul II to Jewish and Catholic theologians taking part in a colloquium in Rome in November 1986:

> Theological reflection is part of the human intelligence and so gives witness to our conscious acceptance of God's will. Honouring our respective traditions, theological dialogue based on sincere esteem can contribute greatly to mutual knowledge of our respective patrimonies of faith and can help us to be more aware of our links with one another in terms of our understanding of salvation.

I might mention in bringing this reflection on theological dialogue to a conclusion that much remains to be done within the Catholic Church to reflect more deeply on the theological implications of the document *Nostra Aetate* for the self-understanding of the Church.

Revd John Pawlikowski of the Catholic Theological Union, Chicago, has suggested that 'without saying it explicitly, the 2221 Council members who voted in favour of *Nostra Aetate* were in fact affirming that everything that had been said about the Christian–Jewish relationship since Paul moved in a direction they could no longer support'.[17]

As we look to the future, it is well perhaps to repeat again that Catholics and Jews must not enter dialogue with the expectation that they will agree on everything. It would be naive of us to think otherwise. We are two distinct faith communities with common roots and a great deal in common, yet with essential differences that must be respected. The process of dialogue requires both a clear understanding of one's own faith tradition and openness to the experience of others. We must not be surprised or disturbed when, on one or other matter that touches our faith or history, we have different opinions or understandings. Neither should sincere criticism upset us, provided that it is objective and framed in a way that does not offend our mutual esteem and respect for one another. Such criticism can be good for us. It helps us to reflect more deeply on our positions or initiatives. This is, of course, very different from certain aggressive criticism with its own agenda and from the activity of pressure groups. These unpleasant activities inevitably provoke a negative reaction and alienate much goodwill, doing immense harm to our dialogue and future relationship.

Let me conclude with some words of the distinguished Rabbi Irving Greenberg which seem to sum up well what I have been trying to say:

> If committed and believing Christians and Jews can discover the image of God in each other, if they can uncover and affirm each other's proper role in the overall divine strategy of redemption, surely the inspiration of this example would bring the Kingdom of God that much closer to everyone.[18]

Sir Sigmund Sternberg, President of the Reform Synagogues of Great Britain and doyen of interfaith encounters and bridge-building, then gave his address:

Sigmund Sternberg

May I begin by paying tribute to the memories of Cardinal John O'Connor and the Lord Coggan, who recently passed away. They were both friends and valiant supporters of interfaith dialogue and we mourn their deaths.

We meet here today still under the impact of the dramatic and never-to-be-forgotten visit by Pope John Paul II to the Jewish State and specifically to Yad Vashem and the Western Wall. These are the only shrines shared by all the Jewish people.

Yad Vashem is the national place of commemoration to the millions of Jews slaughtered at the heart of Europe in the mid-twentieth century. They died only because they were Jews. The Western Wall is the national place of commemoration of the former glory of the Jewish homeland, the ages-old remnant of the Temple Mount where Jews would come to pray on the three pilgrimage festivals of the year. To see the Pope standing there, where the tears and prayers of Jews have been offered down the ages, was indeed a moving occasion. And, in a way no-one could have predicted, the Pope has himself served to link the two places, the Western Wall and Yad Vashem, for the prayer which the Pontiff inserted between the stones of the Western Wall is now enshrined at Yad Vashem, where it can be seen by all.

On the occasion of this conference, it is worth recalling what the Pope said in that prayer, and I quote:

> God of our fathers, you chose Abraham and his descendants to bring Your Name to the Nations. We are deeply saddened by the behaviour of those who, in the course of history, have caused these children of Yours to suffer and, asking forgiveness, we wish to commit ourselves to genuine brotherhood with the people of the covenant.

It was a Christian observer in Israel, Jack Driscoll of the Bat Kol Institute, who made the perceptive observation that, 'by mentioning the Covenant', the Pope ended forever a negative theology which had denied its endurance and affirmed what he had said on previous occasions: that the covenant with the Jewish people was never revoked by God and that the Jewish people remain a people most dear to God.

Friends, I have known few occasions which filled me with so much emotion as when I sat before the monitor at the BBC TV centre that day commenting on the Holy Father's visit to the Kotel. It was paralleled only by the day, a few years ago, when, in company with Cardinal Willebrands, the predecessor of my dear friend Cardinal Cassidy, I was among the party which welcomed John Paul II on his visit to the synagogue in Rome, the first time any pope had entered a synagogue.

I could not help but remember how, as a young Jew growing up in pre-war Hungary, I was once called a 'Christ-killer'. It was my first encounter with Christian anti-Semitism. I was puzzled. I could not make sense of it. I thought of it again when, as a youth, I read the account by Theodor Herzl, the father of modern Jewish statehood, of his visit to Pope Pius X in 1904 to ask his support for a Jewish homeland in Palestine. The Pope told him, in probably the most dismissive terms he could summon: 'If you go to Palestine and settle your people there, we will have priests and churches ready to baptize all of you!'

Nearly a century later, Pope John Paul II visited a very different 'Palestine', one in which a wholly Arab National entity, an embryo republic, lives alongside a sovereign Jewish State of Israel, a place in which Muftis and Chief Rabbis meet the Pope on equal terms as brotherly religions and not, as Pius X predicted, as subjects.

It has been a long march since Herzl's fruitless journey to Rome, a route which crossed continents and took many victims, none so many as the six million Jews of Europe who perished in the Holocaust. Had Herzl been more successful and had civilized society been more alert and concerned, we might not have been heirs to a new and terrible word: genocide.

Curiously, it is religion, that which for so long divided Christians and Jews, which today has become the force uniting us in appreciation of a shared inheritance, an ethic in common, which has as its purpose the healing of the world.

Abraham is father to us both, as indeed he is to the Islamic world, and it is in the light of his readiness to sacrifice in obedience to the divine will that all three faiths today search together for a common goal which yet recognizes their diverse paths.

It has not been easy. But it is increasingly rewarding in terms of the respect engendered one for the other and which finds its latest and welcome expression in our Millennium Conference here in London.

I cannot enjoy the privilege of this platform without expressing my deep appreciation for the support I have consistently received in all my efforts for Jewish–Christian reconciliation from the good Cardinal Cassidy. His role in the Pontifical Commission for Relations with the Jews has been primary in bringing us to this Millennium Conference. It is almost entirely thanks to him that the Vatican established an independent panel of historians to look into the material pertaining to the Holocaust released from its archives. While we await their report – which I hope will be published in the near future – I hope that those with whom the responsibility lies will hold off on the efforts of some to proceed with the beatification of Pius XII. I pray that nothing now will be done, on any side, to upset the positive and forward-looking relationship which has been established between the Church and the Jewish people and which has taken decades to reach the respectful and trusting stage of today.

I know that, here in Britain, we will have a faithful ally in all our efforts to continue the process of reconciliation. Archbishop Cormac Murphy-O'Connor, whom we warmly welcome in our midst today, follows in the steps of a dear and warm friend, Cardinal Basil Hume. We look forward to a continuation of that close and trusting relationship which has been the hallmark of Catholic–Jewish relations in this country in the post-war era.

If I have regrets this evening, it is that I have had so little support in the financing of this conference from those in a position to give it. There is a regrettable sense among many with usually strong social consciousness that 'we can leave it to Siggy'. I can only say to them that they are making a big mistake. I am as mortal as any man and there must be other businessmen who are willing to carry forward the work of dialogue and reconciliation with the Catholic Church in which I have been engaged almost alone for so long.

The historic visit of the Pope to Jerusalem, the huge strides in the improvement of Catholic–Jewish relations, our conference here this week, did not happen by accident. They are the outcome of years of patient and painstaking consultation, dialogue and, yes, sometimes argument. With the visit of the Pope, we reached what Prime Minister Barak called 'a magical moment of truth and a victory for justice and hope'. But like all victories, it must be built upon, its foundations made secure. There was a speech made in this city over one hundred years ago by Henry Edward, Cardinal Manning, the head of the Catholic Church in England, which, on an occasion such as this, is worthy of recall. It was moving and powerful and was made at a meeting called by the Lord Mayor in the Mansion House to protest against the atrocities then being suffered by the Jews of Russia. I would like to end my remarks by quoting something Cardinal Manning said then and which has resonance for us here today:

> There is a book which is common to the race of Israel and to us Christians. That book is a bond between us, and in that book I read that the people of Israel are the eldest people upon the earth – '. . . an imperishable people which, with an inextinguishable life and immutable traditions, and faith in God and the laws of God, scattered as it is all over the world, passing through the fires unscathed, trampled into the dust, and yet never combining with the dust into which it is trampled, lives still a witness and warning to us.' We are in the bonds of brotherhood with it. The New Testament rests upon the Old. They believe in half of that for which we would give our lives. Let us then acknowledge that we unite in a common sympathy.

I do believe that this conference will echo to that message, reinforced so powerfully in our own day by Pope John Paul II, and that our proceedings will have a profound and positive impact on the relationship between our faith communities.

The London Millennium Conference was held under the auspices of the Vatican and the World Union for Progressive Judaism. The opening session was now addressed by the Executive Director of the World Union Rabbi Dr Richard Block:

Richard Block

It is a great pleasure, as President of the World Union for Progressive Judaism, to welcome you to the Millennium Conference on the Theology of Partnership and to thank all those in the Vatican and the World Union's British daughter movements, the Reform Synagogues of Great Britain and the Union of Liberal and Progressive Synagogues, for their dedicated efforts to bring about this conference.

Two traditional Hebrew greetings are 'Baruchim haba'im', 'Blessed are those who come', and 'Shalom aleichem', 'Peace be unto you'. Truly, this is an occasion of blessing, when Catholics and Jews come together in a spirit of partnership and peace to discuss profound matters of shared interest and concern. 'Hineh mah tov u'mah naim, shevet achim gam yachad.' 'How good and pleasant it is when siblings gather together.' Children of the same divine parent, we seek to depart the past millennium, so filled with misunderstanding and pain, and enter a new era of mutual respect and covenantal fulfilment. 'Zeh hayom asah Adonai, nagilah v'nismechah vo.' 'This very day God has made. Let us rejoice and be glad in it.'

This conference is one in which we seek, as His Holiness John Paul II would say, to 'cross the threshold of hope'. Indeed, the transition from the twentieth to the twenty-first centuries is, in some respects, a passage from horror to hope. Both dimensions of our experience and the transition itself are revealed in a story I want to share with you tonight, a true story.

When my children were young, they attended a Jewish day school in Stanford, CT. Our son, Josh, had two close friends who were classmates and twins. Their father had been a 'hidden child' in the Holocaust. His Polish Jewish parents had left him for safekeeping with a Polish Catholic family who took the boy in and sheltered him. The boy's parents asked that if they did not survive the war, he should be sent to relatives in the US, whose name and address they provided before saying goodbye, as it turned out forever, and disappearing into the abyss of the *Shoah*.

When the war was over and the boy's parents did not return, the Catholic couple, who had grown to love the boy, approached their young parish priest and asked if they were obligated to send the boy to his Jewish relatives in America or could they convert him to Catholicism and raise him as their own. The priest instructed them that they must honour the parents' wishes and sadly, but with tremendous integrity and sacrifice, they did. The boy grew up as a proud and committed Jew and was the father of my son's friends, the twins. The priest is elderly now and infirm, but still alive. Two months ago, he arrived in Jerusalem by helicopter, as Pope John Paul II.

In my judgment, John Paul II is the living embodiment of the sacred aspiration and the painstaking search for Catholic–Jewish understanding. During his pontificate we have made more progress in that regard than in the previous 1,950 years. As my friend and colleague Professor Michael Signer of Notre Dame recently wrote me,

> The agenda at the end of Vatican II has been filled in. The Church has denounced anti-semitism; it has moved anti-semitism into the category of a sin; it has established diplomatic relations with Israel; it has come to terms with the memory of Auschwitz in collaborating with Jewish sentiment about the Carmelite convent.

It has done all this, and more, in our lifetimes.

According to Professor Signer, two things have made this possible: first, the attention given by John Paul II, and, second, the hard work in establishing conversations between leaders at the local level. I wish, like Sir Sigmund, to mention, in this regard, the recent death of Cardinal John O'Connor in New York. Cardinal O'Connor was revered, even loved, in the Jewish community. His sincerity, compassion, and good humour made it possible to overcome differences of theology and social policy and develop relationships of respect and meaning between Jews and Catholics. He will be long remembered and greatly missed. In my period of service as a congregational rabbi, I was privileged to participate in two extended Catholic–Jewish dialogues: one in Greenwich, CT, where Father Vincent O'Connor, of blessed memory, was my colleague, teacher and friend; and one in Northern California, where Bishop Pierre DuMaine was my learned Catholic counterpart.

As I see it, our work here is part of the process of transcending, though never forgetting, the painful past, and, though differences remain and misunderstandings persist, of seeking an action agenda for the future, based on shared values, complementary interests, and common hopes. We need to concentrate on continued dialogue and to pursue the implementation of the hard-won gains of recent decades. We must work together on the international level and, perhaps even more importantly, on the national and local levels, where Jews and Catholics work and live. This is where individual bishops and their educational officers and their Jewish counterparts have much to do to make John Paul's breakthroughs real. As Jews, we need to educate and sensitize our own people to the fact that there has been a significant and historic change in Catholic attitudes toward Jews and Judaism, which deserves recognition and acknowledgment.

In all this, patience, persistence, and hard work will be required. For one thing, old attitudes and prejudices die hard, and implementation is always harder than visualization. For another, there are far fewer Jews than Catholics, making it much harder for us to uphold the practical end of a relationship in which we have equal status. But we must do our best.

For the World Union's part, I have asked Rabbi Mark Winer to chair and Rabbi John Levi of Australia to co-chair a World Union rabbinic commission on interfaith relations and I look to them, together with other distinguished colleagues in our movement, some of whom are here tonight, to help the World Union and me fulfil our responsibilities in this area.

Representing some two million Jews in 43 countries, and millions more who identify with our movement, the World Union for Progressive Judaism is the world's largest organization of religiously affiliated Jews. It has a vital role to play and a significant contribution to make in the area of Catholic–Jewish relations. As the World Union's President, I am intent upon seeing to it that we do so. I look forward to sharing the next two days with you, to getting to know you, and to joining with you and others in fruitful joint endeavour. I close with the words of Psalm 90, praying that God will

> Teach us to number our days, that we may gain a heart of wisdom . . .
> And let the graciousness of the Lord our God be upon us; Establish Thou also the work of our hands; Yea the work of our hands establish Thou it.
> Shalom aleichem u'vruchim habaim.

The conference now moved to the Sternberg Centre for Judaism in North West London. It was there that two days of intensive dialogue took place in closed session between equal numbers of Catholic and Jewish scholars. What follows are the key papers, twelve in all, that had been pre-circulated. These have not been significantly changed for this book. In order to allow the maximum time for discussion these papers were not delivered at the conference though each author was given a few minutes to introduce them. Each was followed by a response from a discussant of the partner faith. Once each pair of papers had been launched and two discussants had spoken, discussion and dialogue followed. In almost every case a participant has sought to summarize that discussion. On each day Catholic mass and Jewish daily services were held and all participants attended all services. At the end of the second day two participants bravely attempted spontaneously to provide an agenda for the future emerging from the conference. It is the conference organizers' intention to use their agendas and the full text of this book from which to build further dialogue.

Notes

1. International Catholic–Jewish Liaison Committee, Prague 1990. For the Concluding Statement see *Information Service of the Pontifical Council for Promoting Christian Unity* 75, 1990, pp. 175–7.
2. Holy See's Commission for Religious Relations with the Jews, *We Remember: A Reflection on the Shoah*, Libreria Editrice Vaticana, Vatican City, 1998, II.

3. Ibid., V.
4. C. M. Martini, 'Ricordare oggi per ii futuro', Milan, 18 November 1998 – private copy.
5. Cf. *Information Service of the Pontifical Council for Promoting Christian Unity* 75, 1990, p. 177.
6. Ibid., p. 176.
7. An account of this meeting can be found in *Information Service of the Pontifical Council for Promoting Christian Unity* 87, 1994, pp. 231 ff.
8. Rabbi Eric Yoffie, *Advances and Tensions in Catholic–Jewish Relations: A Way Forward*, The Joseph Klein Lecture on Judaic Affairs, Assumption College, 23 March 2000, published in *Origins* 29/44.
9. Interview given to *L'Avvenire* 28 March 2000.
10. *Nostra Aetate*, No. 4
11. John Paul II, 'Warsaw on the 50th Anniversary of the Warsaw Ghetto Uprising', *Information Service of the Pontifical Council for Promoting Christian Unity* 84, 1993, p. 157.
12. Cf. *Information Service of the Pontifical Council for Promoting Christian Unity* 87, 1994, pp. 234–5.
13. Cf. *Information Service of the Pontifical Council for Promoting Christian Unity* 98, 1998, pp. 168–9.
14. *L'Osservatore Romano*, 30 March 2000, VII.
15. The Joseph Klein Lecture on Judaic Affairs, Assumption College, 23 March 2000. MS, p. 23.
16. 'Central Conference of American Rabbis', *CCAR Journal*, 4, 1999, p. 11.
17. John T. Pawlikowski, OSM, 'Vatican II on the Jews: A Dramatic Example of Theological Development', presented to the 1999 Convention of the Catholic Theological Society of America, Miami, Florida, 12 June 1999.
18. Rabbi Irving Greenberg, ' Judaism and Christianity: Their Respective Roles in the Strategy of Redemption', *Visions of the Other: Jewish and Christian Theologians Assess the Dialogue*, ed. Eugene J. Fischer, New York: Paulist Press, 1994, p. 27.

3

The Theology of Partnership

What is the religious basis on which our partnership is constructed and grounded?

Are Jews and Catholics both in Covenant? How does this work? How do we deal with the history of supercessionism and the doctrines implicit in the words Old and New Testament?

A. Partnership in Covenant

– Tony Bayfield

As families go, I would like to think that mine is a reasonably well-adjusted and loving one. I hope that it warrants the term 'functional' (as opposed to dysfunctional). But then Jewish fathers have a long history of self-deception. Doubtless Abraham thought that Isaac had no inkling of what was about to happen to him: 'God will provide the sheep for the burnt offering, my son.'[1] Isaac quite clearly suppresses his doubts about whom it actually is he has just blessed: 'The voice is the voice of Jacob but the hands are the hands of Esau.'[2] There is nothing like a spot of self-deception for peace of mind. But even I, smiling benignly round the Friday night table, am sufficiently in touch with harsh reality to know the meaning of sibling rivalry.

Lucy, two and three-quarters, tiny and almost drowned by love, lay across the bottom step of the stairs and screamed her head off every time anyone dared to suggest they wanted to go up those stairs to see her brother, Daniel, newly home from the maternity ward. And we thought that we had done everything right! Could Lucy have had intimations of the inner security and humility that are needed to share love? Almost before consciousness had dawned, Daniel came to share at least her ambivalent feelings. Determined always to be first at everything – his first primary school teacher observed that he was so competitive that he even had to be first out of the toilet at break-time – he found it almost impossible to forgive the fact that Lucy had beaten him as the first into life and the family. However much he ran rings round her, nothing could change the stark fact of her primacy in the birth stakes and probably in goodness as well. Miriam was and is simply adored by all of us and her security, born of universal approval, shows. Yet even Miriam at twenty tosses in the casual 'Of course, I'm your favourite', hurriedly pleading 'joke'. But we all know that jokes are the most serious things that we ever make. Twenty-seven years on from Lucy's birth, I look round the *Erev Shabbat* (Friday night) table. The more obvious signs of rivalry have disappeared. They do, thank God, care about each other, relate well to each other, and support each other. The historian Friedrich Heer once described the Jewish people as 'God's First Love', an apposite title.[3] But if I described Lucy as her parents' first love, I suspect you would see a brief flicker on Daniel and Miriam's faces.

Sibling rivalry. I once asked Lucy what she remembered of Daniel's *b'rit*, his ceremonial circumcision. A fraction too quickly she replied 'absolutely nothing'. Memory can be merciful. We Jews do nothing for our first-born daughter's sense of worth and self-esteem by party-ing publicly at the circumcision of our sons. Which is not to advocate female circumcision but is to acknowledge the inequalities that remain within our still patriarchal tradition.

B'rit milah, covenant of circumcision, that most graphic, primitive and enduring of rites, which, for all its lack of choice and inequality, still grips even assimilated and marginal Jewish consciences. 'We bless you the Eternal our God Sovereign of the universe who makes us holy by doing Your commands and commands us to bring our sons into the covenant of our father Abraham.'[4] We Jewish men mark that most contemplated part of our bodies with a profoundly religious sign, a sign that we stand in a covenantal relationship with God.

Scholars tell us that there is an Akkadian word *biritu*.[5] The Akkadian *biritu* and the Hebrew word *b'rit* are cognates. In the ancient world which forms the background to the Genesis narrative the ruler, on ascending the throne, made treaties. There were parity treaties, which stipulated the mutual obligations undertaken by two equal parties. There were promissory pacts, which presumed the inequalities of the parties, but none the less bound the sovereign unilaterally. Out of sheer beneficence, he agreed to the performance of stipulated acts on behalf of his inferiors. In a third type, known as the suzerainty treaty, the sovereign bound his vassals to a set of obligations, which he defined. In return, the sovereign promised nothing, except – implicitly – his protection, conferred in return for the subject's loyalty, trust and performance of the obligations.

It is characteristic of the daring and religious insight of our ancestors, the authors of the *Tanakh*, the Hebrew Bible, that they could seize upon a mundane feature of the social and political life around them and use it as a daring and creative metaphor for their relationship with God. In the Hebrew Bible *biritu* becomes *b'rit*.

Central to this essay, indeed I believe to a theological understanding of the relationship between Jews and Christians (indeed, between those three siblings known as the three Abrahamic faiths), is the conscious and deliberate structuring of the story of *b'rit*, the story which is synonymous with the Jewish faith's account of its encounter with God. The first eleven chapters of the Hebrew Bible unfurl the history of humanity. Before the story fines down to focus on a particular family in its generations and on a particular people, the setting, the backdrop, the context is clearly and explicitly drawn. The context is humanity and we are one small part of suffering humanity and no different and no better or worse for that. At the heart of the story of humanity – its archetypal flirtation with disaster and deeply precarious survival – is Noah, archetypal survivor. Why does Noah plant a vineyard and get drunk? What else would a survivor do, a survivor who has witnessed the almost total destruction of humanity, but try to obliterate the pain of remembering?[6] How does God respond to the pain and survival of Noah? With a rainbow, which is the sign of *b'rit*, of covenant.[7] 'Zot ot habrit asher ani notein beini uveineichem uvein kol nefesh hayah asher itchem l'dorot olam':[8] 'This is the sign of the covenant which I make between Me and You and every living creature that is with you forever.'

This is the first and founding use of *b'rit*, of covenant. Since Noah has already played his faithful part in the survival of humanity, the treaty imposes little or nothing further on Noah and something, a minimal something – never again an all-consuming flood – on God. Yet, what we have is an understanding that all humanity can exist, does exist, in covenantal relationship. Later generations of Jewish teachers went on to define that *b'rit* in terms of the seven Noachide laws,[9] which, to my eyes, now seem minimalist to the point of condescension. But nothing can take away from the fact that the founding, primary use of this daring and defining concept rests between God and all humanity.

The Jewish journey, remembered despite my elder daughter, through the ceremony of circumcision, begins with Abraham, with his call, with his *b'rit* and with the *b'rit* of his son Isaac. But the fulcrum, the defining episode amongst many defining episodes, is set at Sinai. Sinai witnesses the sealing of the covenant between God and the Jewish people in those two climactic chapters of the book of Exodus, chapters 19 and 20. A suzerainty treaty is hammered out. A huge weight of *mitzvah*, of obligation – characterized by one Talmudic rabbi as the full weight of Sinai itself held over the heads of the Jewish people[10] – is imposed. When the narrative is repeated in Deuteronomy the *b'rit* is more one of parity. Judaism constantly embraces paradox and, as so often, both aspects ring true. Those fateful words:

> You stand here, all of you, before the Eternal your God . . . that you should enter into the covenant and consequent obligations to the Eternal your God . . . that God may establish you this day as God's people and that God may be your God . . . Not only do I make this covenant with all its attendant obligations with you, with those who are standing here with us today before the Eternal our God, but I make it also with those who are not here with us this day.[11]

There is no other sentence which reflects more closely my own existential, emotional and intellectual understanding of my Jewish situation. Bound to my suzerain whether I like it or not.

And yet, forever free to question and argue. Let me quote two paragraphs from a brilliant essay on covenant by the American Jewish scholar Arnold Eisen.

> Here lies the terror of the *b'rit* – and its comfort. The awesome creator of mankind is brought in to the human camp, demanding a degree of ethical and ritual purity that mere mortals are hard pressed to achieve. Yet the *mysterium tremendum* is thereby rendered accessible and, to a degree, comprehensible. Israel cannot penetrate the fire and cloud of God's presence, but the people can know what God wants of them. Even more remarkably, they can rest confident that God will submit to the seeming indignity of human conversation. He will negotiate, with Abraham, over the destruction of Sodom, and agree, after the pleading of Moses, to pardon the transgressions of Israel.

God, it seems, has no choice. This is the true daring of the
covenant idea: God, who inscrutably commands Abraham to bind
his son, no less inscrutably binds himself to his own children
through cords of immutable obligation. A moral God who seeks a
moral world, he has created humanity free to disobey. Perforce
a moralist, he is compelled to bargain. Suppose there are fifty
righteous men in Sodom, Abraham asks hesitantly – then, more
boldly, what if there are forty, thirty, twenty, ten? Israel, too, alter-
nately trembles before the father's wrath, appeals to his love, and
presumes upon the net of historical facticity into which he has cast
his lot. Certainly we deserve destruction, the people concede – but
what would the Egyptians say?[12]

The experience of God is powerful and dangerous. That much is a
constant theme throughout Jewish history. Yet there have always
been those who have sought to cultivate the experience, to, as it were,
approach the divine. More often than not such people have been
scarred by the experience.[13] Yet modern progressive Jews like me
speak of continuing revelation and some believe that the presence of
God can be experienced even in a synagogue service! As a rabbi of
nearly 2,000 years ago expressed it: 'Why did God speak to Moses out
of a thorn bush? To teach us that there is no place devoid of the
presence of God, not even a thorn bush.'[14] Or, as Elizabeth Barrett
Browning put it so memorably,

> Earth's crammed with heaven,
> And every common bush afire with God!
> But only he who sees, takes off his shoes . . .[15]

But there are clearly defining moments. Points at which God and
history meet in thundering silence. There are also defining moments
of the reverse kind when God is utterly obscured from history and all
that is visible is the abyss, the *tremendum*.[16] But this paper is about *b'rit*
and that defining, revelatory moment at Sinai when the covenant
between God and the Jewish people was signed, sealed and brought
into force forever.

In recent years, the concept of *b'rit* has come under immense
pressure in Jewish theological writing. There are those who have
sought to strip it of its essential force by questioning the binding
nature of *mitzvot*, the obligations which give the covenant at Sinai its
true character in Jewish thought.[17] There are others who have deemed
the covenant broken by God at Auschwitz and sought to replace it

with a voluntary covenant.[18] But *mitzvot* – as distinct from a list of 613, frozen in time[19] – endure and so does the spectre of Sinai held over our heads.

Then there have been times in the past when others outside of the Jewish people have sought to declare the covenant broken, super-seded, an old testament replaced by a new. Given the many unkind acts portrayed in life and literature the world over under the rubric of sibling rivalry, that should come as no surprise.

I am conscious that what follows in the next few paragraphs draws heavily on an essay that I wrote some years ago.[20] I make no apology because the essay appeared in one of those books that become a rare collector's item almost from the day it was published. I also make no apology because what I have to say seems to me so patently obvious as an existential observation that it has to be reflected in our theology if that theology is to have any integrity.

It is a huge impertinence to try to second-guess the mind of God. Yet I am convinced that whatever else God thinks and wants of me, throwing away my *kipah* and *tallit* and joining the local Catholic Church is not on the Divine agenda. But neither, I am equally con-vinced, does God want all Catholics great and small to swell the membership of the Reform Synagogues of Great Britain. I look at my Christian friends or, rather, I talk to them, witness their lives, and I know that they are moved by faith in much the same way that I am moved by my faith. Let me just personalize this for a few lines in the hope that I can convey something of the quality and intensity of what I feel. A matter of days ago, at the beginning of Easter, I listened to my friend Father Oliver McTernan speaking on *Thought for the Day* on BBC Radio 4 about the threat of nuclear proliferation and arguing for nuclear disarmament – no longer a fashionable subject to talk about in three precious, mass-media minutes – and rooting his defiance in the Easter story and the Easter message. I could and do say the same of two other friends who are 'with us this day' – Sister Margaret Shepherd the indefatigable soul of Christian–Jewish understanding in Britain and Bishop Charles Henderson, equally inexhaustible, faithful and loyal. It is not just the faith and the words and the actions of the person which move me, but the fact that they are rooted in a story which so obviously grounds their life and being. That faith is indisputably real and truthfully grounded in a book, in a story.

Leaving aside the hurt that I feel as a descendant of the Pharisees, I find the book, the story, the New Testament mysterious, challenging, sometimes familiar, sometimes strange, bewildering because it is at times familiar but not quite mine. Like the house next door. Like a coat that looks like mine, but as soon as I try it on I know it isn't and wonder why I thought it was. Which is not surprising because it isn't my book, my story, but my siblings'.

As I said in 'Making Theological Space', I believe that many Christians find in the life, death and resurrection of Jesus as described in the New Testament and in the tradition that flows from those events the fullest disclosure of the nature of God and God's will for them. Such faith involves no necessary error or illusion. Just as Sinai was the central episode of revelation, the covenantal moment for the Jewish people, so too, from my Jewish perspective, is Calvary for Christians and Christianity.

Although this conference and these papers are specifically focused on Jewish/Christian and, in particular, Jewish/Catholic relations, I want to add a footnote, a brief note of extension.

In the book *Dialogue with a Difference*, Rabbi Norman Solomon reflects with extreme kindness and generosity on my 'Making Theological Space' essay.[21] He highlights a book called *Bustan el-Uqul* (*The Garden of Intellect*) by the twelfth-century Jewish Neoplatonist Nethanel Al-Fayyumi. I had not, as Norman knew full well, ever heard of the author or the book let alone read it and was deeply relieved – from the point of view of dented personal pride – to find that even the *Encyclopaedia Judaica* offered but a tiny entry for Nethanel. Solomon's point was this. According to Nethanel each nation receives from its prophet the revelation appropriate to it in the language that it speaks. Not only did Al-Fayyumi show every sign of recognizing Muhammad as a prophet but he also recognized that there were profound religious mysteries within the Qur'an. Solomon concluded,

> Tony's concept of revelation is certainly 'naturalistic'; his emphasis on the social context of religion corresponds to Nethanel's idea that each nation receives an appropriate revelation in its own language; his attitude to the New Testament is not unlike that of Nethanel to the Qur'an; and his concept of Jesus as the way to God for Christians is the counterpart of Nethanel's recognition of Muhammad's prophecy.

Solomon suggests that I have unwittingly reinvented Al-Fayyumi and applied him in richer form to Christianity. Perhaps it is not surprising that my precursor sprang from the medieval Muslim–Jewish world which was more open than its Christian–Jewish counterpart.

There is even something familiar in the way that Muhammad at first addresses the Jewish community with his teachings and only after that address has fallen on unresponsive ears does Islam become its own faith with its own independent, revelatory, covenantal core. Of course, there are profound differences between Jesus and Muhammad, one of which and not the least of which is that Jesus was a Jew.

When God commands Abraham to set out on his world-changing journey what follows is a series of related, connected but different revelatory, covenantal moments, in which three faiths are born and three related peoples are covenanted. Three Abrahamic faiths, three siblings – a sadly dysfunctional family to whose rivalries I shall shortly return.

However, it may be useful at this juncture to look briefly at two related aspects of the theme. I remember vividly the very first time that I acknowledged the New Testament as a book of revelation for Christians, as a document describing what I would characterize as a covenantal experience, and Christianity as a faith involving no necessary error or illusion. A Jewish friend, a gentle, scholarly man, a member of the group within which I was in dialogue, reacted with uncharacteristic anger and hostility. 'You are giving much too much away,' he protested. 'After two thousand years of untold suffering, after all the vicious stereotyping, demonization and persecution, there is much more repentance and restitution to be made before so much can be conceded.' I understand that objection and even experience a certain amount of guilt at 'letting the side down'. But, in the last analysis, theology is not improved by being tempered with political expediency.

A second colleague later chided me more gently, acknowledging revelation in the lives of individual Christians, but denying to the text and the events they portray that same quality. That too I understand. I still feel shocked at myself for giving such acknowledgment to a book which contains so much anti-Judaism, which has served as a proof text for expulsion, forcible conversion and murder. I am not sure that I gain much other than inviting criticism from every side by saying that there are also texts in the Hebrew Bible which I find repugnant. But texts that speak of revelation, whilst bearing the fingerprints of God, are written by human hands as well and are limited, flawed, partial, historically constrained, as are all human beings.[22]

The other issue to which I want to refer is the number of covenants about which I have been speaking. I am familiar with the debate in

Christian circles, which goes under the general heading of single or double covenant theory.[23] For my part, I am clear that there is a covenant with the Jewish people at Sinai, a covenant with the church at Calvary and a covenant with Islam at Mecca. There is also the first covenant with all humanity recalled in the rainbow. Is this the first of four covenants or are the latter three particular strands of the single, original covenant? I don't know the answer to that question and am not sure what the issues are which need unpacking before one could decide. Perhaps our discussion could help me with this particular question.

Now let me offer an interim résumé.

I am arguing that the best metaphor for the relationship between Judaism and Christianity (and Islam) is that of siblings. Each sibling owes its existence and identity to a founding, revelatory experience, depicted in its scriptures. Each revelation establishes a covenant for those who understand themselves to be part of the story, part of the people whose story the scriptures tell. Each revelation, each covenant, each sibling warrants the acceptance, respect and independent space that is every sibling's birthright.

I want now to explore one or two further thoughts which flow from this assertion.

First, I hope that I am not behaving, as one's sibling is often prone to behave by talking excessively my cherished language, from my limited perspective and not listening. Covenant is an enduring theme of Jewish theology and may well not be the best metaphor for a Catholic response. But I am stuck with my own language, think I understand the meaning of 'Testament' and trust that I have read sufficient Catholic theology to be fairly sure that the term 'covenant' is neither repugnant nor devoid of meaning to my sisters and brothers. Incidentally, I ran a computer check on the Qur'an and was interested to find just how many times the word 'covenant' appears in Islam's founding text. Not to mention Noah.

Secondly, I am worried that what I have done is to expropriate the Hebrew scriptures as the soul/sole possession of one sibling, when a second sibling views them as part of its story and a third sibling retells many of the same stories from a different perspective. Let me return to that concern a little later – though I suspect it is an area with which I will need your help in much the same way as over the number of covenants.

Let me tackle at this juncture a third problem. I hope that it is not an absurd instance of human arrogance to pose a question that I have heard from several Jews. If God had really intended a second revelation in Christ (whilst not wishing to invalidate the first revelation or invite Jews to throw in their lot with the people of the second revelation), why on earth would God have wanted to inflict so much pain and suffering on 'God's First Love'? It was hardly kind to set us up to remain faithful to Sinai, reject Calvary and experience the consequences which have led down a road of tears which I have no need to articulate further. I have to say that the question leaves me remarkably unshaken in affirming my thesis, perhaps because the two obvious alternative responses – Jews did miss the boat or Christianity is a huge mistake, seem profoundly, existentially untrue. But I would say this. There is a really curious passage in the book of Exodus, three verses, verses 9, 10 and 11 in chapter 24. They stick out like a sore thumb and all exponents of modern historical criticism deal with them simply by assigning them to 'a different tradition'. Having just been told that only Moses can approach God (and even Moses does not see God, but only experiences where God has been)[24] we suddenly find Moses, Aaron, Nadav, Avihu and seventy elders ascending, seeing God, seeing a pavement of sapphire and eating and drinking with God who, even so, does not raise his hand in disapproval. The passage carries with it the notion of *chutzpah*, of brazen daring, of forcing God's hand, of tearing aside the veil, of entering the Presence not entirely invited. It does indeed stick out like a sore thumb when compared with more familiar passages in which God is completely in control of the moment and the form and the content of revelation. But it really speaks to me. I don't normally quote George Steiner when I am thinking theologically but there is a remarkable passage in one of his essays which underscores this particular theme:

> God suffers gusts of murderous exasperation at the Jews, towards the people who have made Him a responsible party to history and to the grit of man's condition. He may not have wished to be involved; the people may have chosen Him, in the oasis at Kadesh, and thrust upon Him the labour of justice and right anger. It may have been the Jews who caught Him by the skirt, insisting on contact and dialogue. Perhaps before either God or living man was ready for proximity.[25]

It may well be that the picture of human beings as it were forcing the revelatory end, seizing the hem of God's skirt, ascending the mountain into the divine presence unbidden is more congenial to Jewish than to Catholic theology. But perhaps it is not an unacceptable Jewish arrogance to ask whether God had no qualms about, as it were, giving his only son in full knowledge of his son's fate.

Judaism and Christianity (and Islam) place great value on humility. If our texts and traditions are anything to go by, we would all agree with Shakespeare that 'nothing so becomes a man/As modest stillness and humility'.[26] Yet one of the things that strikes me about our two faiths which place such a high value on humility is how lacking in humility we have often been in the claims that we make for ourselves, our revelation, our covenant, our 'truth' – and how scornfully we have treated our sibling in our arrogance (and insecurity?).

I won't rehearse here the various texts that can be quoted to suggest that Judaism has contained more modest[27] tendencies since its early centuries. However, the book of Jonah is remarkable for many things, but the divine concern for the people of Nineveh who are not Jews and whose conversion is not sought is striking. The Torah itself recognizes the Jewish minority status as a fact of life and I do want to quote a passage from the eighteenth-century scholar Jacob Emden, if only to show that I am by no means the lone heretic I might seem!

> The founder of Christianity conferred a double blessing upon the world: on the one hand he strengthened the Torah of Moses, and emphasized its eternal obligatoriness. On the other hand he conferred favour upon the heathen in removing idolatry from them, imposing upon them stricter moral obligations than are contained in the Torah of Moses. There are many Christians of high qualities and excellent morals. Would that all Christians would live in conformity with their precepts! They are not enjoined, like the Israelites, to observe the laws of Moses, nor do they sin if they associate other beings with God in worshipping a triune God. They will receive a reward from God for having propagated a belief in Him among nations that never heard His name: for He looks into the heart.[28]

Nevertheless, there are all sorts of ways in which Jews and Judaism have been hostile to Christianity – from the inclusion of an additional blessing in the *tefilah*, the daily prayer, to refusing to discuss theological matters with Christians. Much stems from fear. Much is rooted in our painful historical experience.[29] But there is something of pride and haughtiness as well. Perhaps it is best understood in terms of the metaphor of lovers, a metaphor which immediately makes one think of the prophet Hosea, of his immensely powerful declaration:

I betroth you to Me forever.
I betroth you to Me with integrity and justice, with tenderness and
     love.
I betroth you to Me with faithfulness and you will know the Lord.[30]

Add to that, the traditional Jewish understanding of the Song of
Songs. In the midst of passion the rest of the world fades away into
nothing and all that exists is I and Thou, or, to put it another way, the
world of lovers is filmed in glorious technicolour and everything
around is mere black and white. Can there have been, could there
possibly be another love like ours? Such passion and devotion is
wonderful and admirable but such intensity is not forever and if it
becomes all consuming it becomes corrupted by hubris. Our two
stories are indeed wonderful, testimonies to the power of love. But
pride, particularly in the claims that have been made to the exclusivity
and superiority of that love, have tarnished it and, sadly, even
corrupted it and betrayed it. I am reminded of a Hasidic aphorism:
Take care of your own soul and another person's body but not of your
own body and another person's soul.[31]
     That great contemporary Jewish scholar Louis Jacobs has a very
revealing comment to make on the subject of humility. He writes:

On the deeper level, the notion is found, especially in Hasidism,
that humility is not the mere absence of pride. Rather it consists
not so much in thinking little of oneself as in not thinking of oneself
at all. When the Hasidim and other Jewish mystics speak of annihi-
lation [*bittul ha'yesh*, abnegation of the self], they are not thinking of
a conscious effort of the will. To try to nullify the self by calling
attention to it is bound to end in failure. Instead, the mystics tend to
suggest, the mind should be encouraged to overlook entirely all
considerations of both inferiority and superiority.[32]

All considerations of both inferiority and superiority. This is not to
suggest that siblings may not be constructively critical of each other.
Far from it, particularly since we are each not self-critical enough.
Why shouldn't doctrines and teaching be subjected to scrutiny
according to shared spiritual and ethical criteria? But claims to be
better, truer, superior, more loved are more than unkind, they lack all
humility and guarantee that the children of Abraham will continue to
disturb the peace of the world as only a dysfunctional family can.
Which takes us back to the theme of siblings. In 1986 the American
scholar Alan F. Segal published a book called *Rebecca's Children:*

Judaism and Christianity in the Roman World.[33] It was an avowedly controversial book, which ended with the following lines:

> In both Judaism and Christianity, the Torah, the national constitution of Judea, was the basis of historical being. Both attempted to preserve it after the collapse of national unity. The fact that they chose such different ways reflected their different social origins in the Judean state and presaged their later roles in history. Their different histories do not alter the fact of their birth as twins in the last years of Judean statehood. They are both truly Rebecca's children, but unlike Jacob and Esau, they have no need to dispute their birthright. It can belong to both of them together.[34]

Segal even had the courage and wit to preface the book with Genesis 25.23: 'Two nations are in your womb; and two people shall be separated from your bowels; one people shall be stronger than the other people and the elder shall serve the younger.'

I have some quibbles with Segal, but they are all at the point where metaphor cannot be stretched too far lest the subtlety of that to which the metaphor points destroys the useful clarity of the metaphor. For instance, I am not sure that twin is as helpful as sibling. Twin is often confused with identical twin and it is extremely unhelpful to think of Judaism and Christianity as identical. It brings with it quite unnecessary pressures and unrealistic expectations. Even sibling has its problems. The phrase 'the three Abrahamic faiths' says something extremely powerful and important whilst still allowing Islam to claim a different mother from either Judaism or Christianity. I am not convinced that the sum total of Jewish and Christian parenting is exactly the same but it doesn't seem useful or helpful to press that subtlety at this juncture.

Segal's central point, that Rabbinic Judaism and Christianity are siblings is absolutely crucial and enormously courageous from a Jewish standpoint. To continue the metaphor of parent and child to which Jews had become accustomed in previous decades was to perpetuate an unconscious polemic which is ultimately unhelpful and demeaning. But that brings us back to the problem that I alluded to earlier, namely, that one cannot simply say, however neat it would be, that the Hebrew Bible is the inheritance of Jews, the New Testament of Christians and the Qur'an of Islam. For Christians, as Segal takes pains to point out, see themselves as profoundly connected to the Old Testament and rightly claim it as their inheritance too. However, the primary Jewish revelation, that covenant with the Jewish people, the

Jewish Calvary or Jewish Mecca, Sinai lies at the heart of the Torah and of the Hebrew Bible.

And Jesus was a Jew. A remarkable Jew.

Perhaps that double complexity, unique to Jews and Christians, does not matter. Suffice to say that whilst we share much, not the least the importance of Sinai, the enduring sense of connection as Israel and the Jewishness of Jesus, we Jews can only ask that Christians remember that the Old Testament varies slightly in order and content from the Hebrew Bible and is often understood and interpreted in different ways. Metaphors can complicate as well as clarify. However, it may just be worth suggesting that Rabbinic Judaism, as it were, moved into the parental house. Which perhaps explains why the Jewish visit to the Christian house is subtly different in quality and feel from a Christian visit to the Jewish house.[35] But nothing detracts from the fact that we are siblings with all the closeness and intensity that accompany that relationship.

The God of Abraham and Sarah, Isaac and Rebecca, Jacob, Rachel and Leah is central to my life. I am convinced that she speaks Hebrew, weeps at the wickedness and suffering of his children, repeats again and again her demand for righteousness and invented chicken soup. This God is not the same as Christ or Allah. And yet, of course, I am also aware of the absurdity of speaking of God as the weeping, Hebrew-speaking inventor of chicken soup – it is just that I can neither think of God or approach God or understand what lies at the heart of our journey without the God of Abraham and Sarah. That great Jewish philosopher Maimonides[36] argued that there is nothing that one can say about God, one can only say what God is not. But that is too hard for me. In the Jewish kabbalistic tradition the counterpoint to my anthropomorphic familiarity is *Ein Sof*, the Without End which points to a recognition of an unnameable and unpossessable reality at the heart of the universe. We are unable to speak of God or approach God except in the language of our stories, our experience, our tradition. Yet both Judaism and Christianity have it in them to glimpse that which is true and real but which is without name or end and lies beyond the particular scriptures, myths and metaphors of our respective faiths.

A few days ago Daniel decided that he had earned a week's holiday. He handed me his season ticket and Miriam and I took a friend to the match. As soon as the match was over Miriam phoned Daniel on my mobile to tell him the score. The following day our friend told me how much he had enjoyed his debut in the Premier League. 'I also enjoyed Miriam's phone call to Daniel', he said. 'You probably didn't notice', he went on, 'at the end of the call she said, "Bye, Daniel, love you." I thought how nice that was.' I mentioned this to Miriam. She looked at me as if to say 'what's all the fuss about', and said, 'But I do love him. He's my brother.' As we Jews say: 'ken yehi ratzon'. May that be God's will for Jewish and Catholic siblings in the new Christian millennium.

And is not all true love founded on mutual respect and valuing, on the equality implicit in each knowing for certain that the other will be accepted for themselves? And does not the love between siblings provide a unique bond for working together in partnership? And does the good parent not avoid favouritism, valuing each sibling for who they are, providing them with the inner security to be both humble and confirming, and binding each in a covenant of love forever?

Notes

1. Gen. 22.8.
2. Gen. 27.22–29.
3. Friedrich Heer, *God's First Love: Christians and Jews over Two Thousand Years*, London: Weidenfeld and Nicolson, 1967.
4. Blessing recited by the father at the circumcision of his son.
5. See, for instance, Arnold Eisen, 'Covenant', in Arthur A. Cohen and Paul Mendes-Flohr, eds, *Contemporary Jewish Religious Thought*, New York: Free Press, 1988, p. 107.
6. See Gen. 9.20. I am indebted to Rabbi Professor Jonathan Magonet for this insight.
7. Gen. 9.9.
8. Gen. 9.12.
9. These go back to Mishnaic times and are traditionally enumerated as the prohibitions of idolatry, blasphemy, sexual sins, murder, theft, eating limbs torn from a live animal and the injunction to establish a legal system.
10. The reference here is to the Talmudic text in which it is suggested that God held Sinai over the heads of the Israelites in order to gain their agreement to the Covenant. I don't think that my equation of the weight with *mitzvot* is too much of a liberty.
11. Deut. 29.9–14. It is worth noting that the widely expressed traditional rabbinic understanding of 'those who are not here today' is that it refers to the descendants of those present and to proselytes.
12. Eisen, 'Covenant', pp. 108–9.
13. The classic text is the account of four rabbis who 'enter Pardes'. One dies, one goes mad, one becomes a heretic and only the fourth, Rabbi Akiva, emerges unscathed. See also Louis Jacobs, *The Jewish Mystics*, London: Kyle Cathie, 1990.
14. *Exod. R.* 2.9.

15. Elizabeth Barrett Browning, *Aurora Leigh*, Bk. vii.

16. The reference here is to the remarkable book by Arthur A. Cohen, *The Tremendum*, New York: Crossroad, 1981.

17. This is the standard accusation against forms of Judaism which stress autonomy but leave no scope for obligation. For Liberal or Progressive Judaism with obligation, see Eugene Borowitz, *Renewing the Covenant*, Philadelphia: JPSA, 1991; Tony Bayfield, *Sinai, Law and Responsible Autonomy*, London: RSGB, 1993.

18. For instance, the American scholar and teacher Rabbi Irving Greenberg, *Voluntary Covenant*, New York: National Jewish Resource Centre, 1982.

19. See my 'MANNA', *Manna* 63, Spring 1999.

20. Tony Bayfield and Marcus Braybrooke, eds., *Dialogue with a Difference*, London: SCM Press, 1992. See my introduction, pp. 3–7, and chapter 'Making Theological Space', pp. 15–28.

21. Norman Solomon, 'The Third Presence: Reflections on the Dialogue' in Bayfield and Braybrook, *Dialogue with a Difference*, pp. 151–3.

22. I hope that I am not being either offensive or unhelpful by utilizing an understanding of the nature of the text which may not be acceptable to some Jews and many Catholics.

23. I acknowledge particularly the stimulating writing in this area of my good Catholic friend Dr Gavin D'Costa.

24. The traditional Jewish understanding of Ex. 33.23.

25. George Steiner, 'A Kind of Survivor', in *Language and Science*, reproduced in George Steiner, *A Reader*, London: Penguin Books, 1984.

26. Shakespeare, *Henry V*, III. i. 3–4.

27. I am not sure whether it would have been more helpful or clearer to use the vogue term 'pluralist'.

28. Quoted in Louis Jacobs, *A Jewish Theology*, London: Darton, Longman and Todd, 1973 p. 286 f.

29. Whilst not wanting to be sidetracked into the details of the past, I would like to acknowledge briefly two things. First, both Jews and Christians should read and think about studies of the first and second Christian centuries. In, for instance, James D. G. Dunn's, *The Partings of the Ways*, London: SCM Press, 1991, I am struck both by the Jewish resentment of the new infant and the inevitability of the parting(s) on the four issues that Dunn sets out. Secondly, we must acknowledge the enormous influence of the imperial world into which Christianity was born on its self-perception and role. If Judaism had become the official religion of the Roman Empire, as it nearly did, who knows what might have happened between the siblings in subsequent centuries.

30. Ho. 2.21–22.

31. Menahem Mendel of Kotsk (1787–1859).

32. Louis Jacobs, *The Jewish Religion*, Oxford: Oxford University Press, 1995, p. 256.

33. Alan F. Segal, *Rebecca's Children: Judaism and Christianity in the Roman World*, Cambridge, MA: Harvard University Press, 1986.

34. ibid p 181.

35. Miriam, my younger daughter, adds this. 'Four people brought me up, my parents and my two older siblings. You are all part of me in a way that, perhaps, I am not part of you.'

36. Spain, twelfth century.

Discussant

– Joann Spillman

It is a privilege and a delight to respond to Rabbi Tony Bayfield's paper because it displays the author's depth of thought, generosity of spirit and lively sense of humour. I fear one rarely finds these qualities united in a single author! In the paper, Rabbi Bayfield suggests the use of two images that can provide both Jews and Christians with effective metaphors for understanding: the images of covenant and of siblings. In the course of his paper, Rabbi Bayfield invites us to explore these images and he asks whether the image of covenant works as well for Catholics as it does for Jews. He also takes notice of the debate among Christians engaged in the Jewish–Christian Dialogue over whether to affirm a single covenant shared by Jews and Christians or to affirm two, partner covenants. He asks for clarification of this issue and inquires what theological issues are at stake in this debate among Christian theologians. In the course of his paper, Rabbi Bayfield reminds Christians that, as they read and interpret their Old Testament, they should be cautious and remember that the Old Testament varies slightly in order and differs somewhat in content from the Hebrew Bible and is understood and interpreted by Jews and Christians in different ways.

In my discussion this morning, I wish to respond to Rabbi Bayfield's two proposals and also comment upon some of the issues that he raises in the course of his paper. First, his proposals: I enthusiastically endorse his suggestions to use the images of covenant and siblings because both are powerful metaphors, deeply rooted in the Jewish and Catholic religious imaginations. In answer to the question of whether covenant works as well for Catholics as for Jews, I can only reply in the affirmative. The image of covenant is prominent in both Testaments of the Christian Bible, is often used in the history of Christian doctrine, appears frequently in Christian prayers and liturgy – especially Catholic liturgy, and is prominent in recent Church documents on Catholic–Jewish relations.

I affirm Rabbi Bayfield's proposals with admiration and gratitude. In light of the long, sad history of Christian anti-Judaism, they are especially generous and courageous. I am also pleased to affirm these images because both can be gender inclusive. While covenant may be problematic because the sign of covenant is circumcision, it can be an inclusive image. 'Siblings' is unquestionably inclusive of women and men. Women are often relegated to the fringes of discussions of theology, even within the Jewish–Christian dialogue, and it is a pleasure to see images that include women.

However, there are some problems with both images. For Jews and Christians, siblings are bound to bring to mind the many biblical stories of sibling conflict, from Cain and Abel forward. The image of covenant also presents challenges because of its ambiguity. For years I have been studying Christian and Jewish theologians who use the term 'covenant' and I find myself often puzzled by what the word means and implies. Since I know far more about Christian theology than Jewish theology, I will focus my observations on Christian writers. I have found that various Christian theologians use the term 'covenant' in differing ways. Even though their uses of the term may be similar, there are clearly pluralities of Christian understandings of covenant. While the term covenant is frequently used in Christian theology, it never became a standard category in theology nor did it become a technical term with a precise meaning. Thus one can find a doctrine of creation, sin or redemption in virtually all systematic/constructive Christian theologies, but one does not find a corresponding doctrine of covenant in most such theologies. While one can find entries for 'creation', 'sin,' and 'redemption' in virtually all dictionaries of Christian theology, one does not usually find an entry for 'covenant'.

While I know far less about Jewish theology than Christian theology, what I have read leads me to suspect that there is also a plurality of meanings of covenant in Jewish theology.

Moreover, when Jews and Christians use the term, they do so in the context of different religious traditions. This makes it likely that there are important differences between the Jewish understandings of covenant and the Christian understandings. So when Jews and Christians affirm a single shared covenant or two partner covenants, they are likely to be affirming different claims. This is to be expected since both groups of theologians are making their affirmations *from within* their two – often, quite different – faith communities.

In the course of his paper, Rabbi Bayfield took notice of the Christian debate over the single and double covenant perspectives and wondered what theological issues are at stake in this debate.[1] I will venture a brief response to his question. I believe that debate arises primarily because Christians are divided over how best to express their appreciation of their biblical heritage, especially as found in the teachings of Paul. Theologians of recognition[2] are also divided over whether to stress the continuity and shared heritage of Judaism and Christianity (best captured by the image of one covenant) or to stress the distinctiveness and uniqueness of each faith tradition (best rendered by the image of two covenants).

Rabbi Bayfield cautions his Christian conversationalists to be careful when interpreting the Old Testament. He reminds us that the Old Testament differs slightly in order and (for Catholic and Orthodox Christians) in content from the Jewish Bible. I endorse his warning and wish to reinforce it. Jews and Christians read their common texts quite differently. They identify different passages and themes as most important and find different emphases in the shared stories. Both Jews and Christians read the Hebrew scriptures while 'looking forward', that is they read with the help of and even through the eyes of later developments. Jews look forward to the Talmud and later developments: Christians look forward to Christ and later developments. It is sometimes the case that Jews and Christians read their shared scripture so differently that it is hard to recognize the common text.

In connection with this point, may I suggest the recent book by the late Paul van Buren, *According to the Scriptures?*[3] There is much in this book that is not of interest to us here and much that is controversial. I direct your attention, however, to van Buren's claim that Christians developed their approach to the Hebrew scripture as they fashioned their early faith statements. Van Buren holds that the early *kerygma* and the Old Testament (the Hebrew scriptures as interpreted by Christians) emerged together. As van Buren phrases it, the 'discovery of the gospel' and the 'invention of the Old Testament' occurred together. Thus, from the beginning of Christianity, the Christian reading of the Old Testament is just that – a Christian reading. Honesty demands that Christians make a very clear distinction between the Old Testament and the Jewish Bible.

As Rabbi Bayfield developed his paper, he continually referred not only to the Jewish–Catholic dialogue but also to the Jewish–Christian dialogue. Indeed he placed the Jewish–Catholic dialogue within the larger Jewish–Christian dialogue. I appreciate his insight, because the need to build bridges of understanding with Judaism is an imperative shared by Catholics and other Christians. Moreover there are important issues in the Jewish–Protestant dialogue and Jewish–Orthodox dialogue which do not arise for Catholics. In this area, as in others, I respond to Rabbi Bayfield's essay with gratitude and delight.

Notes

1. Readers interested in this debate will find comprehensive discussions of it in the works of John Pawlikowski including: *What Are They Saying about Christian–Jewish Relations?*, New York: Paulist Press, 1980, *Christ in the Light of the Christian–Jewish Dialogue*, New York: Paulist Press, 1982. *Jesus and the Theology of Israel*, Wilmington, DE: Michael Glazier, 1989, and 'Single or Double Covenant?: Contemporary Perspectives', *Peace, in Deed: Essays in Honor of Harry James Cargas*, ed. Zev Garber and Richard Libowitz, Atlanta, GA: Scholars Press, 1988. Among theologians championing the one-covenant approach are Monika Hellwig, A. Roy Eckardt and Norbert Lofink; among those championing the two-covenant perspective are James Parkes, Rosemary Ruether and John Pawlikowski. While he places the category of Covenant at the centre of his theology, Paul M. van Buren's position is too complex to place in either group. In his trilogy, *A Theology of the Jewish–Christian Reality*, New York: Seabury Press, 1980, 1983, 1988, he tended toward the one-covenant model in Vol. I and toward the two-covenant model in Vol. III.
2. I propose 'theology of recognition' as a convenient designation for that Christian theology that recognizes the enduring role of Judaism in God's plan for salvation and thus sees Judaism as genuinely revelatory and salvific. As of now, there is no generally accepted name for this type of Christian theology. See my 'The Image of Covenant in Christian Understandings of Judaism', *Journal of Ecumenical Studies*, Winter, 1998, p. 64, for the proposal to use the term 'theology of recognition'.
3. Paul M. van Buren, *According to the Scriptures: The Origins of the Gospel and of the Church's Old Testament*, Grand Rapids: Eerdmans, 1998.

B. Partnership in Covenant

– Clemens Thoma

Kinship between Jews and Christians must be recalled. After a lot of misunderstandings, disagreements and accusations in past times Jews and Christians must be conscious of their common ground, the covenant. We Christians must attempt to prove that our identity is based on the vocation of God into the neighbourhood of the people of the first covenant. We Christians have to acknowledge that we belong to the infinite God and that he has invited us to be a partner – in addition to the Jewish people – and that Christ is our representative. Jesus the Jew is the mediator of the peoples of the world in the face of the Jewish people. But nearly until now the Jewish-Christian covenant-community was an unfortunate enterprise. The main reasons: anti-Semitism and partially anti-Christianism. So we have to reconsider the covenant of God with Israel. We have to reconceptualize the religious world.

Before we venture near such difficult questions, first we should shortly outline the meaning of 'covenant' and 'partnership' in the Jewish and Christian–Jewish contexts and then illustrate our definitions with examples which Jewish historical tradition values as fundamentally important for relations with non-Jewish religions and ethnic groups. Hereafter, we shall be able to see a light trace which will bring us nearer to an answer. First of all, it must be emphasized that the point is to build a 'bridge theology which maintains the theological integrity and validity of both religious traditions'.[1]

Covenant

Covenant (*b'rit*, *diathêkê*, *foedus*, *pactum*, *Bund*) is an expression of mysterious partnership between God and the people of Israel. God is the founder, the one who calls, Israel is the responding partner.

According to Daniel 11.28–30, the acknowledgement of the *b'rit kodesh*, the covenant of sacredness, means fidelity to Israel's jeopardized religion. The covenant of sacredness is the sign God sets when Jews resist seductions and menaces of Gentile polytheists and rulers. He who keeps and saves the covenant of sacredness in obedience through times of affliction belongs to Israel. We cannot do without the basic concept of covenant if we want to characterize Judaism under a religious and social viewpoint. The Hebrew Bible deals with God as a partner, on one side, and the people of Israel or an especially chosen person, on the other side. The covenant as an agreement between God and Israel or a representative of Israel contains the election he made of the Jewish people and its declaration of belief in him; God makes promises, and the people is bound to keep the commandments.

The solemn words of the covenant contracted in Deuteronomy 26.16–19 apply to every book of the Old Testament:

This day the Lord your God commands you these statutes and ordinances. You shall therefore be careful to do them with all your heart and with all your soul. You have declared this day concerning the Lord that he is your God and that you will walk in his ways, and keep his statutes and his commandments and his ordinances and will obey his voice. And the Lord has declared this day concerning you that you are a people for his own possession, as he has promised you and that you are to keep all his commandments, that he will set you high above all nations that he has made, in praise and in fame and in honour and that you shall be a people holy to the Lord your God.

Every covenant contracted between God and Israel absolutely requires the people to recognize the Lord as its king. God is Israel's ruler and partner. The obedient, hopeful person is the partner God addresses. This point is especially emphasized in connection with the Sinai covenant, the most important one in Jewish religious tradition. As an advance concession, God overcame Israel's enemies and saved the Israelites (Ex. 14–15). To bring its own contribution to the covenant, Israel acknowledged God's lordship and promised him fidelity: 'All that the Lord has spoken we will do and we will be obedient' (Ex. 19.8; 24.3–7).

Before the congregation of the people of Israel contracted its covenant with God on Mount Sinai, two other covenants were in force. They were important, not only for the contracting parties, but also for humanity's future at large. I mean God's covenants with Noah (Gen. 9.8–17) and with Abraham (Gen. 15 and 17).

Noah's covenant

Noah's covenant (Gen. 9.8–17) is in force for every human being. God vouches for the continuance of life on earth. People shall multiply, respect human beings and restrain from murdering and from shedding human blood. Later on, Noah's seven commandments were deduced from his covenant. They suit biblical expectations: you shall not worship idols, blaspheme, shed blood, carry on illicit sexual relations, rob, or eat a limb torn from any living animal. The positive (seventh) commandment requires an orderly justice administration to be set up.[2] Noah's covenant is meant for Israel and for the rest of the human race. It ties people and religions together. It also suggests that special elections and separations are not necessarily combined with obliging covenants. What is more, the whole of humanity is admonished to keep with the creator a covenant of at least seven points which especially aim to ban grave menaces to other persons, the breakdown of legal systems and perverse worship of God. Noah's covenant therefore binds Jews and Christians and has to be discussed between them as partners.

Abraham's covenant

God's covenant contracted with Abraham can be seen from some viewpoints as the concentration of all biblical covenants. Ben Sirah's wording (Ecclus. 44.19–21) points to such an interpretation:

> Abraham was the great father of a multitude of nations and no one has been found like him in glory. He kept the law of the Most High and was taken into covenant with him. He established the covenant in his flesh and when he was tested he was found faithful. Therefore the Lord assured him by an oath that the nations would be blessed through his posterity, that he would multiply him like the dust of the earth and exalt his posterity like the stars and cause them to inherit from sea to sea and from the river to the ends of the earth.

According to this view, God's covenant with Abraham is a binding agreement which rests on both partners' probation and hope. To be sure, it is not confined to them. On the contrary, it becomes a graceful gift to an unlimited number of descendents who are born into it. Its

ray of hope affects many more people. Humanity at large is entitled to
say or to presume it is involved in Abraham's covenant, because only
the whole human race is so numerous that it can be compared to 'the
dust of the earth' and 'the stars'. Conversely, if somebody were to
assert that a person does not form part of Abraham's covenant, then
he would defame God's generosity and magnanimity. Therefore,
Abraham's covenant also belongs to Jewish–Christian dialogue.

Different covenants

Many specialists have already added up the number of biblical
covenants with the forefathers, namely, the patriarchs, Moses, David,
the prophets and the people of Israel. According to a passage from the
Talmud (*b. Sot.* 37a–b), it is not necessary to count precisely the
number of covenants. The author explains Deuteronomy, and
especially its twenty-seventh chapter, in which 'all Israel' is ordered
'to declare with a loud voice' certain blessings and curses. This
liturgical act exhorts the people of Israel to 'hear the statutes and the
ordinances, which I [= God] speak in your hearing this day, [and to]
learn them and be careful to do them' (Deut. 5.1). By reason of the
numerical values of these passages and of other ones (for instance
Deut. 28.64), the Talmud deduces that the Bible contains forty-eight
covenants. Furthermore, it holds the view that God on Mount Sinai
spoke of the covenants in general terms, whereas he discussed their
details, and the question of additional covenants, with Moses in the
tabernacle of covenant. In this respect, Rabbi Akiva says: 'General
and particular truths were spoken on Mount Sinai, repeated in the
tabernacle of covenant, and tripled in the Plains of Moab. The Torah
therefore does not contain any mizwa (prescription) which was not
contracted upon by forty-eight covenants' (*b. Sot.* 37b).

   This Talmudic passage offers some possibilities of internal Jewish
and Jewish–Christian dialogue. God has contracted many covenants
with people. One of them shines – occasionally, at least – in each
person who keeps a Torah-prescribed *mitzvah*. God's covenant
concerns everyone who answers it with 'yes', and everyone who does
something this covenant stipulates. This is a path of hope for
Christians for their own creed as well. In the first chapter of
II Corinthians, Paul describes Christ as the human guarantee that
God shows himself and that his revelation includes *mitzvot*:

   As surely as God is faithful, our word to you has not been Yes and
   No. For the Son of God, Jesus Christ, whom we preached among

you . . . was not Yes and No; but in him is always Yes. For all the promises of God find their Yes in him. That is why we utter the Amen through him, to the glory of God. But it is God who establishes us with you in Christ and has commissioned us. He has put his seal upon us and given us his Spirit in our hearts as a guarantee. (II Cor. 1.18–22)

Equally important is Galatians 4.4–5: 'When the time had fully come, God sent forth his Son, born of woman, born under the law, to redeem those who were under the law, so that we might receive adoption as sons.' Every covenant is a divine 'yes' and mysteriously happens together with a human 'yes'. God's 'yes', as well as 'amen' as its human echo, are indispensable expressions of loyalty to the Lord as the source of the covenants. Still more important is the Talmudic statement that there are many covenants and that a new one comes into being every time a Torah-prescribed *mitzvah* is kept.

You cannot conceive Christianity unless you hold that Christ did observe Jewish law. This does not mean that Christians are no longer obligated by any commandment of the Old Testament. They are just exempt from such prescriptions as circumcision and Temple sacrifice. It is essential for the Christian creed that Jesus kept the whole Jewish law vicariously for humanity at large and so became the representative of Jewry for Gentiles as well. Christians have to bear in mind that he was a law-abiding Jew. It is equally important to remember the Jewish and Christian doctrine that God's covenants with the forefathers, Israel, and the nations of the world can be multiplied.

Partnership

It is a fundamental Jewish and Christian dogma that we and the whole creation have been made in God's image: Genesis 1.26–27 and 5.1; II Cor. 3.18; James 3.9. Hence the ideal of *imitatio Dei*. In this respect, one usually quotes a rabbinical comment to Deuteronomy 11.22 (*Sifre* 49):

God is called merciful – be merciful, too! The Holy One, blessed be He, is called gracious – be gracious, too! As it says: 'The Lord is gracious and merciful' (Ps. 145.8) . . . God is called righteous, as it says: 'The Lord is righteous; he loves righteous deeds' (Ps. 11.7) – be righteous, too! God is called merciful, as it says: 'I am merciful, says the Lord' (Jer. 3.12) – be merciful, too! That is why it says: 'Every one who is called by my name, whom I created for my glory' (Isa. 43.7).

And it says: 'The Lord has made everything for its purpose' (Prov. 16.4).

The Rabbis used to read many Torah statements as exhortations to imitate God. They understood covenant as a partnership between God and Israel that imposed on both sides corresponding duties. God is ready to cooperate with Israel; this is emphasized in connection with Deuteronomy 7.12: 'The Lord your God will keep with you the covenant and the steadfast love which he swore to your fathers to keep'. Today, we call this cooperation between God and human beings 'covenantal nomism'.[3]

Members of God's people are therefore his active substitutes and partners. On his behalf and as his representatives, they work for one another and against every form of idolatry and misanthropy. The Torah as a binding document defines each party's keeping of his agreements and duties.

In the days of the Temple, the high priest had to prepare for a long time with his brethren before he held the solemn ritual on the Day of Atonement. During the whole service, he understood himself as a substitute and messenger (*shaliach*), not only of God, but also of certified experts in law and tradition (*b. Yom.* 19a–b; *b. Ned.* 35b; *b. Qid.* 23b). On behalf of both authorities, he confessed sins as follows:

O Lord! I have sinned before thee, I and my house. O Lord! Forgive the wrongdoings, the transgressions, the sins which I have committed and transgressed and sinned before thee, I and my house! As it is written in the Torah of Moses thy servant: 'For on this day shall atonement be made for you, to cleanse you; from all your sins shall you be clean before the Lord' (Lev. 16.30). And they answered him: Blessed be the name of his glorious kingdom for ever and ever! (*m. Yom.* 3.8; *b. Yom* 35b)

This ritual throws light upon the meaning and connection of the way Judaism understands offices. The human office-bearers – high priest, priest, Bible exegetes and the people of Israel – are God's representatives; on his behalf, they certify remission of sins and they praise the Lord. He always acts together with persons. Jews and Christians can find here matters relevant to a great many theological and historical colloquies. Let me point to mercy as a central item. Mercy, forgiveness and turning to the Lord are parts of the covenant. Every office-bearer is in God's service. So holds the New Testament as well; it says in Romans 11.27: 'And this will be my covenant with them when I take away their sins.' This sentence bases itself on at least four passages of the Old Testament: Isa. 27.9, Isa. 59.20–21, Jer. 31.33–34 and Ps. 14.7. The earthly purpose of the covenant is the 'tikkun ha-olam', the repair and perfection of the world and of its inhabitants.

Attractive communities

Communities of covenant have a great attraction and influence on persons who are in doubt or whose religious practices lack shape and who hope to experience the *b'rit* with God and its human resonance.

Converts

According to biblical tradition, the peoples of the world often menace Israel, but the Chosen People will overcome them with God's help; converts will join Israel and many representatives of the Gentile nations will be friendly to it. This hope is based on a most important prophecy. In Isaiah 49.6, God says to Israel: 'it is too light a thing that you should be my servant [just] to raise up the tribes of Jacob and to restore the preserved of Israel. I will give you as a light to the nations, that my salvation may reach to the ends of the earth.' In the last days, according to Ben Sira 48.10, Elijah's task will be 'to turn the heart of the father to the son and to restore the tribes of Jacob'. In Old Testament times, it was hoped that Israel would grow and become stronger as well as more attractive for all nations of the world.

According to rabbinical tradition, Jethro's example shows how converts can bring luck to Israel. The Torah writes (Ex. 18.1): 'Jethro, the priest of Midian, father-in-law of Moses, heard of all that God had done for Moses and for Israel his people, how the Lord had brought Israel out of Egypt.' *Midrash Shemot Rabbah* 27.3 explains this passage with the following parable:

> A bird flew away from a hunter and alighted on a king's statue. This excited the hunter's admiration. He shouted at the bird: 'What a wonderful flight you have performed!' Something similar happened to Balaam, when he shouted enthusiastically at Jethro: 'Enduring is your dwelling place and your nest is set in the rock' (Num. 24.21).

The 'nest in the rock' means Israel under the protection of God whom the Bible calls 'the Rock'. This parable describes Jethro, the father-in-law of Moses, as the archetype and model of all converts to

Judaism. He heard of the Lord's wonders for the benefits of Jews as well as of Baalam's curses. Jewish tradition explains Jethro's conversion to Judaism as a flight from a threatening ruin to God's protecting presence. Converting means a flight from hostile attacks as a result of divine guidance. The Jethro parable encourages conversion amongst people who are attracted to it: it stimulates Jews to a firm faith.

The Rabbis' exegesis sees Pharaoh's daughter as a convert as well: *b. Megillah* 13a reports that she opposed the idols of her father's house and rescued little Moses from the Nile, so that 'he became her son' (Ex. 2.10). According to several Jewish traditions, one can consider as Jews persons who bring about a future for the Jewish people or rescue Jews from death and undoing.[4] Conversion to Judaism has many forms and aspects. Non-Jewish persons who save Jews are Jews. They are the successors of Pharaoh's daughter: she became a Jewish person by rescuing the child Moses.

God's presence

Judaism and Christianity can both rouse hope in the human heart. For instance, Ezekiel 37.26–28 describes as follows God's attitude towards the reunified tribes of Israel and Judah:

> I will make a covenant of peace with them; it shall be an everlasting covenant with them; and I will bless them and multiply them, and will set my sanctuary in the midst of them for evermore. My dwelling place shall be with them; and I will be their God, and they will be my people. Then the nations will know that I the Lord sanctify Israel, when my sanctuary is in the midst of them for evermore.

According to this passage, as well as many other ones, the people of Israel is an exemplarily blessed and peacemaking body and the Lord dwells in its very midst and core. This community which includes both him and a human group has attracted and still attracts many people.

Christianity, too, appeals to lonely and searching men and women. The New Testament reports a saying of Jesus which points in the same direction (Matt. 11.28–30):

> Come to me, all who labour and are heavy laden, and I will give you rest. Take my yoke upon you, and learn from me; for I am gentle

and lowly in heart, and you will find rest for your souls. For my yoke is easy, and my burden is light.

According to the last phrase of the Gospel of Matthew the resurrected Christ is with his Jewish and non-Jewish disciples 'always, to the close of the age' (Matt. 28.20). Judaism and Christianity as bodies, each one along its own lines, both testify to God's gracious, forgiving presence. A dialogue between Jews and Christians about religious experiences in this respect would help develop the inner structure of both groups.

Final remarks

Pope John Paul II deposited on 26 March 2000 at the Western Wall of the Jerusalem Temple a piece of paper. The content of this paper is:

> God of our fathers, you chose Abraham and his descendants to bring your Name to the Nations: We are deeply saddened by the behaviour of those who in the course of history have caused these children of yours to suffer, and asking your forgiveness, we wish to commit ourselves to genuine brotherhood with the people of the Covenant. We ask this through Christ our Lord.

With this prayer and with this gesture the Pope emphasized especially four points: (1) the Western Wall of the Temple is a place of God's special presence, of the *Shekhinah*; (2) the Pope witnesses the Covenant between God and the Jewish people; (3) the Pope professes that the God of Israel, the God of the Covenant, is the God who grants our prayers; (4) and the Pope appeals to Christians to recall the kinship with the Jewish people. Christians should acknowledge and celebrate the bond between Jews and Christians.

Not only at the Western Wall of the Temple but also during his whole journey through the Near Orient the Pope repeated again and again his faith in the God of Israel as the God of the covenant. His main religious message was that the covenant is the basis of peace and friendship.

The conference of the Swiss Bishops in April 2000 published a declaration in which the Bishops declared that, the *b'rit* of God with the Jewish people is a Christian article of faith, a Catholic Creed. If we don't accept this *b'rit* we cannot prevent anti-Semitism now and in the future. Some Swiss Catholic leaders are planning a sort of national council, to acknowledge and to confirm this article of Christian faith.[5]

I hope my observations will stimulate the dialogue between Jews and Christians. We must talk together about our partnership with God. Our Jewish partners live in his covenant with Israel. Christ has committed his disciples and followers to that alliance. It is important to be aware that there is a valid partnership between God and the human contracting parties. But the primary concern is probably to arouse again consciousness of God's presence in the midst of all those communities which have undeservedly and for nothing (*hinnam*) come by grace only into his covenant.

Notes

1. Michael B. McGarry, *Christology after Auschwitz*, New York: Paulist Press, 1977, p. 61f.; Michael Siegner, 'One Covenant or Two: Can we Sing a New Song?', in John T. Pawlikowski and Hayim Gorem Perelmuter (eds), *Reinterpreting Revelation and Tradition: Jews and Christians in Conversation*, Franklin WI: Sheed & Warch, 2000, pp. 3–23; Friedrich Avemarie, *Tora und Leben, Untersuchungen zur Heilsbedeutung der Tora in der frühen rabbinischen Literatur*, Tübingen: Mohr/Siebeck, 1996, 575 f.
2. See David Flusser, 'Noachitische Gebote: Judentum' *Theologische Realenzyclopedie* eds Gerhard Krause, Gerhard Müller, Berlin, 1976, pp. 582–5; in the New Testament: Acts. 15.19 f.; in the early church: *Did.* 6.1–3.
3. Following Ed. P. Sanders, *Paul and Palestinian Judaism: A Comparison of Patterns of Religion*, London: SCM Press, 1977.
4. See Clemens Thoma, *Theologie jüdisch–christlicher Begegnung: Das Messiasprojekt*, Augsburg: Pattloch Verlag, p. 55 f.
5. Erklärung der Schweizer Bischofskonferenz zum Verhalten der katholischen Kirche der Schweiz zum jüdischen Volk während des Zweiten Weltkrieges, Fribourg, 14 April 2000.

Discussant

– Tovia Ben-Chorin

1. Professor Thoma's paper, 'Partnership in Covenant', makes possible an existential dialogue based on religious experience, Jewish and Christian, since it underlines the covenantal relationship between the creator and the created. That attribute – creator – which I see as a fundamental element in that covenantal relationship from a Jewish point of view is missing in the paper. This fact does not in any way detract from the excellent presentation, well founded on Jewish and Christian sources. The obvious question is: does the covenantal relationship, which begins vertically, develop, by definition, horizontally? Does it develop between one group of believers (religion) and another group of believers (religion)?

   The last prophet in the Hebrew Bible, who doesn't actually have a name but is called simply My Messenger (Malachi), recognizes that the One God of Israel can be worshipped and recognized by non-Jews, that is to say, those who are within the Noachide Covenant. 'For from where the sun rises to where it sets, My name is honoured among the nations, and everywhere incense and pure oblation are offered to My name; for My name is honoured among the nations – said the Lord of Hosts' (1.11).

2. In the covenantal situations recorded in the Hebrew Bible, starting with Noah, and ending with the renewed covenantal relationship to be, with Israel (Jer. 31), the initiative always emanates from God, but, as I humbly believe, represents not only God's *hesed* (grace) towards man but, in the words of Abraham Heschel, 'God in search of man'. The covenant is made with Abraham, the first believer in God and the first patriarch of Israel, but also *Av Hamon Goyim*, the father of many nations (Gen. 17.4 and 5). (This promise is given to him after the birth of Ishmael but before his name-change from Abram to Abraham.)

3. The covenantal relationship is not always a situation of choice but,

as the Rabbis acknowledged, may well involve compulsion. As the Talmud in *Shabbat* 88a describes it, the Almighty hung the mountain of Sinai over the Israelites like a pail and said to them, 'if you accept the Torah, it is a good thing and if not, this place will be your grave'. Moreover, only the individual can break away from the Covenant (Deut. 30); the group is committed forever. Does Christianity experience a similar dialectic?

4. Shared scripture and a long historical involvement, not always by choice, has forced Jews and Christians into a *yachdav* (together) relationship, best but not only described by Amos in 3.3: 'Do two walk together unless they have been destined (to do so)?'

5. As a religio-social system, Judaism and Christianity contain within themselves a repentance mechanism which demands self-criticism, continuing evaluation, acknowledgment of failure and sin and, finally, atonement and rebuilding. This is a response to a world in which a new idol worship endangers man's existence as a human being created in the image of God. Globalization, on the sole basis of economics – profits and losses – does not leave space for prophetic vision or human needs. We, the representatives of the Covenantal Faith – *Yirei Adonai* (those who hold God in respect) – we, the Children of Abraham (which of course includes Islam), must ensure that God's image remains within the human community.

Discussion recorder

– Andrew Goldstein

Rabbi Tony Bayfield added to his paper: he is often asked why as a rabbi should he spend so much time on Jewish–Christian dialogue? He believed faith and religion was at the heart of existence. Yet differences, pride and arrogance, lack of humility had all too often led one religion to claim superiority over others, had led to conflict and wars. This must make God weep. He reiterated the theme, developed in his paper, of Christians and Jews being siblings . . . and pointed to the story of Esau and Jacob being reconciled – 'and he kissed him and they wept' – but going their separate ways. We need to kiss and weep and move on in partnership.

Professor Dr Clemens Thoma explored the nature of the covenant and the covenant of God with Israel. He quoted David Flusser who explored the innermost motive of Paul . . . and concluded that Paul's motive was to bring the covenant to the 'nations' in response to Isaiah's (49.6) call that Israel become a 'light to the nations'. Paul gathered the nations into the covenant of Israel. The Noachide covenant had originally united all peoples of the world, and Pope John Paul II's recent letter in the Western Wall went further, for there he talked of 'the people of the covenant' uniting Jews and Catholics in the same covenant. A recent statement by Swiss Bishops had united Jews and Christians in the same covenant, thus anti-Semitism was a sin. Ben Sirah (44.19–21) had long ago called Abraham 'the great father of all nations' . . . we are all united as the children of Abraham (presumably thus extending to Muslims).

Professor Joann Spillman, commenting on Rabbi Bayfield's paper, endorsed the metaphor of 'siblings' and then queried the effectiveness of the concept of covenant for Jews and Catholics . . . and concluded it was deeply relevant. There are many references to covenant in Catholic writings. In fact she had over 800 Christian documents exploring covenant and it was even more prominent in Catholic writings than in Protestant. She questioned whether there was a single or double covenant.

Rabbi Tovia Ben-Chorin started by dedicating his thoughts to his late father who had been involved in dialogue long before it was popular. Commenting on Professor Thoma's paper, Rabbi Ben-Chorin thought that the concept of 'creator' was missing in the paper. He thought it easier to think of God as creator than imagining God's glory. He thought there was no problem for Jews in seeing God making a covenant with Jews and with Christians, but harder to see Jews and Christians within the same covenant. He did point to various verses in the Hebrew Bible that see God as being the God of all people (e.g. Mal. 1.11 – 'from where the sun rises to where the sun sets My name is to be praised . . .'). He then urged us to consider Jeremiah 31 – it was one thing to muse on covenants past, but we need to consider Jeremiah's idea of a future covenant with all peoples.

In the discussion that followed, Professor Elliot Dorff commended the sibling metaphor . . . but said that once it had been applied to children, now we are challenged to love each other as adults. Rabbi David Rosen said Jews had to ask themselves if they can seriously consider Christians as part of Israel. Christians must ask if they believe that Jews finally have an equal covenantal relationship with God: a Jew can get into Heaven, but is the best they can hope for grade 1B? Dr Eugene Fisher thought the word covenant should be seen as a verb not a noun: it was an on-going concept, not just an event in the past. He thought the best metaphor for the relationship of Jews and Christians was of root and branch. The Old Testament biblical inheritance was the root, and Judaism and Christianity two branches growing from it (he was not sure how Islam fitted into this metaphor).

Dr Guy Stroumsa thought that siblings were a good way of describing the relationship, but Jews had to cope with a new way of thinking. Increasingly historians talk of two religions developing at the same time, that is, post-70CE: Rabbinic Judaism and Patristic Christianity (and maybe also Gnosticism). Jews think they are direct inheritors of the Pharisees, whereas Rabbinic Judaism, developing after the sea-change of the destruction of the Temple, was a new religion.

Revd Dr John Pawlikowski also posited this theory of co-emergence and said it took well over a century for the process of separation of the two religions to take place. This new concept challenges the traditional Christian evangelical stance, the belief that salvation comes only through Jesus Christ. Rabbi Mark Solomon accepted the co-emergent view and added that Rabbinic Judaism may have been greatly effected and affected by emerging Christianity. He also questioned the place of covenant in Judaism. It may have been found in the Bible, and now we are discussing the concept again, but, he argued, in between Jews rarely discussed the idea. Instead *mitzvot* and Torah were the important concepts – doing God's will, not debating the nature of the relationship. The Noachide Covenant was not much debated in rabbinic literature and was not a concept of which we could nowadays be proud.

Rabbi Elizabeth Sarah also agreed that Judaism and Christianity were born at the same time and noted the times: Judaism was born in the aftermath of great disaster amidst despair at the loss of the Temple, and its development was soon hampered by the conversion of the Roman Empire to Christianity. Dr Susannah Heschel also accepted this idea: we now must admit that Judaism was shaped by emergent Christianity and go beyond the nineteenth century, well-meaning notion that Christianity is a branch of Judaism.

How do we each understand chosenness and election? What place does each faith leave for the other – and, indeed, for others? How do we see our own 'specialness' and that of the other?

C. Understanding Election

– Elliot Dorff

The biblical doctrine that God chose Israel has been a prevailing theme in Jews' self-image, giving them both a sense of divine favour and divine mission. At the same time, that doctrine has motivated hatred of Jews, for non-Jews see the doctrine of the Chosen People as the ultimate expression of Jewish cliquishness and chauvinism, and, as such, it has certainly been an obstacle to mutual understanding and good relations between Jews and non-Jews. How can Jews be honest to themselves and their own tradition on this matter and yet create good relations with people of other faiths?

While this is an obvious problem for us now, it should be noted that it was not much of a problem to Jews living in societies not structured by the principles of the Enlightenment. That includes the majority of the world's Jewish population until 1945. In such societies, Jews were second-class citizens, at best, and they were treated to gentile hostility, injustice, and even rape, pillage and death. Under such conditions, Jews did not have to go very far to see themselves as morally superior to those among whom they lived, and the doctrine of God's election of Israel served to confirm their impression. We were living in exile and in depressed circumstances 'because of our sins', as the High Holyday liturgy affirms, but God himself proclaims in the Torah that even when he is most angry with us, He will ultimately take us back:

> And yet for all that, when they are in the land of their enemies, I will not reject them, neither will I abhor them, to destroy them utterly and to break My covenant with them; for I am the Lord their God. But I will for their sakes remember the covenant of their ancestors, whom I brought forth out of the land of Egypt in the sight of the nations, that I might be their God; I am the Lord.[1]

This doctrine gave Jews through the centuries not only hope for a better future and continuing motivation to remain Jews in the face of adversity; it also gave them the mission to persist in what they perceived as God-given ways of behaviour and belief as a model for other nations. Given the long history of this doctrine, then, and the critical role it played in assuring the continuity of both Judaism and the Jewish People to this day, the election of Israel is not a tenet that Jews can dismiss lightly.

What, then, raises questions in Jews' minds about this belief today? Two factors are most important in motivating this reassessment. First, Enlightenment ideology created nations that, at least in theory and to a greater or lesser degree in fact, treated Jews as equal citizens with full rights to participate in all aspects of society. That put the relations between Jews and non-Jews on a completely new footing. Now the non-Jewish world was not automatically filled with morally and intellectually benighted louts who would like nothing better than to harm Jews; it instead consisted of people who believed in 'self-evident' truths, to quote the United States' Declaration of Independence, 'that all men are created equal, that they are endowed by their Creator with certain unalienable rights, and that among these are life, liberty, and the pursuit of happiness'. It took some two hundred years for those beliefs to become anything like reality even in the United States, where they were perhaps most fervently pursued, but the many steps taken by the United States and by other Western countries during that time to live according to the new ideology made Jews living in those countries rethink their understanding of non-Jews and their relationship to them. The fact that these changed political realities also enabled Jews in increasing numbers to enter universities and to study secular philosophy and the religions of the world made it even harder for them to hold on to the view that only Judaism had something to offer humanity and that all other religions and peoples were inherently inferior.

If these political changes made Jews think twice about the biblical doctrine of election, the religious changes instituted most forcefully by the Second Vatican Council made them rethink that doctrine yet again. If Catholics and, after them, a number of Protestant denominations were adopting positions that recognized other religions – and especially Judaism – as valid paths to God and if at least some denominations of Christianity were even abandoning attempts to convert Jews, then how could we retain a doctrine that seemed increasingly not only old-fashioned, but downright mean? Moreover, elements of Judaism itself seemed to soften the exclusivism involved in the doctrine of election. After all, even classical Judaism portrayed non-Jews as the creatures of God with a covenant of their own given to all children of Noah.[2] Moreover, contrary to most other religions, Judaism is not missionary, for, as the talmudic Rabbis say, 'the pious and virtuous of all nations participate in eternal bliss'.[3] That is, according to Judaism you do not have to be Jewish to be 'saved', contrary to many forms of Christianity to this day.[4] But if Christians were changing their claims to being the exclusive route to God while yet reaffirming their belief in Christianity, perhaps we Jews needed to find a way to assert our own belief in Judaism without denigrating those of other faiths as unqualifiedly as the doctrine of election in its historical meaning had entailed.

In this paper, then, I will first review the primary elements in the classical doctrine of election as developed in the Hebrew Bible, the literature of the Rabbis of the Talmud and Midrash, and in the thought of a few Jewish thinkers of the Middle Ages. I will then describe some modern reinterpretations of the doctrine. Finally, I will suggest some thoughts about reshaping the doctrine for our time in a way that takes into account the new political and religious realities of Jewish relationships to non-Jews and yet preserves the Jewish commitment to Judaism.

The Components of the Classical Doctrine of Election

One important linguistic key to the classical doctrine of election is that while the Bible many times describes God as choosing (*bahar*) and as loving (*ahav*) Israel,[5] it never describes Israel as 'a chosen people' (*am nivhar*). The closest it gets is to describe Israel as an *am segulah*, a precious people. This should already alert us to the fact that for the Bible God's choice of Israel does not confer on them an indelible characteristic they inherit biologically and cannot lose; it rather is God who chooses Israel and finds Israel precious – but only as long as Israel acts in the way that God wants. This inherently conditional nature of the Election is already clear the first time that God announces it to the entire People Israel standing at Sinai:

> Now, then, if you will obey Me faithfully and keep My Covenant, you shall be My treasured possession among all the peoples. Indeed, all the earth is Mine, but you shall be to Me a kingdom of priests and a holy nation.[6]

And yet God creates not only a contractual relationship with Israel on a quid pro quo basis, but also rather a covenantal relationship. Thus, as I have noted above, God's choice of Israel is not dissolved by Israel's failure to abide by the terms of the Covenant, for even as God punishes Israel the covenantal relationship persists.

In human terms, God's choice is less like a contract for specific performance and more like a covenant of marriage. As such, the Covenant articulates some, but not all, of the mutual purposes and activities between the covenanting partners, for those would be worked out in the course of the relationship. Moreover, unlike most contracts, which have a specified task and duration, this relationship would encompass all areas of life and last forever. No wonder, then, that even though the Covenant described in the Torah has many of the features of suzerainty treaties of ancient times between a people and its leader,[7] the Bible also describes the relationship it creates as being like one between a husband (God) and his wife (Israel)[8] or between a father (God) and his first-born son (Israel).[9] Fitting such a relationship, Israel is commanded to love and be faithful to God[10] just as much as God, as Israel's lover, loves Israel and does for it acts of loyalty and loving-kindness (*hesed*).[11]

There are several implications of this loving relationship between God and Israel. First, God chose Israel to abide by his commandments in their full form – 613 by traditional count instead of the 7 given to all humanity. This means that Israel bears special responsibility: 'You alone have I singled out of all the families of the earth. That is why I will call you to account for all your iniquities.'[12] As the ones acting according to God's full list of desires, Israel is to be 'a kingdom of priests and a holy nation' and 'a light of nations'.[13] When Israel fails to abide by God's commandments, God will punish her,[14] but no matter how bad her deeds God will eventually forgive her.[15] Ultimately God will redeem her from all her oppressors[16] and will bring a Messianic time when peace will reign in nature as well as among humans and all peoples will learn Torah from the People Israel re-established in Zion.[17] Thus the biblical concept of the Chosen People is intimately connected to its concepts of Covenant, love, responsibility, punishment and exile from the Promised Land, forgiveness, and messianic redemption.

These themes are expanded and made even more central in rabbinic literature. Picking up on the Bible's depiction of God and Israel as husband and wife, Rabbi Akiva interprets the biblical book, Song of Songs, as love poems between God and Israel rather than between human lovers.[18] Moreover, Jews are commanded to wrap themselves in *tefillin* each morning as a graphic symbol of renewing their wedding bands with God. *Tefillin* are leather straps affix on the arms and head boxes that contain parchments with biblical passages proclaiming God's oneness. The four passages on the parchments are placed in one compartment in the box on the arm and in four separate compartments in the box on the forehead. Just as Jews reaffirm their marriage with God each day, so too, in the rabbinic imagination, God dons *tefillin* daily. This then leads to the obvious question:

Rabbi Nahman bar Yitzhak said to Rabbi Hiyya bar Avin: 'Just what is written on the *tefillin* of the Master of the Universe?' He replied, 'And who is like Your people Israel, a unique nation on the earth [whom God went and redeemed as His people, winning renown for Yourself for great and marvellous deeds, driving out nations before Your people whom You redeemed from Egypt. You have established Your people Israel as Your very own people forever; and You, O Lord, have become their God]' (I Chronicles 17.21–22).

Does the Holy One really take pride in Israel's praises? He really does, as it says in the verse: 'You have affirmed this day that the Lord is your God' (Deuteronomy 26.17) and in the following verse it states: 'And the Lord has affirmed this day that you are, as He promised you, His treasured people [who shall observe all His commandments and that He will set you, in fame and renown and glory, high above all the nations that He has made; and that you shall be, as He promised, a holy people to the Lord your God]' (Deuteronomy 26.18–19). The Holy One says to the Children of Israel: 'You have revealed My unique Oneness in the universe, and I shall make you unique in the world.' 'You have revealed My unique Oneness in the universe': this is apparent from the verse (contained in the *tefillin* worn by Jews), 'Here O Israel, the Lord is our God, the Lord is One' (Deuteronomy 6.4). 'And I shall make you unique in the world', as the verse says, 'And who is like Your people Israel, one nation on the earth' (I Chronicles 17.2 1). Rabbi Aha, the son of Rabba, said to Rabbi Ashi: 'This teaching [as applied to God's *tefillin*] we can understand as relevant to the parchment of one of the compartments [in the head *tefillin*]. But what about the other three?' He replied, . . . [They contain the following verses:] 'For what great nation is there' (Deuteronomy 4.7) . . . Or what great nation . . .' (Deuteronomy 4.8), which are similar, occupy one compartment. 'Happy are you, O Israel' (Deuteronomy 33.29) and 'Who is like your people Israel' (I Chronicles 17.21) – these [two verses on a similar theme] are found in another [second] compartment. 'Or has any god ventured [to go and take for himself one nation from the midst of another by prodigious acts . . . as the Lord your God did for you in Egypt before your very eyes?]' (Deuteronomy 4.34) – in another [third] compartment. 'And He will set you, in fame and renown and glory, high above all the nations that He has made, and you shall be, as He promised, a holy people to the Lord, your God' (Deuteronomy 26.19) – in another [fourth] compartment. And all of these verses are written in the [one compartment of the] *tefillin* of [God's] arm.[19]

For the Rabbis, then, God has chosen Israel because Jews proclaim God's unity to the world. God also, according to other rabbinic sources, has chosen Israel because of her humility: 'How I love you, for even at the moment I raise you to greatness, you efface yourselves'.[20] One source makes this even more explicit:

'It is not because you are the most numerous of peoples that the Lord set His heart on you and chose you . . .' (Deuteronomy 7.7). Not on account of your overwhelming numbers, nor on account of your performing more commandments than they do – for the [other] nations engage in [performing – divine] precepts, and yet are less obligated to do so than you and so aggrandize My name to a greater degree than you do [by performing my commandments]. 'Indeed you are the smallest of peoples . . .' (Deuteronomy 7.7): Your merit lies in that you hold yourselves very humbly before Me, and for this I love you, as it states, 'I have loved you,' says the Lord, 'but I have hated Esau' (Malakhi 1.2) . . . And it is written, 'And it shall be at the end of days, that the mountain of the Lord shall be established at the top of the mountains . . .' (Isaiah 2.2). This is the meaning of the verse, 'Though your beginnings were troubled, your end will be very great' (Job 8.7).[21]

And while that source maintains that God's love for the people Israel has nothing to do with their performance of the commandments, other rabbinic sources maintain just the opposite, that indeed the motive for God's love is Israel's faithful acts of obedience:

Why did the Holy One, blessed be He, choose Israel? Because all the [other] nations repudiated the Torah and refused to receive it, but Israel agreed and chose the Holy One, blessed be He, and His Torah.[22]

Indeed, the Rabbis tell an expanded version of this story, in which God offers the Torah to all the powerful nations of the world, one by one, but when each one asks God what the Torah contains and discovers that it forbids something that they were notorious for doing, they each reject it. When God, with no other choice, finally offers the Torah to the puny People Israel, they do not even ask what it contains – a mark of either complete trust in God or utter foolishness! – and say instead, 'na'aseh ve'nishmah', 'We shall [agree to] do it, and [then] we shall listen [to what it demands].'[23] In the end, though, God loves Israel even romantically because she becomes beautiful through observing God's commandments:

'You are beautiful, my love, you are beautiful' (Song of Songs 1.15): You are beautiful through the commandments, both positive and negative, beautiful through loving deeds . . .'[24]

Conversely, the Rabbis were convinced that 'Gentiles are addicted to licentiousness',[25] and the prayer they created for leaving the house of study has them thanking God

that You have set my lot among those who sit in the house of study and the synagogue and have not set my lot with those who frequent the theatres and circuses; for while I labour to inherit Paradise, they labour for the pit of destruction.[26]

There are several results of God's choice of Israel. First, the trials that the People Israel suffer, including exile from the Promised Land, are to be seen as the chastisements of a loving father, in line with a verse from the biblical book of Proverbs: 'For the Lord chastises the one He loves, just as a father rebukes the son he loves.'[27] Israel's diminished state is therefore not proof of her rejection by God but, on the contrary, evidence of God's continuing love and care.[28] Indeed, God himself, according to the Rabbis, accompanies Israel into exile and will return to the Promised Land with them.[29] Ultimately, God will not destroy Israel through punishment; on the contrary, 'When the Children of Israel stood at Mount Sinai and received the Torah, the Holy One said to the Angel of Death, "You can have sway over all the other nations, except this one, for they are My portion." '[30]

Second, it is for Israel's sake, according to the Rabbis, that God cares for the world:

If not for Israel, rain would not fall on the earth, and the sun would not shine, since it is in their merit that the Holy One illumines this world, and in time to come the nations of the world will see how bound up the Holy One is with the Jewish nation.[31]

Third, according to some rabbinic sources, God hopes through Israel to spread the Torah to all nations, and therefore 'Moses expounded the Torah in seventy languages' and 'even a Gentile who obeys the Torah is equal [in God's eyes] to the High Priest'.[32] On the other hand, some rabbinic sources declare that the Torah was God's gift meant only for the People Israel,[33] that much of God's instruction (Torah) for the People Israel was put in oral form and not in writing 'so that the nations could not falsify it, as they had done with the Written Torah, and say that they are the true Israel',[34] and that, because of Gentile (probably mostly Christian) distortions of the Torah, 'A Gentile who occupies himself with the study of Torah is deserving of death.'[35] Thus the rabbinic record is deeply divided on whether or not that most treasured evidence of God's choice of the People Israel, his gift of the Torah, was to be shared with non-Jews, and a similar ambivalence applies to prospective converts to Judaism.[36] Still, the accepted doctrine during talmudic times and thereafter was that God had given the Covenant of Noah to every human being, and the righteous of all peoples, as defined by the seven commandments of that Covenant, will inherit the bliss of the hereafter.[37]

Finally, while Israel may be despised by other nations now, in the Messianic future they will be rewarded by God with the reunion of all Jews in the land of Israel, the rebuilding of Jerusalem, the restoration of Jewish autonomy, and general prosperity. In fact, non-Jews will then seek to convert to Judaism to take advantage of Jews' new status but will not be allowed to do so because their motive will only be self-serving.[38]

The Rabbis not only expanded the meaning of the doctrine of election in the ways described above, they also made it part of the Jew's daily round. The liturgy that the Rabbis created is replete with mention of God's choosing us Jews. Specifically, that doctrine is repeated in the blessings that each person called to the Torah recites, in the blessings over wine sanctifying the beginning and ending of each Sabbath and Festival, in the middle section of the *Amidah* for Festivals, in the blessing before the *Sh'ma* recited each morning and evening, and in the *Alenu* prayer that ends every service. Thus this tenet is not something buried in the rabbinic literature that only the intellectually elite would know; it rather pervades the daily life of the Jew.

Some Medieval Versions of the Doctrine of Election

Given the prominence that the Rabbis afforded the doctrine of election, it is surprising that, according to Professor Menachem Kellner of the University of Haifa, 'not one of the medieval writers who listed principles of faith included it in their lists'.[39] Medieval Jewish thinkers certainly did include some of the components of the doctrine – God, revelation, commandments, redemption, and a Messianic future – and they clearly believed in Israel's chosenness, but the doctrine as such never becomes a matter of the medieval thinkers' definition of the fundamental faith commitments of Judaism.

Still, Jews lived daily with the distinctions between Israel and the nations. Not only did their liturgy affirm such distinctions but also their very lives did, for the non-Jews among whom Jews dwelled lived their lives according to very different beliefs, values and patterns of behaviour, and they often discriminated against, threatened, or killed Jews for upholding the Jewish tradition. Thus consciousness of the distinctions between Jews and non-Jews was hardly something that had to be affirmed as a matter of faith: it was simply a fact of life.

As Professor Jacob Katz of Hebrew University has pointed out,[40] there were primarily two theories offered by medieval Jews to explain the differences. Rationalists like Saadia Gaon (892–942) and Moses Maimonides (1135–1204) maintained that Israel's chosenness consisted of her possession of, and obedience to, the Torah. As Saadia put it, ' Our nation of the Children of Israel is only a nation by virtue of its laws.'[41]

Another strain, though, for which Katz finds roots in the Midrash but which was developed substantially by Yehudah Halevi (1075–1141) and especially by the *Zohar* and the later mystical tradition, sees the chosenness of Israel as an essential quality of the nation, as part of their very being. Halevi, for example, dubs Israel 'the pick of mankind', and he thus thinks it impossible for any non-Israelite to convert to Judaism.[42] Chosenness is, for this mystical strain, a biological characteristic that cannot be shared with others even if Jews wanted to do so. This seems grossly racist to us, but, as Professor Bernard Goldstein of the University of Pittsburgh has pointed out, in fairness to this school, we must note that during the Middle Ages conflicting national and religious groups each advanced their own claims to nobility and belittled the character and status of their opponents: Spanish Christians affirmed their superiority over Jews and Muslims; Muslims affirmed a similar superiority over Christians and Jews; and Arab Muslims even affirmed their superiority over non-Arab Muslims. In each case, at least some proponents of such claims maintained them not alone on theological or moral grounds, but on the inherent, essential character of the people transferred biologically.[43] Thus it is not surprising that we find at least a few voices like that of Halevi claiming Jewish superiority to Christians, Arabs and North Africans in an essentialist, biological mode. Unfortunately, some of that same attitude has characterized the reactions in our own day of some Jews – usually those least secure in their Jewish knowledge and identity – to Jews by choice, claiming that converts can never be 'real' Jews – even though they often know and practise more of Judaism than those born Jews making such claims!

Clearly the rationalist school of thought has at least theoretically more room than the essentialist school for good interfaith relationships, for rationalist theories make chosenness dependent upon the acceptance of specific beliefs and/or actions. In Maimonides's case, Israel was chosen to teach the world about God's existence and unity, and so conversion to Judaism was possible and, in his case, considerably easier than some contemporary Orthodox rabbis would make it. Still, even these thinkers were not interested in stretching beyond their own Chosen People very much, for they see the other nations and religions as constant threats. Maimonides, for example, says that

> all the nations, instigated by envy and impiety, rose up against us in anger, and all the kings of the earth, motivated by injustice and enmity, applied themselves to persecute us. They wanted to thwart God, but He will not be thwarted. Ever since the time of revelation every despot or ruler, be he violent or ignoble, has made it his first aim and final purpose to destroy our Torah and to vitiate our religion by means of the sword, by violence, or by brute force.[44]

Furthermore, in arguing against Islam, Maimonides specifically invokes the language of the Chosen People:

> When God spoke to Abraham, He made it amply clear that all the blessings that He promised and all his children to whom He will reveal the Law and whom He will make the Chosen People – all this is meant only for the seed of Isaac. Ishmael is regarded as an adjunct and appendage in the blessings of Isaac.[45]

And in the uncensored ending of his code, the *Mishneh Torah*, he says this about Jesus:

But if he does not meet with full success, or is slain, it is obvious that he is not the Messiah promised in the Torah . . . Even of Jesus of Nazareth, who imagined that he was the Messiah, but was put to death by the court, Daniel had prophesied, as it is written, 'And the children of the violent among your people shall lift themselves up to establish the vision; but they shall stumble' (Daniel 11.14). For has there ever been a greater stumbling than this? All the prophets affirmed that the Messiah would redeem Israel, save them, gather their dispersed, and confirm the commandments. But he caused Israel to be destroyed by the sword, their remnant to be dispersed and humiliated. He was instrumental in changing the Torah and causing the world to err and serve another besides God . . . Jesus of Nazareth and the Ishmaelite [Mohammed] who came after him only served to clear the way for King Messiah, to prepare the whole world to worship God with one accord . . . Thus the Messianic hope, the Torah, and the commandments have become familiar topics – topics of conversation [among the inhabitants] of the far isles and many peoples, uncircumcised of heart and flesh . . . But when the true King Messiah will appear and succeed, be exalted and lifted up, they will forthwith recant and realize that they have inherited naught but lies from their fathers, that their prophets and forebears led them astray.[46]

This is hardly the foundation for good interfaith relations!

Nevertheless, during the Middle Ages the most forthcoming Jewish advocate of open relations with Christians was also a strong advocate of Maimonides – namely, Rabbi Menahem Me'iri (1249–1306). He specifically declared that Christians were not to be classified as idolaters, despite the doctrine of the Trinity, the Eucharist, and frequent bowing down to graven images in Catholic practice. Moreover, as Jacob Katz has pointed out, in contrast to some of his predecessors, Me'iri did not confine his remarks to the context of whether Jews could engage in business with Christians; he instead applied his analysis to all relations between Jews and Christians.[47] He, though, was the exception to the rule.

Given the often hostile attitude that Christians took toward Jews during the Middle Ages, it is not surprising that Jews were not eager to open themselves to an appreciation of Christianity. Indeed, in that context, the fact that Maimonides, in the passage quoted above, coupled his denunciation of Jesus and Mohammed as false prophets with the thought that they nevertheless performed the valuable function of preparing the larger world to think about

God, the Torah, the commandments and the Messiah is nothing short of astonishing.

Modern Jewish Interpretations of Chosenness

As indicated at the beginning of this paper, the new circumstances in which Jews found themselves after the Enlightenment led them to probe their tradition for new ways to interpret their tradition that could provide a more sanguine view of non-Jews while still affirming their Jewish commitment and identity. The most common way to do this in the nineteenth century in Western Europe and North America was to emphasize the universalistic parts of the Jewish tradition. For someone like Hermann Cohen, an important German Jewish theologian of the late nineteenth and early twentieth centuries, Judaism taught the world ethical monotheism and continues to do so in the present. In the Messianic future for which Judaism yearns, though, all peoples of the world will embrace ethical monotheism and, in that sense, everyone will be 'chosen'. This was also the view of American theologians associated with the Reform movement at that time – people like Isaac Meyer Wise and Kaufmann Kohler. This view diminished both the intensity and the importance of the whole doctrine of a Chosen People; indeed, except for the pride of being the first to bring ethical monotheism to the world, one wonders why anyone who accepted this approach would want to be distinctively Jewish any more.

While there have been Jews in the United States since 1654, a large wave of Jews arrived from Eastern Europe between 1881 and 1923. Specifically, the Jewish population in the United States went from approximately a quarter of a million at the beginning of that period to 4.2 million at its end – a seventeen-fold increase.[48] While 'the first generation' (those who were adults in the first three decades of the twentieth century) simply tried to eke out a living in America, the second generation (those born in the United States and adults between 1930 and 1955) had a clear agenda to find a way to be accepted in their country and yet remain Jews. Toward that end, as Professor Arnold Eisen of Stanford University has pointed out, the concept of chosenness 'was the single most popular theme of discussion' in that second generation, for three reasons: (1) they wanted to be integrated into the modern world and not be seen as a people apart any longer; (2) the doctrine of election had historically led to much suffering, a tie all too evident in the Holocaust and the anti-Semitism Jews suffered in the United States in those decades; and

(3) the Puritan definition of America itself as a chosen people and a promised land had permeated American self-consciousness and therefore provided an opening for Jews to feel part of America.[49]

Most of the rabbis writing in that generation identified Jewish ideology with American ideology, making both the United States and the Jewish People two peoples chosen by God for the values they shared. One notable exception was Mordecai M. Kaplan, who asserted that the Chosen People concept should be abandoned and should be replaced with the conviction that each community in the world had its own vocation to carry on its own distinctive culture. Moral norms are embedded in nature for Kaplan, and so communities that do immoral things, like the Nazis, would stand indicted under a universal, moral critique. Aside from immorality, though, each society in the world had not only its own right to live but also a duty to maintain and foster its own distinctive contribution to world civilization.[50] Kaplan maintains this, in part, because he is a deist, and so God, lacking a will, cannot choose anyone. Part of what motivated Kaplan, though, was his desire to rid Judaism of the chauvinism involved in the concept of chosenness, including invidious comparisons with other cultures and inflated claims about one's own. Kaplan's replacement of God's choice of the Jewish people with a more even-handed approach asserting the worth of every culture, though, did not provide Jews with enough of a motivation to remain Jewish in the face of overwhelming pressures to assimilate, and so not many Jewish thinkers followed his lead in this.

In fact, as Eisen describes, the third generation of American Jews (those who were adults between 1955 and 1980) generally re-embraced the doctrine of chosenness, albeit with a greater sense of its mystery and therefore a less well-defined sense of its meaning and implications. One major exception to that trend is Richard Rubenstein, who, in his 1966 book *After Auschwitz*, maintained that the Jewish belief in being the Chosen People was one of the factors that led to the Holocaust and should be abandoned; we should instead understand ourselves, very much in Kaplan's mode, simply as one people among many others.[51] For most others writing in those years, though, the belief in being the Chosen People reappeared with gusto. The sense of isolation that Jews felt in the days before Israel's Six Day War made Jews doubt the reality of universalistic promises. Events that occurred after Eisen's book was written have reinforced that sense. So, for example, Jewish women attending international Jewish women's conferences often find themselves on the defensive for having a Jewish national life in Israel (whether they are Israelis or not), so much so that their comradeship with other women on the feminist agenda all but gets lost in the hostility expressed toward them. Moreover, Jews have become increasingly interested in the life of the spirit and in theology in the last few decades, and so a concept as deeply rooted as election is inevitably part of the agenda.

Even Orthodox thinkers like Hebrew University Professor David Hartman, though, are concerned to state that election should not mean chauvinism. Thus, in the Introduction to his 1985 book, *A Living Covenant*, he states the view for which he argues in the rest of the book:

> I argue strongly for the significance of Jewish particularity, not for its uniqueness. The covenantal election of Israel at Sinai, which is a central theme in this work, should not be understood as implying a metaphysical claim regarding the ontological uniqueness of the Jewish people. I do not subscribe to the view that a serious commitment to the God of Israel and Torah requires one to believe that the Jewish people mediate the only authentic way for the worship of God. I make no claims regarding all the non-Judaic ways of giving meaning and significance to human life.[52]

And one Orthodox rabbi, Irving Greenberg, has articulated a radically new view of Covenant, according to which God was the primary actor in the Covenant in biblical times, but after the destruction of the Second Temple God and Israel became equal partners, and, after the Holocaust, Israel is the primary determiner of the content of the Covenant. Under that theory, the very notion of God's choosing Israel continues, just as the relationship between spouses may change over time, but it has become considerably altered, perhaps to the point of Israel choosing God more than God choosing Israel.[53]

My Own Restatement of the Concept of Election

What, then shall we make of election in our own day? Building on the approach in my 1991 article on Covenant,[54] I would like to suggest that Jews' belief in election in our time must reflect the historical, philosophical and theological points that I made there.

Specifically, both Judaism and Christianity have changed over time, and therefore any historically authentic version of a belief in election must reflect that development. From a philosophical point of view, none of us can match God's omniscience and therefore we must make the claims of our convictions with a substantial degree of humility and respect for others who think differently. That is reinforced in the case of election by Jewish theology, according to which God wants us humans to conceive of and worship the divine in different ways.

These points, taken together, would mean that I, contrary to Hartman, would indeed make claims about other religions: I would say that they are what God wants. That, in fact, is why I as a Jew should not missionize among non-Jews. We can guess why God wants multiple ways of thinking about the transcendent element of our experience and appreciating it: Maimonides, as we have seen, and Franz Rosenzweig long after him both thought that Christianity's mission was to take the Jewish message to the world (although Rosenzweig thought much less well of Islam).[55] Whether they are right or not, Judaism demands respect for other religions.

It does not, however, require us Jews to give up our commitment to Judaism; on the contrary, it demands that we resist any efforts on the part of other religions or the secular world to convince us to drop our Jewish convictions and practices or change them into some mutated form, such as 'Jews for Jesus' do. Moreover, we both can and should evaluate the strengths and weaknesses of other approaches; we should not assert that all ways to think about God and to acknowledge the divine are equally good. At the same time, we should trust our commitment to our own tradition enough to subject it to the same kind of analysis of its strengths and weaknesses: that is not only the honest and fair thing to do, but the deeply religious thing to do, for that process of self-evaluation can only strengthen one's understanding of our tradition and loyalty to it. After all, the Torah calls us 'the Children of Israel', and Jacob does not become Israel until he wrestles with God.

How, then, should we think of ourselves? Clearly Jews and Catholics, like people of any faith, will affirm their own convictions minimally as being right for them. Many will go beyond that relativistic claim. Some will go to the other extreme, maintaining that their own faith is the only right one. I want to take a middle ground. Specifically, I want to acknowledge that my own commitment to Judaism is, at least in part, a function of the accident of my birth into a Jewish home and my upbringing there. Judah Halevi was certainly right in this: part of what makes us committed to our own religion is that it is familiar and that it includes attachments to people in our family and community whom we know and love. A mature commitment to one's religion, though, should also confront what it stands for. When people do that, I would hope that they would say that, after careful analysis and judgment, their own faith asserts better than any other what is true and good for human beings – at least as far as they can tell. It is that last phrase that is the important one, for it acknowledges that while we can know enough about life to make assertions about what to believe and do and while we can argue for them and even, if necessary, lay down our lives for them, we can never know, as God does, what is ultimately true and good. Therefore we must be, on the one hand, forthright in affirming our convictions of belief and action and, on the other, open to the enduring possibility that we are wrong. Moreover, we should also be open to learning from others, precisely for the epistemological and theological reasons that I develop in the other article.

One way to get at our feelings of chosenness and at the factors that lead us to see our tradition as true and good is to ask, 'What aspects of my tradition make me proud?' In my case, I am most proud of Judaism's moral seriousness. That includes its careful, talmudic analysis of moral problems to see all their sides, of its insistence on translating good intention to action, and of its overriding compassion for the poor and downtrodden. I am also proud of its strong emphasis on education, both general and Jewish. And I am, third, proud of its thick sense of community, requiring us all to take care of others as extended members of our family.

Do other traditions have these elements in them? Undoubtedly some other religions have some of these traits, and some have them all. Moreover, some other religions and secular philosophies have very positive aspects to them that Judaism does not have. Along with most American Jews, for example, I will acknowledge openly that we learned about the notion of individual rights from Western liberalism and that that concept is critically important to how we understand ourselves today as Americans *and as Jews*. Thus pride in my own religion should not blind me to what I can learn from others; on the contrary, it should prompt me to seek out what they have to offer.

Thus chosenness, as I understand it, does not imply chauvinism at all; it instead involves a faith that Judaism has it right, as it were, that it provides the truest and best recipe for thought and action that I know, while still recognizing that equally bright and morally sensitive people have adopted other traditions. This position is, as I explore elsewhere, neither relativism nor absolutism, but relativity: that is, it assumes that both reality and moral norms are objective, but we can only know them from our own perspective.[56]

In the end, then, chosenness communicates the special feelings that we have for our own traditions. Those feelings have been nurtured, in part, by long personal experience within the tradition and by the associations and love we have for the community committed to it. In those with examined faith, they are also fostered by their own analysis of, and commitment to, what it affirms. The trick is to remember that we are human beings making these judgments and that other equally bright and moral people can make other judgments. We then can all wrestle with each other and with God, as Jacob did in order to become Israel.

Notes

1. Lev. 26.44–45.
2. *b. Sanh.* 56–60.
3. *Sifra* on Leviticus 19.18.
4. The very idea of being 'saved' means different things in Judaism and Christianity. In Christianity salvation is from sin and from the damnation that sin incurs. Judaism believes too strongly in free will to maintain that we could ever be saved from sin and still remain human. Thus when biblical figures or we ourselves in Jewish liturgy ask God to 'save' us, it is to save us from difficult straits in life, whether they be physical, emotional, political, or something else. To do what God wants of us and to merit a place in the World to Come, according to classical Judaism, Jews need to abide by the Jewish tradition and God's Covenant with Israel and non-Jews need to abide by the Noachide Covenant.
5. Some examples of God's choosing the People Israel: Deut. 4.37; 7.6–11; 10.15; 14.12; 32.9; Isa. 14.1; 41.8–9; 44.1–2; 48.10; 49:7; Ezek. 43.27; Hos. 14.5; Mal. 1.2; 2.11; Ps. 32.12; 35.4; 47.5; 149.4. Some examples of God's loving the People Israel: Deut. 4.37; 7.8, 13; 23.6; Jer. 12.7; 31.2; Hos. 2.21–22; 3.1; Ps. 103.4.
6. Ex. 19.5–6.
7. For examples of such documents, cf. James B. Pritchard, ed., *Ancient Near Eastern Texts Relating to the Old Testament* (Princeton, NJ: Princeton University Press, 1950), pp. 159–61 (Lipit-Ishtar Lawcode) and pp. 163 ff. (The Code of Hammurabi – see especially the prologue on pp. 164–65 and epilogue on pp. 177–80). Good secondary reading on this includes George Mendenhall, 'Ancient Oriental and Biblical Law' and 'Covenant Forms in Israelite Tradition', in *The Biblical Archeologist Reader*, no. 3, eds, Edweard F. Cambell, Jr., and David N. Freeman, Garden City, NY: Doubleday, 1967, chs. 1 and 2; D .J. McCarthy, *Old Testament Covenant: A Survey of Current Opinions*, Oxford: Basil Blackwell, 1973, and Delbert R. Hillers, *Covenant: The History of a Biblical Idea*, Baltimore: Johns Hopkins University Press, 1969.

   Moshe Weinfeld has noted ('Covenant', *Encyclopedia Judaica* 5.102 1) that the idea of a covenant between a god and a people is unknown in other religions and cultures; it was a special feature of the religion of Israel. That makes sense when we remember that it was only the religion of Israel that demanded exclusive loyalty to its deity, and hence it was only in Israel that the covenant model was appropriate, for suzerainty covenants also demanded exclusive loyalty to the sovereign.
8. E.g., Jer. 2.2–3; Hos. 2, esp. vv. 18 and 21–22.

9. Ex. 4.22; Deut. 14.1; 3 2.6; Isa. 63.8; Hos. 11.1.
10. Deut. 6.5; 11.22.
11. Examples of God known for loyalty and loving-kindness (two meanings of the word *hesed*): Ex. 20.6; 34.6, 7; Num. 14.18; Deut. 5: 10; 7.9. See note 5 above for sources on God's love for Israel.
12. Amos 3.2. Cf. Prov. 3.12.
13. Ex. 19.6; Isa. 49.6; cf. 42.1–4 and 51.4–5.
14. See, for example, Lev. 26; Deut. 28; Lam. (entire).
15. For example, Lev. 26.41–45; Num. 14.19; Deut. 4.31; II Kings 13.23; Ezek. 20.17; Hos. 14.5; Lam. 3.32; Dan. 9.18–19; Neh. 9.19, 27, 28, 31.
16. Ex. 15.13; Deut. 30.3; Isa. 11.11–16; 63.9; 66.13; Ps. 44.27.
17. Isa. 2.1–4; 11.1–10; Mic. 4.1–6.
18. Cf. *m. Yad.* 3.5; *t. Yad.* 2.4; *b. Meg.* 7a.
19. *b. Ber.* 6a–6b. Cf. also *Mekhilta* to Exodus 15.2 (36b).
20. *b. Ḥul.* 89a.
21. *Midr. Tanh., Parashat Ekev*, par. 3, on Deut. 7.7.
22. *Num. R.* 14.10; cf. *b. 'Abod. Zar.* 2b.
23. *Sifre Deut.* par. 343 (142b); *Num. R.* 14.10. The sources are citing Ex. 24.7, in which the people strangely first agree to 'do' what God says and then agree to 'hear' it; cf. also Ex. 19.8, where they agree to carry out the demands of the Torah even before they have been revealed in chapters 20 ff., 24.
24. *Song of Songs Rabbah* 1.63 on Song of Songs 1.15. For other examples, see *m. Ab.* 3.14; *Mid. Tanh., Parashat Bamidbar*, par. 26; etc.
25. *b. Yeb* 98a.
26. *J. Ber.* 7d. This prayer is still used after the completion of study of a tractate of Talmud and, in an abbreviated form, in some versions of the early morning liturgy.
27. Prov. 3.12.
28. See, for example, *b. Pes.* 87b; *b. Meg.* 29a; *Exod. R.* 1.1; *Midr. Ps.* (ed. Buber) on Psalm 94 (Rabbi Eliezer ben Jacob's interpretation of Prov. 3.12); *Midr. Prov.* (ed. Buber), section 13.
29. *b. Meg.* 29a.
30. *Exod. R.* 32.7; *Pesiqta deRab Kahana*, section 46. Cf. *b. Ab. Zar.* 4a; *Leviticus Rabbah* 27.6; *Otzar Hamidrashim* (ed. Eisenstein), p. 97, section 18. The Rabbis even maintain that 'Whoever rises up against Israel is as though he rose against the Holy One, blessed be He' (*Sifra* to Lev. 19.2), and, conversely, 'Whoever helps Israel is as though he Helped the Holy One, blessed be He.' Similarly, 'Whoever hates Israel is like one who hates Him' (*Sifre Numbers*, par. 84 [22b]).
31. *Midr. Tanh., Parashat Terumah*, par. 9. According to *b. Šab.* 88a, 'The Holy One, blessed be He, made a condition with the works of creation and said to them, "If Israel accepts the Torah, you will endure; if not, I will reduce you again to chaos." ' Cf. also *Esther Rabbah*, Introduction (*Petihtah*), par. 11.
32. Seventy languages: *Genesis Rabbah* 49.2; cf. *b. Šab.* 88b. The Torah for everyone: *Sifra* to Leviticus 18.5.
33. E.g., *b. Ber.* 7a.
34. *Numbers Rabbah* 14.10; cf. *Tanh. Buber, Ki Tissa* 34 [58b].
35. *b. Sanh.* 59a.
36. Sources expressing a positive attitude toward converts include *b. Šab.* 31a;

b. Pes. 87b; *Mek.* to Exodus 22.20; and, ultimately, the first source that describes the method for conversion (*b. Yeb.* 47a–47b). In contrast, 'Proselytes are as troublesome to Israel as a sore' (*b. Yeb.* 47b).

37. *t. Sanh.* 13.2. In contrast to Israel's Torah, which, by traditional count, consists of 613 commandments, the Noachide Covenant God makes with all the other nations of the world consists of seven laws, six prohibitions and one positive commandment: the prohibitions against murder, idolatry, blasphemy, adultery/incest, robbery, and devouring a limb torn from a live animal, and the positive commandment to establish an equitable legal system (*b. Sanh.* 56–60). While any non-Jew who abided by those laws would inherit a portion in the World to Come, some sources depict the gentile nations as rejecting even that abbreviated set of demands: *Sifre Deuteronomy* par. 343 [142b].

38. *Bavodah Zarah* 3b. Cf. *Leviticus Rabbah* 36.2. For more sources on the doctrine of election in rabbinic sources, see Yosef Ginsburg, ed., *He Loves His People Israel: An Anthology of Sources,* Jerusalem: Shamir Publications, 1997; A. Cohen, *Everyman's Talmud,* New York: E. P. Dutton, 1949; Schocken, 1975, pp. 58–66; C. G. Montefiore and H. Loewe, *A Rabbinic Anthology* (Philadelphia: Jewish Publication Society, 1960 [first published in 1938]), pp. 58–85.

39. Menachem Kellner, 'Chosenness, Not Chauvinism: Maimonides on the Chosen People,' *A People Apart: Chosenness and Ritual in Jewish Philosophical Thought,* ed. Daniel H. Frank, Albany: State University of New York Press, 1993, p. 51.

40. Jacob Katz, *Tradition and Crisis: Jewish Society at the End of the Middle Ages,* New York: Schocken, 1971, pp. 26–7.

41. Saadia Gaon, *Book of Beliefs and Opinions,* trans. Samuel Rosenblatt, New Haven: Yale University Press, 1948, Book 3, Chapter 7 (p. 158). Maimonides held the same view: 'God has singled us out by His law and precepts, and our preeminence over the others was manifested in His rules and statutes' (Maimonides, 'Epistle to Yemen', *Iggerot ha-Rambam* [*The Letters of Maimonides*], ed. and trans. Ya'akov Shilat, Jerusalem: Ma'aliyot, 1988, p. 97. Menachem Kellner convincingly points out that Maimonides' view of election was based on his Aristotelian views of human psychology and that it emerges in many of his writings; see Kellner, 'Chosenness', pp. 51–75, esp. n. 27.

42. Judah Halevi, *The Kuzari,* trans. Hartwig Hirschfield, New York: Pardes, 1946. See especially Book 1, pars 27, 95; Book II, pars 30, 34, 36–42; Book IV, par. 23.

43. Cited by Kellner in his article, 'Chosenness, Not Chauvinism' (see n. 39 above), in n. 14, p. 70.

44. Maimonides, *Crisis and Leadership: Epistles of Maimonides,* trans. A. S. Halkin, Philadelphia: Jewish Publication Society, 1985, p. 97.

45. Ibid., p. 108.

46. Isidore Twersky, *A Maimonides Reader,* New York: Behrman House, 1972, pp. 226–7. Twersky prefaces these paragraphs with this comment: 'The following is the uncensored version of the end of [the Book of] Kings [in Maimonides' *Mishneh Torah*], ch. XI.'

47. Jacob Katz, *Exclusiveness and Tolerance: Studies in Jewish–Gentile Relations in Medieval and Modern Times,* London: Oxford University Press, 1961; New York: Schocken, 1962, pp. 114–28.

48. Nathan Glazer, *American Judaism,* 2nd edn, Chicago: University of Chicago

Press, 1972, pp. 60, 82–3.

49. Arnold Eisen, *The Chosen People in America: A Study in Jewish Religious Ideology*, Bloomington: Indiana University Press, 1983, pp. 4–7. The quotation is on p. 4.

50. Mordecai M. Kaplan, *Judaism as a Civilization*, New York: Schocken, 1934, 1967, pp. 233 f., 246–59; 439–47; *The Meaning of God in Modern Jewish Religion*, New York: Behrrnan, 1937, 1962, pp. 96, 102 ff.; *Questions Jews Ask, Reconstructionist Answers*, New York: Reconstructionist Press, 1956, pp. 35, 413, 501 ff. For a discussion of Kaplan's theory, see my article, 'The Meaning of Covenant: A Contemporary Understanding', *Issues in the Jewish–Christian Dialogue: Jewish Perspectives on Covenant, Mission, and Witness*, eds. Helga Croner and Leon Klenicki, New York: Paulist Press, 1979, pp. 40–6. See also S. Daniel Breslauer, *The Ecumenical Perspective and the Modernization of Jewish Religion*, Missoula, MT: Scholars Press, 1978.

51. Richard Rubenstein, *After Auschwitz*, Indianapolis: Bobbs-Merrill, 1966, chs. 1–3, esp. pp. 58, 69–71.

52. David Hartman, *A Living Covenant: The Innovative Spirit in Traditional Judaism*, New York: The Free Press, 1985; Woodstock, VT: Jewish Lights, 1997, pp. 3–4; cf. pp. 12, 18, 90, 93, and 96–8.

53. Irving Greenberg, *The Jewish Way*, New York: Simon & Schuster, 1988, ch. 3, esp. pp. 87–93.

54. Elliot N. Dorff, 'The Covenant as the Key: A Jewish Theology of Jewish–Christian Relations', *Toward a Theological Encounter: Jewish Understanding of Christianity*, ed. Leon Klenicki, New York: Paulist Press, 1991, pp. 43–66.

55. Franz Rosenzweig, *The Star of Redemption*, trans. William H. Hallo, New York: Holt, Rinehart, and Winston, 1971 (first published in German in 1921), pp. 164–6, 171–3, 199–204. For a description and evaluation of Rosenzweig's views, see my article, 'The Covenant: How Jews Understand Themselves and Others,' *Anglican Theological Review* 64:4, October, 1982, pp. 481–501.

56. I explain this more in my book, *Knowing God – Jewish Journeys to the Unknowable*, Northvale, NJ: Jason Aronson, 1992, esp. ch. 2.

Discussant

– Margaret Shepherd

Key issues for my faith

The idea of 'chosenness' is central in Christianity and is linked closely to the church's understanding of itself as 'People of God', with its responsibility to be 'salt of the earth' and 'light of the world', contributing to the building of the Kingdom of God.

The essence of chosenness is seen as the gratuitous act of God to enter into a relationship with humankind, primarily with Israel and then, par excellence, through Jesus Christ.

Different aspects of election in the church's history

The first community of Christian believers saw itself as heir to the assembly (*ekklesia* in the Septuagint) of the Chosen People before God, above all, the assembly on Mount Sinai, where Israel received the Law and was established by God as his holy people. There was the tendency for this early Christian community to define itself as the 'new' or 'true' people of God, replacing Israel.

Ancient promises were seen to be fulfilled in Christ. Through him, redemption from sin, estrangement from God, had been made possible for the whole human race. He was accompanied in this drama by the community of his followers.

The early church had to clarify its relationship to the People of Israel. We see several different understandings of this in the New Testament:

1. Luke–Acts: the Christian community understood itself as the Church of Jews and gentiles. The reconciliation of these two groups symbolized the redemption of the whole of humanity. With tension in the church between Hebrew and Hellenistic Christians, the church saw itself as a 'new people', beyond Jews and gentiles. This essentially negated the future of the Jewish people.

2. Matthew: here, stress is laid on the unfaithfulness of 'old Israel', and its infidelity to the Covenant, reaching its peak in the rejection of Jesus. Jews are no longer to be considered God's people. His Covenant with them has been dissolved. A new Covenant had been made in Jesus – to extend to all who believe in his name. The church is the new People of God, replacing the People of Israel. It alone inherits Israel's promises and blessings. This view was very influential in other parts of the New Testament, with the Church Fathers and with the self-understanding of the Middle Ages.

3. Paul's letter to the Romans: this refers to the old prophetic idea of the 'remnant' which remains faithful. For Paul, this is Jesus himself and the community of believers. The promises are extended to the gentiles. But for Paul, the Jewish people remain chosen, to be reconciled before the end of time with the church of Jesus.

Later in the Middle Ages and beyond, the church was to focus more and more on the fate of individual Christians, their salvation, faith, their being chosen by God.

Vatican II saw a radical shift, with its teaching that God's saving grace is operative everywhere. No one is left without means of salvation. In the Constitution on the Church, *Lumen Gentium*, the single dominant biblical image of the church is that of the People of God. It also recognizes that salvation is possible even apart from explicit faith in Christ. Jews are affirmed as God's Chosen People; God is recognized as present in the worship and life of the synagogue, the Church's integral links with the Jewish people are strongly emphasized. Catholics are invited to enter into dialogue with Jews, to purify preaching, catechetics and theology from anti-Jewish trends and destructive myths.

After his visit to the Rome Synagogue in 1986, Pope John Paul II spoke of Judaism as 'our elder brother' and of Jews as 'irrevocably the beloved of God'.

In the three major Vatican documents, *Nostra Aetate* (1965), Guidelines (1974) and Notes for Preaching and Catechesis (1985), there was a distinct development in understanding.[1] In *Nostra Aetate* the Church was presented as the new People of God; in Guidelines there is an avoidance of such supercessionist implications; and then in Notes we see that the Jews are to be presented as 'the people of God of the Old Covenant, which has never been revoked by God', quoting Pope John Paul II at Mainz in 1980. Here the Jewish people is referred to as 'a chosen people' and it speaks of '. . . the people of God of the Old and the New Testament'.

Reflecting the amazing change in Catholic–Jewish relations, Cardinal Etchegaray said, in 1983, 'as in the parable, neither of the two sons can gain possession of the entire inheritance; each one is for the other, without jealousy, a witness to the gratuity of the Father's mercy'.[2]

So, in the early church, divine election referred to the church's place in history. Later, until modern times, chosenness referred to personal salvation. Today, there is the attempt to move beyond preoccupation with the individual to the destiny of humankind. Human history is seen as the locus of divine grace, humanity as a whole destined for salvation and glory.

Rabbi Dorff's paper provides the Jewish context of the understanding of chosenness in which the Christian understanding is situated. It is rooted in the biblical notion of divine election of the Jewish people, a sign of God's favour and of his mission for his people. This has sustained them through a perilous history, with a persistent belief in the way God intended them to behave, serving as an example for others. This has been a fundamental element in Jewish self-understanding, developed in rabbinical literature and pervading every aspect of Jewish life. Rabbi Dorff speaks of modern Jewish interpretations of chosenness with their emphasis on universalism, but latterly there has been a restatement of the importance of a sense of election, seen as a mystery. He challenges us to consider how today, in the light of a changed relationship between Jews and Christians we can both rethink this doctrine.

The following are key questions for further discussion:

1. How can the chosenness of the Jewish people be reconciled with the chosenness of the Christian church?
2. If humanity itself can now be called the chosen 'People of God', what is the relationship between the church, the Jewish people and the whole of humanity?
3. How can the church and the Jewish people both witness to the election of humankind itself, to God at work in the struggle of people for justice and community, a more human social order?
4. Are we Jews and Christians being called to a new sense of mission in our world, while still affirming our identity as chosen people(s) of God, retaining our distinctiveness as Jews, as Christians?

5. What do we understand by Jewish or Christian particularity, not uniqueness?
6. As Judaism and Christianity have changed over time, what does election mean to each of our faith traditions today?
7. As Fr John Pawlikowski reminds us in his paper, the writings of Pope John Paul II emphasized that Jews and Christians remain linked in their very basic identities. How does this relate to the theme of chosenness?

Notes

1. *Declaration on the Relationship of the Church to Non-Christian Religions (Nostra Aetate*, No. 4), Ecumenical Council Vatican II, 28 October 1965; *Guidelines and Suggestions for Implementing the Conciliar Declaration Nostra Aetate No. 4*, Vatican Commission for Religious Relations with the Jews, 1 December 1974; *Notes on the Correct Way to Present the Jews and Judaism in Preaching and Catechesis in the Roman Catholic Church*, Vatican Commission for Religious Relations with the Jews, 24 June 1985.
2. Roger Cardinal Etchegaray, intervention at a Plenary Session of the Bishops on Reconciliation, Rome, 4 October 1983, cited in H. Croner, ed., *More Stepping Stones to Jewish–Christian Relations*, New York: Paulist Press, 1985, p. 61.

D. Understanding Election

– Edward Ondrako

We have been asked three questions. How do we understand chosenness and election? What place does each faith leave for the other, for others? How do we see our own 'specialness' and that of the other?

Question 1: Understanding Election Today

Election in General

The idea of chosenness and election is sacred by the nature of the subject. Webster's *Encyclopedic Unabridged Dictionary of the English Language* (1996 edn) defines 'chosen' as selected from the several; preferred, such as my chosen profession. Webster gives the theological definition of chosen simply as 'elect'. Finally, Webster includes the Chosen People as the Israelites. The reference is to Exodus 19. The Webster definition has no mention of elect in the New Testament, a curious lacuna.

In Exodus 19.5, the Lord attaches a double stipulation to being chosen. He instructs Moses: 'tell the people of Israel . . . if you will obey my voice and keep my covenant, you shall be my own possession among all peoples'. In this text, the people of Israel must obey God and keep his Covenant. Disobedience and infidelity have dire consequences. To obey the voice of the Lord and to keep his Covenant are poles apart from radical autonomy, a competitive struggle in the name of equality, and the quest for power or self-assertion so characteristic of modern thought. Instead, to obey the voice of the Lord and to keep his Covenant requires self-mastery. One obeys because one is chosen by God who does not repress a person's humanity. Obedience deepens one's humanity through intelligent and free reflection. By obeying God and keeping his Covenant, a person achieves unity of mind, body and spirit.

The obedience of faith enables a person to become truly human and truly free. Moreover, living in the obedience of faith enables the chosen, the elect, to live together in a world with countless other persons, who may not share the same understanding of being chosen. They can participate in life and grow together because to obey God and to keep his Covenant does not suppress one's individuality or individual freedom. For the believer, individual freedom serves and sustains the common good and the community of participants or partners support the individual as he or she grows into human integrity and maturity. This, in short, is a personalist view of election.

Specific Definition of Election

In 1967, Xavier Léon-Dufour edited the *Dictionary of Biblical Theology*, a translation of *Vocabulaire de théologie biblique*, originally published in Paris in 1962. In this he wrote that without election it is impossible to understand anything about God's plan for human beings: 'The experience of election is that of a destiny different from that of other peoples, of a unique condition due not to a blind concatenation of circumstances or to a series of human successes, but to a deliberate and sovereign initiative of Yahweh.'[1] Awareness of this divine activity starts with the beginning of Israel as the people of Yahweh. This awareness is inseparable from the Covenant which draws its meaning from the mystery of God's love in choosing Israel.

The earliest confessions of divine choice in the Hebrew scriptures (Deut. 26.1–11; Judg. 24.3, 15; Ex. 34.9 and 19.5) reflect a faith found still earlier in one of Balaam's oracles: 'How can I curse whom God has not cursed?' (Num. 23.8 f.). Léon-Dufour observes that the 'election of the people seems to be prepared for by a series of previous elections, and it is constantly developed by the choice of individuals newly chosen' (p. 116). The unique plan of God unfolds in continuity with these early confessions. Therefore, those called before Abraham (Abel, Noah, Shem), and after him, the patriarchs, the prophets, priests and levites, all attest to a continuity between their election and the election of Israel. Besides choosing his people, Yahweh has chosen the earth and holy places for himself. God has chosen the mountain of Zion (Ps. 78.68; and 68.19); and the temple of Jerusalem (Deut. 12.5) (pp. 116–17).

Election: Origin, Purpose, Result

Léon-Dufour explained election around the root *bhr* (b☐h☐r) in Deuteronomy.

1. The *origin* of election is a gratuitous initiative of God: 'It is you whom Yahweh your God has chosen' (Deut. 7.6), and not you who chose him. The explanation of this grace is love; no merit, no excellence justifies it. Israel is the last of the peoples, 'but . . . Yahweh has loved you' (Deut.7.7f.). Election creates a close relation between God and his people: 'You are sons' (Deut. 14.1). Yet this parentage has nothing natural about it, as is often the case between the divinity and its believers in paganism. It is the result of Yahweh's choice (Deut. 14.2) and expresses the transcendence of him who is always 'the first to love' (I John 4.19).

2. The *purpose* of election is to constitute a holy people, consecrated to Yahweh, 'raised above all nations in honour, renown, and glory' (Deut. 26.19), making the grandeur and the generosity of the Lord radiate among the peoples. The Law, by the barriers it sets up between Israel and the nations, is the means to assure this holiness (7.1–6).

3. The *result* of an election which sets Israel apart from other peoples is to bind her to a destiny that has nothing in common with theirs: either extraordinary prosperity or unparalleled misfortune (Deut. 28). The word of Amos remains the charter of election: 'From among all the families of the earth I have known only you; therefore I will punish you for all your iniquities' (Amos 3.2). [2]

Election and Rejection

Cycles of election and rejection are seen in the Hebrew scriptures. God chastises his people but does not renounce them. The unfaithful bride is repudiated for her sins but the election continues in a new form (Isa. 6.13). In fact, God calls the new Israel 'my elect' (Isa. 41.8; 43.20; 45.4); or 'my elects' (Isa. 43.10; 65.9, 15, 22). For example, God chose Cyrus to be conqueror 'for the sake of Israel, my elect' (45.5). Finally, the Servant, one who is neither priest, king, nor prophet is called 'my elect' (Isa. 42.1).

In this context, the Matthean text: 'Many are called, but few are chosen' (Matt. 22.14) is challenging. Matthew is conscious of the problem of the unworthy in Judaism. The parable of the marriage feast (Matt. 22.1–14) is one of three (Matt. 21.23–27 and 28–32) that address the issue of the importance of Jews and gentiles who have come to believe in Jesus to live in a worthy manner.[3]

Election and Jesus

In the New Testament, the title 'God's elect' is rarely given to Jesus (Luke 9.35; 23.35; probably John 1.34). When it is used, it is at a solemn moment such as at his baptism. One hears a voice from the cloud, saying, 'This is my Son, my Chosen; listen to him!' (Luke 9.35). At his crucifixion, the rulers scoffed at him, saying, 'He saved others; let him save himself, if he is the Christ of God, his Chosen One!' (Luke 23.35). Even though Jesus never uttered the name Chosen One or Elect, he has the clearest conviction of his election. 'Let us go on to the next towns, that I may preach there also; for that is why I came out', he told Simon and those who were searching for him (Mark 1.38). In response to the Pharisees, Jesus said, 'Even if I do bear witness to myself, my testimony is true, for I know whence I have come or whither I am going, but you do not know whence I have come or whither I am going' (John 8.14). After healing the sick man at the pool of Bethzatha on the Sabbath, Jesus said: 'The Son can do nothing of his own accord, but only what he sees the Father doing; for whatever He does, that the Son does likewise' (John 5.19). A little later he added: 'If you believed Moses, you would believe me, for he wrote of me' (John 5.46).

Jesus, God's elect, in turn, chose twelve to work closely with him. He said, 'You did not chose me, but I chose you and appointed you that you should go and bear fruit and that your fruit should abide' (John 15.16a). In the elections of Matthias (Acts 1.24) and Paul (Acts 9.15), one sees that the church is being built on witnesses. In a sermon after the resurrection of Jesus, Peter said, 'God raised him on the third day and made him manifest; not to all people, but to us who were chosen by God as witnesses, who ate and drank with him after he rose from the dead' (Acts 10.4 1).

Election and the Church

Catholics hold that this divine election is continued in the Church. The Matthean parables of the two sons, wicked tenants, and marriage feast (Matt. 21 and 22) are not dealing with the replacement of Israel by the church or of Jews by gentiles, but about worthy living.[4] The choices made by the leaders of the Christian communities confirm God's choices and acknowledge God's Spirit (Acts 6.3). The Spirit is the one guiding the twelve to impose their hands upon the deacons, the seven men who were to help the widows so that the twelve would not neglect preaching the word of God. The same Spirit helped the Church of Antioch to designate Paul and Barnabas to do his work

(Acts 13.2 ff.). The early church understood diverse charisms in their midst as a further manifestation of election to make up a community.

Catholics hold that God's choice explains the gift of faith and the openness of a person to accept the Word. Human wisdom alone does not provide the answer. Individuals come together in community by God's choice. At Jerusalem Peter said,

> Brethren, you know that in the early days God made choice among you, that by my mouth the Gentiles should hear the word of the gospel and believe. And God who knows the heart bore witness to them, giving them the Holy Spirit just as he did to us; and he made no distinction between us and them, but cleansed their hearts by faith. (Acts 15.7–9)

In I Peter 2.9–10 one finds a fitting summary for this elect as *ekklesia*:

> You are a chosen race, a royal priesthood, a holy nation, God's own people, that you may declare the wonderful deeds of him who called you out of darkness into his marvellous light. Once you were no people; once you had not received mercy but now you have received mercy. Because of this election, the individual is willing to endure everything for the sake of the elect, that they also may obtain salvation in Christ Jesus with its eternal glory.

Recapitulation: Chosen or Rejected: Do We Have It Right?

The long and troubled history of Jewish–Catholic relations cries out for those involved in sincere dialogue today to 'get it right'. The development of the ideas of chosenness, election and rejection have to show whether their ideas have been a true development or a corruption of the original idea of election.

In sum, the divine choice of Abraham was irrevocable, a blessing for all. The focus of the entire Old Testament remained on the divine promise. At the same time, this divine promise is not a denial of the possibility of real guilt, nor the consequences of real guilt, rejection of divine blessing. For Catholics, Abraham's election is fulfilled in Jesus.

> He [Jesus] is our peace, who has made us both one, and has broken down the dividing wall of hostility, by abolishing in his flesh the law of commandments and ordinances, that he might create in

himself one new man in place of the two, so making peace, and might reconcile us both to God in one body through the cross, thereby bringing the hostility to an end. (Eph 2.14–16)

Is it possible for one who is chosen or elect to freely repudiate being chosen by God? What are the consequences for such free choices? Amos wrote: 'I will punish you for all your iniquities' (3.2). Jesus was stern with the foolish maidens who ran out of oil for their lamps: 'I do not know you' (Matt. 25.12). Does Jesus annul their election? The words of Amos and Jesus suggest 'just punishment' for individual rejection, but not the annulment of divine election. The chastisement of the individual maidens is because of their shortsightedness and failure to prepare for the bridegroom.

Léon-Dufour gives an important Catholic interpretation (p. 119). He raises this rejection of the maidens to the realm of eschatology. The rejection 'I do not know you' no longer belongs to time but to the necessity of every human being to make spiritually free, definitive decisions about death, judgment, heaven and hell. The rejection of Jesus did not fall on the Jewish people. While there is sin in their history, that is, their rejection of God's elect, or their stumbling on the rock that had been chosen and placed by God (Rom. 9.32 f.), they remain, 'according to the election, beloved because of their fathers' (11.28). Their error, as that of the nations in the Old Covenant, is provisional and providential (11.30 f.). As long as the Lord has not come, they are called to conversion. God has the power to graft them in again. All Israel will be saved (11.23–27).

Paul's Mystical Musings

In chapter 11 of his letter to the Romans, Paul asks: has God rejected his people? 'By no means! I myself am an Israelite, a descendent of Abraham . . . God has not rejected his people whom he foreknew' (11.1–2). Paul then develops his reasoning about the remnant. 'At the present time there is a remnant, chosen by grace. But if it is by grace, it is no longer on the basis of works; otherwise grace would no longer be grace' (11.5–6). Immediately, there is a transition to the question: 'what then? Israel failed to obtain what it sought. The elect obtained it, but the rest were hardened' (11.7). Then he asks: 'have they stumbled so as to fall? By no means! But through their trespass salvation has come to the Gentiles, so as to make Israel jealous' (11.11). Paul then develops the theme of jealousy, rejection and reconciliation. He uses images of dough and of branches being broken off from the richness of the olive tree, warns those who might be tempted to boast that they are secure as branches on the tree, and takes note of the kindness and severity of God. Paul celebrates the power of God to graft these natural branches that have been broken off because of unbelief back into their own olive tree.

Then, in a compelling mystical summary, he writes:

Lest you be wise in your own conceits, I want you to understand the mystery, brethren: a hardening has come upon Israel, until the full number of the Gentiles come in, and so all Israel will be saved, as it is written, 'The Deliverer will come from Zion, he will banish ungodliness from Jacob; and this will be my covenant with them when I take away their sins'. As regards the gospel they are enemies of God, for your sake; but as regards election they are beloved for the sake of their forefathers. For the gifts and the call of God are irrevocable. (11.25–29).

After recalling that the gifts and the call of God are irrevocable, Paul ponders that 'God has consigned all men to disobedience, that he may have mercy upon all' (Rom. 11.32). In other words, Paul has reached the end of his speculative reflection on how the chosen or the elect could not accept Jesus as Lord. In the following verse, he leaves a somewhat mystical musing: 'O the depth of the riches and wisdom and knowledge of God! How unsearchable are his judgments and how inscrutable his ways!' Then, with more than a hint of intellectual and spiritual humility, he concludes: 'for who has known the mind of the Lord, or who has been his counsellor? Or who has given a gift to him that he might be repaid?' (11.33, 35).

These theological insights of Paul have their roots in his first letter to the Thessalonians: 'For we know, brethren beloved of God, that he has chosen you; for our gospel came to you not only in word, but also in power and in the Holy Spirit and with full conviction' (1.4–5). A few lines later, he wrote:

We were gentle among you, as a nursing mother cares for her children. With such affection for you, we were determined to share with you not only the gospel of God but our very selves as well, so dearly beloved had you become to us. (1.7–8)

The image of a nursing mother taking care of her children seems a fitting end to the first question about how one understands chosen-ness and election. Because of a special relationship, unlike any other two religions, might Jews and Catholics be to each other as a nursing mother is to her children? My historical-theological and pastoral intuitions as university chaplain answer affirmatively.

Question 2: What place does each faith leave for the other, for others?

Place is defined as a particular portion of space, whether of definite or indefinite extent. All would agree that the space Jews and Catholics have for each other, for others, has been pummelled by historical factors. Today, historians have a tall order to try to report on what really happened, how a progressive estrangement in the first century of the Common Era spun out of control. Partners in dialogue need to build on history.

Shortly after Vatican II, Yves Congar made reference to an evocative description, the 'hierarchy of mistakes'. This elicits reflection on mistakes that were more damaging than others in the relations between Jews and Catholics. Understanding problem and mystery, in this context, may assist partners in dialogue to avoid historical and theological pitfalls and to build a new place, that is, new space for each other.

Problem and Mystery

In *The Mystery of Being*, Gabriel Marcel makes a helpful distinction.

> A problem is something which I meet, which I find complete before me, but which I can therefore lay siege to and reduce. But a mystery is something in which I myself am involved, and it can therefore only be thought of as 'a sphere where distinction between what is in me and what is before me loses its meaning and validity'. A genuine problem is subject to no appropriate technique by the exercise of which it is defined; whereas a mystery, by definition, transcends every conceivable technique. It is, no doubt, always possible (logically and psychologically) to degrade a mystery so as to turn it into a problem, but this is a fundamentally vicious proceeding, whose springs might perhaps be discovered in a kind of corruption of the intelligence.[5]

As the church looks into the depths of herself as mystery, she links her people to the stock of Abraham. In the groundbreaking decree,

Nostra Aetate (The Declaration on the Relationship of the Church to Non-Christian Religions), the Vatican Council Fathers said: 'Sounding the depths of the mystery which is the church, this sacred council remembers the spiritual ties which link the people of the new covenant to the stock of Abraham' (#4).[6]

Insights on the church, sacred scripture, the church in the modern world, and on religious freedom, from Vatican II, find expression in *Nostra Aetate*, The Council Fathers raised their own consciousness about the problems between the two faiths.

> The church of Christ acknowledges that in God's plan of salvation the beginnings of its faith and election are to be found in the patriarchs, Moses and the prophets. It professes that all Christ's faithful who as people of faith are daughters and sons of Abraham (see Gal. 3, 7), are included in the same patriarch's call and that the salvation of the church is mystically prefigured in the exodus of God's chosen people from the land of bondage. On this account the church cannot forget that it received the revelation of the Old Testament by way of that people with whom God in his inexpressible mercy established the ancient covenant. Nor can it forget that it draws nourishment from that good olive tree onto which the wild olive branches of the Gentiles have been grafted [see Rom. 11.17–24]. The church believes that Christ who is our peace has through his cross reconciled Jews and Gentiles and made them one in himself [see Eph. 2.14–16]. (*Nostra Aetate* #4)

The Council Fathers taught: 'it is true that the church is the new people of God, yet the Jews should not be spoken of as rejected or accursed as if this followed from holy scripture' (*Nostra Aetate* #4). Without this understanding through the ages, a hierarchy of mistakes were made. The Council Fathers concluded: 'All must take care, lest in catechizing or in preaching the word of God, they teach anything which is not in accord with the truth of the Gospel message or the spirit of Christ' (*Nostra Aetate* #4).

In 1993, recalling the Uprising of the Warsaw Ghetto, Pope John Paul II wrote:

> As Christians and Jews, as children of Abraham, we are called to be a blessing for the world [cf. Gen. 12.2 ff.] especially by our witness in faith to God, the source of life, and by our commitment to work together for the establishment of true peace and justice among all peoples and nations. Taking up the way of dialogue and mutual

collaboration, we deepen bonds of friendship and trust among ourselves and offer to others a sign of hope for the future.[7]

Pope John Paul II and a Theology of abuses by the Church

How might Jews and Christians be a blessing for one another when many obstacles exist? Many find it very difficult to understand the distinction between the church as spotless bride of Christ and the individual members who are sinful, in need of conversion to the Lord and in need of repentance and reparation. Yet, it is a central distinction in which a theology of abuses of the church has developed. This distinction is pivotal to the present and future development of a theology of partnership.

In *Tertio Millennio Adveniente* (1994), Pope John Paul II spoke of the abuses by the church. He does not cover up or diminish the mistakes of those who sullied the face of the church. He is not afraid of the truth. By taking such a stand, Pope John Paul II has sent a clear message to Catholics to educate themselves about the past and present. It is part of the hope he preaches and teaches to hold that education leads toward wisdom, while wisdom leads toward virtue, and virtue is a solid foundation for partnership. Pope John Paul II wrote:

> The Church should become more fully conscious of other children, recalling all those times in history when they departed from the spirit of Christ and his Gospel and, instead of offering to the world the witness of a life inspired by the values of faith, indulged in ways of thinking and acting which were truly forms of counter-witness and scandal. (*Tertio Millennio Adveniente* #33)[8]

He builds on the belief that the church is holy because of her incorporation into Christ. Nevertheless, 'the Church does not tire of doing penance: before God and man she always acknowledges as her own her sinful sons and daughters'. He echoes the profound conviction of *Lumen Gentium* that besides pursuing the path of penance, the church is always in need of and pursues renewal (cf. *Lumen Gentium* #8). In sum, he states that the church needs a clear awareness of what has happened to her for ten centuries. 'She cannot cross the threshold of the new millennium without encouraging her children to purify themselves, through repentance, of past errors and instances of infidelity, inconsistency, and slowness to act' (*Tertio Millennio Adveniente* #33). The pontiff is convinced of the power of honest acknowledgment of the weaknesses of the past, not as a force for loss of faith, but as a help for strengthening faith. Pope John Paul II is confident in its spiritual power. He asks for the church to change its mentality and certain attitudes, offers a source of new teaching for the future, and gently suggests that the sins of the past may be temptations for the present.

The list of sins which the pontiff has pointed out require a greater commitment to repentance and conversion. His focal point is the sins which 'have been detrimental to the unity willed by God for his people' (#34). Citing the Vatican Council's Decree on Ecumenism, he admits that people on both sides are to blame. Nevertheless, 'such wounds openly contradict the will of Christ and are a cause of scandal to the world' (*Unitatis Redintegratio* # 1.3). While this concern is about Christian unity, the pontiff is clear that unity is a gift, a gift from the Holy Spirit. Catholics 'are asked to respond to this gift responsibly, without compromise in our witness to the truth, generously implementing the guidelines laid down by the Council and in subsequent documents of the Holy See' (*Tertio Millennio Adveniente* #34).

Unity is a gift of the Holy Spirit. Therefore, the presence of the Holy Spirit in the hearts of all people of good will is a sacred insight of the Catholic Church which is the foundation of its openness to people of other religions, not only to other Christians, but to all people who have religious sensibilities. This understanding and respect, humble awareness and devotion to the power of the Holy Spirit, assists Catholics in their examination of conscience and in their promotion of initiatives to overcome divisions of the past.

Pope John Paul II calls for repentance for the acquiescence given to intolerance and even the use of violence in the service of truth. His education of Catholics to this painful chapter of the Church's history, in my view, has been unparalleled in modern history:

> It is true that an accurate historical judgment cannot prescind from careful study of the cultural conditioning of the times, as a result of which many good people may have held in good faith that an authentic witness to the truth could include suppressing the opinions of others or at least paying no attention to them. Many factors frequently converged to create assumptions which justified intolerance and fostered an emotional climate from which only great spirits, truly free and filled with God, were in some way able to break free. (*Tertio Millennio Adveniente* #35)

This quintessential insight about accurate historical judgments is full of promise. For example, as a third generation American of Slovak ancestors, I have been researching Slovakia's sorrowful history during World War II. The painful questions about Hitler, President Tiso and the Jews may not be reduced into a teacup. I find hope with Pope John Paul II's insight into identifying great spirits, truly free and filled with God. Rabbi Abraham Abba Frieder of Nitra, Slovakia, the spokesperson for the Jewish Community throughout the war, who appealed to Dr Tiso not to resign as president when he wanted to in 1940, is one of them. Bishop Jan Vojjtašš vak of Spišš, one of the first to hear what was really happening at Auschwitz, and who took action, is another.

It is one thing to say that Slovak history was very complex and needs objective historical study. Problems of prejudice, deception, anti-Judaism, anti-Semitism, and the struggle for individual and national survival were all mixed. It is another to say:

> Yet the consideration of mitigating factors does not exonerate the Church from the obligation to express profound regret for the weaknesses of so many of her sons and daughters who sullied her face, preventing her from fully mirroring the image of her crucified Lord, the supreme witness of patient love and humble meekness. From these painful moments of the past a lesson can be drawn for the future, leading all Christians to adhere fully to the sublime principle stated by the council: 'The truth cannot impose itself except by virtue of its own truth, as it wins over the mind with gentleness and power'. (*Dignitatis Humanae* #1, in *Tertio Millennio Adveniente* #35)

Vatican II: Apathy or Reception

In *Tertio Millennio Adveniente*, Pope John Paul quickly gets to the heart of each Catholic's conscience, 'Christians need to place themselves humbly before the Lord and examine themselves on the responsibility which they too have for the evils of our day' (#36). Religious indifference, the loss of the transcendent sense of human life, confusion in the ethical sphere, even about the fundamental values of respect for life and the family, the influence of the climate of secularism and ethical relativism are points he makes for examination of conscience. He does not hide the fact that there is an increasing lack of religion as he sees it, and as the fathers at Vatican II saw it.

Gaudium et Spes, the Church in the Modern World, addresses various kinds of atheism and its causes. Human beings exist for communion with God and that capacity begins at birth. Those who consciously strive to drive God from their hearts and avoid all questions of religion must answer for themselves. What Vatican II reminds Catholics of and what is echoed by Pope John Paul II is the fact that 'believers can have more than a little to do with the rise of atheism' (*Gaudium et Spes* #19; *Tertio Millennio Adveniente* #36).

> To the extent that they are careless about their instruction in the faith, or present its teaching falsely, or even fail in their religious, moral or social life, they must be said to conceal rather than to reveal the true nature of God and of religion. (GS #19)

The Holy Father identifies a problem for many Christians that 'the spiritual life is passing through a time of uncertainty which affects not only their moral life but also their life of prayer and the theological correctness of their faith' (TMA #36). He warns about erroneous theological views. What was known as a *pietas fidei*, or *obsequiosum religiosum*, that is, a prayerful, intellectual humility and practice of the obedience of faith, has given way to a crisis of obedience in respect to the Church's *Magisterium*.

The Pope laments the lack of discernment that became acquiescence by many Christians when totalitarian regimes violated human rights. He regrets the responsibility of many Christians for grave forms of injustice and exclusion. 'How many Christians really know and put into practice the principles of the Church's social doctrine?' he asks.

In sum, question two asks about the place each faith leaves for the other, for others. The Pope's experiences at Vatican II, his pastoral sensibilities, his visits around the world, but above all his prayer, gave the world *Tertio Millennio Adveniente* and its emanation, *Memory and Reconciliation* (12 May 2000). Creating brotherhood is creating place, 'definite and indefinite space'. His candour and loyalty elicits a theology of partnership, study and dialogue. Dialogue, 'accompanied by careful discernment and courageous witness to the truth, remain(s) valid and call(s) us to a greater commitment' (TMA #36).

I have no doubt that Pope John Paul II's brief prayer at the Wailing Wall is a new definition of 'place'.

> God of our fathers, you chose Abraham and his descendents to bring Your Name to the Nations. We are deeply saddened by the behaviour of those who in the course of history have caused these children of Yours to suffer, and asking forgiveness, we wish to commit ourselves to genuine brotherhood with the people of the Covenant.

Question 3: How Do We See Our Own Specialness and That of the Other?

Jews and Catholics have a mysterious spiritual link that is special. Special is being a particular one; particular, individual, or certain, such as a special number, or a special reserve vintage of wine. Special does not have the same meaning for the relationship between Catholics and members of any other religion. Spiritual link has to do with issues such as salvation. Besides salvation, specialness touches the delicate question of what happens to persons who are chosen but live in an unworthy manner.

'Outside the church there is no salvation'

'Outside the church there is no salvation' is a teaching from the time of the Fathers of the church. Improperly understood, it is an obstacle to the development of a theology of partnership. A narrow interpretation risks replacing Israel with the church and the Jews with gentiles. The Catholic Church today articulates her claim 'outside the church there is no salvation' with broad and careful nuances. In brief, she teaches that it is a total contradiction to the truth of God's love to predestine anyone to be lost, but to live in an unworthy manner exacts a price for the elect.

To recapitulate, election (b□h□r) is an act of God in the Old Testament. Election signifies the call of *Yahweh* and Israel's response. Election is because of God's love and not because of any merit. Responsibility comes with election. Failure to be responsible brings punishment. Distortion of a proper understanding of election brings unrealistic security in *Yahweh*'s protection. Election has an opposite. Non-election is a consequence of failure to act responsibly, i.e. to recognize the divinity of *Yahweh* and to listen to Him.

Eklegesthai (to choose) in Mark, Luke, John and the Acts of the Apostles has the context of the divine act of Jesus choosing the apostles.

> God chose what is foolish in the world to shame the wise, God chose what is weak in the world to shame the strong, God chose what is low and despised in the world, even things that are not, to bring to nothing things that are, so that no human being might boast in the presence of God. (I Cor. 1.27–28).

As in the Old Testament, antecedent election in the New Testament brings the responsibility of the elect. Fidelity through eschatological

tribulations is expected of the elect because the elect live conscious
that nothing can separate them from the love of Christ. No adversary
can triumph over God although at times it may seem that the adversary is winning. In time, the term elect seems to have become a
conventional term for Christians. In sum, the proper emphasis of
election is always on God's plan of salvation. It is a misrepresentation
to focus on the polarity of election and non-election or reprobation.
Finally, election in the New Testament imposes a consciousness of
mission.[9]

From St Justin to the Council of Florence-Ferrara in 1442

'Outside the church there is no salvation' is a teaching affected by
historical conditioning. In his *Dialogue* with Trypho the Jew, St Justin
held that Jews who observed the law of Moses would be saved as well
as anyone who did what was good, holy, and just (2CE). St Ireneus
taught that God provides for all who have lived virtuously in their
own generation and feared and loved God. St Clement taught God is
saviour of all (3CE). Origen preached that God provides people with
occasions for practising virtue and doing what is right. St John
Chrysostom said:

> You cannot say that at that time (before his coming) Christ was
> unknown, because he was not known by all, but only by the upright
> and the virtuous, any more than you can say that today he is not
> being adored by men, on the grounds that now not all have come to
> adore him.[10]

In sum, salvation, even of those who did not know him, had always
been through Christ.

Christians who had fallen into heresy or schism and grave sins
received stern warnings of no salvation outside the church (cf. St
Ignatius of Antioch and St Ireneus (*PG* 7.966–967 and *PG* 12.841–842).
St Ambrose, St Gregory of Nyssa, and St John Chrysostom argued
that the faith had been spread to all peoples. Those who refused to
accept it should blame themselves.[11] St Augustine (d. 430) and St
Fulgentius of Ruspe (d. 533) wrote about predestination. St Fulgentius
wrote:

> Most firmly hold and by no means doubt, that not only all pagans,
> but also all Jews, and all heretics and schismatics who die outside
> the Catholic Church, will go to the eternal fire that was prepared for
> the devil and his angels. (*PL* 65.704)

These teachings remained to the Council of Florence in 1442 and beyond. Whoever interpreted their ambiguities in a wooden manner caused chaos.

From Development of Doctrine to a Cautious Theology

John Henry Newman took a view that may help Jews and Catholics through any chaotic interpretation of 'outside the church there is no salvation'.[12] In 1843, he preached a sermon to the faculty at Oxford on the theory of development.

> The absence or partial absence, or incompleteness of dogmatic statements is no proof of impressions or implicit judgments, in the mind of the Church. Even centuries might pass without formal expression of a truth, which had all along been the secret life of millions of souls. (*University Sermons* #15 p. 323)

In 1845, his *Essay on the Development of Doctrine* gave seven notes or criteria to study the development of a particular doctrine in the context of the whole history of the development of doctrine: preservation of type, continuity of principles, the power of assimilation, logical sequence, early anticipation, preservative additions and chronic continuance. When William Ewart Gladstone, the former English Prime Minister, challenged the Church on papal infallibility, Newman answered in the *Letter to the Duke of Norfolk*, 1874, with a synthesis of these notes. The doctrine of papal infallibility cannot be understood apart from freedom, conscience and authority. Newman defended the reasonableness of the definition of infallibility as already existing in the Catholic Church, and the logical step to accept it with qualifications. He argued for a generous loyalty towards ecclesiastical authority and an authority exercised with a wise and gentle minimism. With such an attitude, Newman could accept the dogma that 'outside the church there is no salvation' as one which no Catholic can ever think of disputing.

> The main sense is, that there is no other communion or so-called Church, but the Catholic, in which are stored the promises, the sacraments, and other means of salvation; the other and derived sense is, that no one can be saved who is not in that one and only Church. But it does not follow, because there is no Church but one, which has the Evangelical gifts and privileges to bestow, that therefore no one can be saved without the intervention of that one Church (*Letter to the Duke of Norfolk*, p. 335).

In fact, Newman relied on Pius IX's doctrine of invincible ignorance (10 August 1863).

We and you know, that those who lie under invincible ignorance as regards our most Holy Religion, and who, diligently observing the natural law and its precepts, which are engraven on the hearts of all, and prepared to obey God, lead a good and upright life, are able, by the operation of the power of divine light and grace, to obtain eternal life.

Prudent Minimizing

Newman introduced his idea of prudent minimizing. 'Who would at first sight gather from the wording of so forcible a universal, that an exception to its operation, such as this, so distinct, and, for what we know, so very wide, was consistent with holding it' (p. 336). No private or unauthorized person ought to impose any interpretation of dogmatic statements upon the consciences of others beyond the legitimate sense of the words because all general rules have exceptions. He wrote:

To be a true Catholic a man must have a generous loyalty towards ecclesiastical authority, and accept what is taught him with what is called pietas fidei, and only such a tone of mind has a claim, and it certainly has a claim, to be met and to be handled with a wise and gentle minimism. (p. 339)

Change: Linguistic, Theological and Philosophical

At the beginning of this third Christian millennium, one asks: had Catholics understood and lived with the spirit that Newman described, how different might the last century have been? The last 2,000 years? The one hundred years since Newman's death in 1890 have shown significant linguistic, theological and philosophical changes. As we meet in London, more positive changes are happening.

Turning Point

The definitive turning point came at Vatican Council II. *Lumen Gentium* (The Dogmatic Constitution on the Church) made a dramatic leap and development in the Church's self-understanding and her view of the specialness of others. The statement that 'The Church of Christ subsists in the Roman Catholic Church' (*Lumen Gentium* #8) still is heard as a clap of thunder. It leaves open the question of who and how others are related to Christ.

The next paragraph (#14) says:

> relying on scripture and tradition, it teaches that this pilgrim church is required for salvation. Christ expressly asserted the necessity of faith and Baptism. Therefore, those could not be saved who refuse to enter the church, or to remain in it, while knowing that it was founded by God through Christ as required for salvation.

It was a severe reminder of judgment for failures for those who are sons and daughters of the Church because of their exalted status.

> A person who does not persevere in charity, however, is not saved, even though incorporated into the church. Such people remain indeed in the bosom of the church, but only 'bodily' not 'in their hearts'. (#14)

Specialness and the Spirit of Lumen Gentium

Paragraphs (#15) and (#16) of *Lumen Gentium* are a summary of specialness. Paragraph (#15) emphasizes the Church's attitude towards other baptized groups

> who are honoured by the name of Christian, but do not profess the faith in its entirety or have not preserved unity of communion under the succession of Peter. The Spirit stirs up desires and actions in all of Christ's disciples in order that all may be peacefully united, as Christ ordained, in one flock under one shepherd.

Paragraph #16 is a summary of the specialness of those who have not yet accepted the gospel. The Church recognizes that they are related to the People of God in various ways, especially those who received the first covenant and election.

> There is, first, that people to whom the covenants and promises were made, and from whom Christ was born in the flesh (see Rom. 9.4–5), a people in virtue of their election beloved for the sake of the fathers, for God never regrets his gifts or his call (see Rom. 11.28–29). But the plan of salvation also includes those who acknowledge the Creator, first among whom are the Moslems: they profess to hold the faith of Abraham, and together with us they adore the one,

merciful God, who will judge humanity on the last day. Nor is God remote from those who in shadows and images seek the unknown God, since he gives to everyone life and breath and all things (see Acts 17.25–28) and since the Saviour wills everyone to be saved (see I Tim. 2.4). Those who, through no fault of their own, do not know the Gospel of Christ or his church, but who nevertheless seek God with a sincere heart, and, moved by grace, try in their actions to do his will as they know it through the dictates of their conscience – these too may attain eternal salvation. Nor will divine providence deny the assistance necessary for salvation to those who, without any fault of theirs, have not yet arrived at an explicit knowledge of God, and who, not without grace, strive to lead a good life. Whatever of good or truth is found amongst them is considered by the church to be a preparation for the Gospel and given by him who enlightens all men and women that they may at length have life. But very often, deceived by the Evil One, people have lost their way in their thinking, have exchanged the truth of God for a lie and served the creature rather than the Creator (see Rom. 1.21 and 25). Or else, living and dying in this world without God, they are exposed to ultimate despair. This is why, to procure the glory of God and the salvation of all of these people, the church, mindful of the Lord's command, 'preach the Gospel to every creature' (Mark 16.15) takes great care to encourage the missions.

Common Mission

A theology of partnership beckons Jews and Catholics to a common mission to raise the moral consciousness of culture, to confront the religious indifferentism of societies and to help people to find a new horizon of spiritual union. This has been Pope John Paul II's constant message since 1979.

Conclusion

What a dramatic progression in understanding chosenness and election in the sixty-three years between *Mit Brennender Sorge* (1937), when Pius XI confronted the Nazi myth of race and blood, perhaps in terms too cautious, and *Memory and Reconciliation: The Church and the Faults of the Past* (2000). In Pius XI's encyclical, 14 March 1937, the term 'elect' is almost hidden in a strong condemnation of the errors of Nazism. On 12 March 2000, the Day of Pardon, while asking for forgiveness, the Holy Father committed himself and Catholics to genuine brotherhood with the people of the Covenant.

I lament that the 'purification of memory' envisioned by Pope John Paul II was not part of Catholic sensibilities in 1937. I deplore statements meant to be strong but which seem weak in hindsight, whatever the motive. I rejoice when I witness a Day of Pardon, with all its ramifications for the future. The Day of Pardon is the result of the rich spiritual insight from a key architect of *Gaudium et Spes*. He knows that our *mysterious* spiritual link invites partnership in a way known to God.

> The Christian is certainly bound both by need and by duty to struggle with evil through many afflictions and to suffer death; but, as one who has been made a **partner** in the paschal mystery, and as one who has been configured to the death of Christ, will go forward, strengthened by hope, to the resurrection. All this holds true not only for Christians but also for all people of good will in whose hearts grace is active invisibly. For since Christ died for everyone, and since all are in fact called to one and the same destiny, which is divine, we must hold that the holy Spirit offers to all the possibility of being made **partners**, in a way known to God, in the paschal mystery'. (GS #22)

May the true spirit of Vatican II and the return to the sources for Jews be like a lens to help both understand election. May their discoveries at Vatican II and in Jewish Heritage be like a prism to see the spectrum of colour in a common, shared space. May continual study and understanding of election form the strong cable of 'specialness' for building an unbreakable bond of spiritual unity.

Appendix: Congregation for the Doctrine of the Faith, *Mysterium Ecclesiae* (1973)

Summary of how the Church reconciles apparent contradictions in the development of doctrine.

Difficulties [in the transmission of divine revelation by the Church] arise also from the historical condition that affects the expression of revelation. With regard to this historical condition, it must first be observed that the meaning of the pronouncements of faith depends partly upon the expressive power of the languages used at a certain point in time and in particular circumstances. Moreover, it sometimes happens that some dogmatic truth is first expressed incompletely (but not falsely), and at a later date, when considered in a broader context of faith or human knowledge, it receives a fuller and more perfect expression. In addition, when the church makes new pronouncements it intends to confirm or clarify what is in some way contained in sacred scripture or in previous expressions of tradition, but at the same time it usually has the intention of solving certain questions or removing certain errors. All these things have to be properly interpreted. Finally, even though the truths which the church intends to teach through its dogmatic formulas are distinct from the changeable conceptions of a given epoch and can be expressed without them, nevertheless it can sometimes happen that these truths may be enunciated by the sacred magisterium in terms that bear traces of such conceptions . . . In addition, it has sometimes happened that certain formulas in the habitual usage of the church have given way to new expressions which, proposed and approved by the sacred magisterium, presented more clearly or more completely the same meaning.[13]

Notes

1. Xavier Léon-Dufour, ed., *Dictionary of Biblical Theology*, New York: Desclee, 1967, p. 115.
2. Ibid., p. 117.
3. Cf. Raymond Brown, *An Introduction to the New Testament*, London: Doubleday, 1997, pp. 196–7.
4. Ibid., p. 196.
5. Gabriel Marcel, *Le Mystère de L'Etre* (2 vols), Paris: Aubier-Montaigne, 1963–4; trans. G. S. Fraser, *The Mystery of Being* (2 vols), South Bend, Ind.: Gateway, 1977, pp. 211–12.
6. Texts for the Vatican II decrees cited in the pages that follow (*Nostra Aetate, Lumen Gentium, Unitatis Redintegratio, Gaudium et Spes* and *Dignitatis Humanae*) are taken from Austin Flannery, ed., *Vatican Council II: The Sixteen Basic Documents, A Completely Revised Edition in Inclusive Language*, Northport, NY: Costello, 1996. (The practice is to cite paragraph numbers (#) rather than pages.)
7. Eugene Fisher and Leon Klenicki, eds, *Pope John Paul II–Spiritual Pilgrimage*: *Texts on Jews and Judaism, 1979–1995*, New York: Crossroad, 1995, p. 27.
8 *Tertio Millennio Adveniente* [On the Coming of the Third Millennium], Apostolic Letter of John Paul II, 10 November 1994 (Libreria Editrice Vaticana, Vatican City), Washington, DC: US Catholic Conference, 1994.
9. Cf. J. McKenzie, *Dictionary of the Bible*, London: Macmillan, 1965, pp. 227, 228.
10. Cited in F. Sullivan, *Salvation Outside the Church*, New York: Paulist Press, 1992, pp. 14–17.
11. Ibid., pp. 18–27.
12. See J. H. Newman, *Fifteeen Sermons Preached before the University of Oxford, 1826–1843* (1918 edn); *Certain Difficulties Felt by Anglicans in Catholic Teaching, vol. 2: Letter to the Duke of Norfolk, 1874* (1910 edn); *An Essay on the Development of Christian Doctrine, 1845* (1910 edn); London: Longmans, Green & Co, 1910, 1918.
13. *Acta Apostolica Sedis 65*, Vatican City: The Vatican, 1973, pp. 402–3.

Discussant

– David Goldberg

May I begin my saying how much I enjoyed reading this paper: It was logical, elegant, clear and concise. If I could briefly summarize the major arguments as I understand them, they would be as follows. Dr Ondrako asks three questions:

1. How do we understand chosenness and election?
2. What place does each faith leave for the other, for others?
3. How do we see our own 'specialness' and that of the other?

Dr Ondrako refers to the specific definition of election in the Bible:

> The experience of election is that of a destiny different from that of other peoples, of a unique condition due not to a blind concentration of circumstances or to a series of human successes, but to a deliberate and sovereign initiative of Yahweh (p. 85).

It is worth commenting in parenthesis that when Rabbi Dorff discusses election from the Jewish perspective, he makes two fundamental points:

1. That those 'called' both before and after Abraham attest to a continuity between their election and the election of Israel.
2. The purpose of election is to constitute a holy people. The means to assure this holiness is The Law.

Dr Ondrako pursues the following line of thought:
In the New Testament the title 'God's Elect' is rarely used of Jesus himself. It is the twelve disciples whom he elects to work with him who are 'The Chosen of God'. For Catholics, this divine election is continued in the Catholic Church. The original election of Abraham is fulfilled in Jesus. This raises the theological problem of what are the consequences for the individuals, or people, who repudiate being

chosen? Xavier Leon-Dufour (Dictionary of the Bible) gives an important Catholic interpretation: 'The rejection of Jesus did not fall on the Jewish people. While there is sin in their rejection of God's elect . . . they remain, according to the election, beloved because of their fathers.' The apostle Paul muses on this issue in Romans XI and in his first Letter to the Thessalonians. It is in that Letter that he uses the image of the nursing mother taking care of her children, which Dr Ondrako suggests is a fitting metaphor for understanding chosenness and election in the context of the Jewish/Catholic relationship. But I feel bound to ask, which religion is the mother, and which the child? – Perhaps the metaphor of two siblings under God's love might be more appropriate.

Dr Ondrako summons the evocative description of Yves Congar about the 'hierarchy of mistakes' that has bedevilled Jewish/Catholic relations. *Nostra Aetate* was a ground-breaking decree, in that it taught that while the church is the new people of God, the Jews should no longer be spoken of as rejected or accursed. The presence of the Holy Spirit in the hearts of all people of goodwill is the foundation of the church's openness to other religions. On his recent visit to Jerusalem and the Western Wall, the Pope's prayer affirmed a commitment to genuine brotherhood with the (Jewish) people of the Covenant.

The final section of Dr Ondrako's paper considers the controversial doctrine that 'outside the church there is no salvation'. A too narrow definition of that statement jeopardizes the development of a theology of partnership. The proper emphasis of election should always be on God's plan of salvation. It is a limiting misrepresentation to focus on the polarity of election and non-election or reprobation. The view of John Henry, Cardinal Newman, and his theory of the development of the idea of 'prudent minimizing' is perhaps pertinent in helping Jews and Catholics to a positive interpretation of the doctrine. Together Jews and Catholics have a common mission to raise the moral consciousness of culture and to confront the religious indifference of societies. The paschal mystery is not only for Christians, but also for all people of goodwill in whose hearts grace is visibly active:

'Since all are in fact called to one and the same destiny, which is divine, we must hold that the Holy Spirit offers to all the possibility of being made **partners** in a way known to God in the paschal mystery' (Pope John Paul II , *Gaudium et Spes*).

Thus is a link forged between 'election' and 'specialness' that results in an unbreakable bond of spiritual unity.

Discussion recorder

– Peter Keenan

Rabbi Dorff argued that the 'biblical doctrine that God chose Israel has been a prevailing theme in Jews' self-image, giving them both a sense of divine favour and divine mission'. He noted, however, that this doctrine of election has contributed also to hatred of Jews by those who, for whatever reason, have understood it – then and now – as an 'expression of Jewish cliquishness'. Rabbi Dorff delineated two important reasons why modern Judaism is looking once again at the doctrine of election: the results of the heritage of the Enlightenment and the consequent Christian re-estimation of Judaism in the light of the Second Vatican Council's teachings (1962–5). His remaining comments can be summarized in the observations that election continues to be an important element in the contemporary Catholic–Jewish dialogue, but one which needs to be understood in a dynamic manner. In other words, the theological concept of 'tradition' is one which 'cannot be frozen in time'; of its very nature, it is open to development. It follows, therefore, that we are to be modest in the religious claims that believers make, understanding that there is a moral duty to look beyond concepts like election, to ensure that they are not interpreted in an insensitive, exclusivist manner.

Fr Ondrako spoke also in positive terms of the importance of understanding the nature of tradition in both faith communities. With reference to the concept of theological development, he suggested that a possible fruitful approach to the study of this key issue would be to understand it in terms of the Pauline metaphor of the nursing mother, in such a manner that Catholics and Jews are able to explore the metaphor in a relationship of mutual trust and tolerance, contributing thereby to the building of 'new space for the other'. Fr Ondrako argued that the documents of the Second Vatican Council (1962–5), most particularly *Lumen Gentium* and *Gaudium et Spes*, are a rich source of theological material which can provide a basis for continuing Catholic–Jewish dialogue in the twenty-first century.

In her response to Rabbi Dorff's paper, Sr Margaret Shepherd noted that, in any discussion of election/chosenness, it is imperative to remember that Jews and Christians are, on the one hand, charged with the task of reconciling their shared (but not mutually exclusive) claims to 'chosenness' and, on the other, with the challenge of understanding how this sense of election relates to the wider religious – and also secular – world.

Rabbi David Goldberg, responding to Fr Ondrako's paper, remarked that it was indeed helpful to investigate the subject of election in terms of examining the meaning of 'space' and 'specialness' with regard to the two faith traditions. Such an approach, rooted in the notion of biblical election, supported the attempt to develop in our time a 'theology of partnership', though Rabbi Goldberg was not convinced by Fr Ondrako's use of the writings of John Henry Cardinal Newman (d. 1900) as one possible means to that end. Rabbi Goldberg thought that a more fruitful avenue for development would be to explore further the sibling metaphor, addressing it in the context of establishing whether the metaphor's 'identities' are as clear-cut as first suggested by Rabbi Bayfield.

Delegates' responses to the four speakers agreed with the main thrust of the arguments presented, both in the position papers and in the respondents' spoken observations. A number of speakers agreed with Rabbi Goldberg's observations, noting that the sibling metaphor, helpful as it is, will need to be developed further or replaced entirely as part of the on-going Catholic–Jewish dialogue. Others spoke eloquently of the connection between the Jewish understanding of election in relation to the centrality, for Christians, of the paschal mystery: these experiences, for they transcend conceptualization, participate in a profound awareness of mystery; it is this experience (fundamental, for example, to Saul of Tarsus's sense of religion) which is common to the two faith traditions, one which – in different, but complementary, ways – Jew and Christian must together explore. This undertaking is an ethical imperative in the light of the truth that the two faith communities are called to respond to God's elective call. How, at the dawn of a new millennium, we are to work towards the fulfilment of such a vision, *after Auschwitz*, is a challenge for those of this generation committed to the dialogue. A number of contributors opined that our success in this endeavour will bear fruit, not in the short term, but in the hearts and minds of the next generation of Catholics and Jews who, in the memorable words of (Blessed) Pope John XXIII (d. 1963), embrace one another as 'their brother, Joseph'.

Such an aspiration, easily articulated, is one which, given the almost 2,000 years' history of little meaningful dialogue between Jews and Christians, is indeed very difficult to realize, and more than one speaker noted in this context how the idea of being chosen is capable of a number of not always complementary interpretations. Is it, for example, possible for a Jew or a Christian to lose – or cast away – their election?

In similar but different ways, therefore, speakers endorsed the understanding that there is indeed 'a way forward', but that it is by no means easy. It is one which will require the service of a multiplicity of metaphors, if Jews and Christians are together to plumb the rich theological depths of election. It was agreed also that such an enterprise will be fruitful only if both religious traditions eschew any simplistic notion of particularism (whilst recognizing that election continues to be a relevant theological concept), a phenomenon all too common when some Jews and Catholics interpret election to mean an exclusivist, fundamentalist-type understanding of religious commitment. One speaker articulated passionately the conviction that it is now time to challenge in unambiguous terms the claim of the 'religious right', in both religions, to speak for the faith traditions of which they are members. It was argued, and Conference agreed, that this is a matter requiring urgent attention. It was agreed further that this imperative needs to be understood with reference to the world religions in general, and Islam in particular. It was acknowledged that this is no easy task, and Cardinal Cassidy remarked that, in this and related matters, we need to remember that the dialogue is at a very early stage, but one which is a quantum leap ahead of where we were a generation or so ago: to paraphrase the words of Abraham Lincoln (in a very different context), 'Jew and Catholic may be walking forward together slowly; never again shall we stumble alone backwards.' On this note, the deliberations concluded.

4

The Context of Partnership

What is the background against which our partnership is forged?

How do we read our texts in the light of modernity? How do we deal with those texts which may cause offence to our partners? How do we deal with texts that appear to run contrary to what we regard as the fundamental values of our respective traditions? How do we deal with texts which may be read as licence for violence or bigotry? How do we approach and read the sacred writings of the other?

A. Reading our Sacred Texts Today

– Jonathan Magonet

I am conscious of the background experience that I bring to the topic and the need to be careful in extrapolating from that experience to a wider context. My particular framework is twofold: lecturing in the Hebrew Bible to rabbinic students and degree students at the Leo Baeck College; and over thirty years' experience of co-organizing a Jewish–Christian Bible Study Week in Germany. This latter has led to a variety of dialogue activities in that country, including teaching courses on the Hebrew Bible in university and theological settings as well as at the Kirchentag and Katholikentag. Though all these opportunities have also given me access to people from different countries and I am familiar with some of the literature in the field, the scene I know best is the German one and that must inevitably provide the basis to what I have to say.

   My engagement with the Hebrew Bible began with my own studies at Leo Baeck College under Dr Ellen Littman, *zikhronah livrakha* ('may her memory be for a blessing'). Though primarily an historian, particularly of nineteenth-century German Jewry, she was invited to teach Bible at the college from its inception. While methodologically she was bound to the Historical-Critical school she was simply an enthusiast for the Hebrew Bible, with a particular love of the prophet Jeremiah, a love she conveyed to her students. Whatever it was that she sparked off in me, I became her designated successor and, having acquired my Ph.D. at Heidelberg, returned to teach. My own approach at the time was somewhat out of phase with current scholarship and it only became evident some years later that we were at the beginning of a new kind of literary reading of biblical texts that has now become something of a growth industry. As I have indicated elsewhere,[1] it has also signalled a return to biblical studies of many Jewish scholars, as if, with a sigh of relief, we can finally look for meaning, however elusive, in the biblical materials and, consciously or unconsciously, leap the centuries back to classical Jewish forms of biblical commentary.

At the risk of adding a romantic note, during my studies at Leo Baeck a well-known Jewish bookshop, Shapiro-Valentine, in the East End closed down. When I visited the sale, the bookseller, the historian Professor Chimen Abramsky in another guise, persuaded me to buy a couple of volumes of Midrash (traditional Jewish biblical exegesis). When I purchased them, even without being able to read, let alone understand, their content, I felt a sudden burden of responsibility to ensure that the tradition they incorporated did not end in this ignominious way, but that I, I alone if necessary, had to somehow teach and hand them on. Though I have never taught those exact texts, I think that the desire to communicate the content of the Hebrew Bible and the rich tradition of Jewish biblical scholarship, as well as my own understandings, has been a primary motivating force in my subsequent career. That is to say, it is the Hebrew Bible as a living, communicating library of books that has interested me, with all the different scholarly methods seen as 'handmaids' to that primary purpose of interpretation and teaching. Those who helped me see this in those early stages were people like Rudolf Stamm and Werner Peiz, the former a German Protestant pastor, and the latter a German Jew who became an Anglican minister and then a sociologist. Both in their different ways pushed me back to the text in the quest, first of all, to try to understand it and then make it available in all its fascination to others.

This brings me to my first question, to the title of this discussion and the phrase 'sacred texts'. A more comprehensive view of Judaism would have to include under the generic term 'Torah', the Talmud, the Midrashic collections, the legal codes, the philosophical and the mystical writings. However, if we confine ourselves to the texts which, in the rabbinic phrase, 'defile the hands', then the Hebrew Bible is the core. Here the tradition distinguishes between the Pentateuch, the first text to be designated as 'Torah', which is the direct revelation of God, and the Prophets and Writings which are inspired by God but which reflect different degrees of human influence in their composition.

As a progressive Jew, shaped by the Enlightenment and an historical way of viewing my tradition, I accept that a long period of composition lies behind the Torah itself, even if I remain agnostic about the precise way it came about.[2] So I am effectively caught between the certainties and to some extent the dogmatic requirements of Jewish tradition and the distancing, not to say scepticism, of modern scholarly approaches. Thus almost everything I have to say about the authority of the Hebrew Bible has to be prefaced with an 'as if': this is what the tradition prescribes, and I may choose to accept it or not. Similarly my conclusions about the meaning of any passage, having reviewed as many interpretations, classical and modern, as possible, is to talk of 'degrees of probability' in understanding it. The 'assured results of scholarship', no less than the assertions of traditional Jewish commentaries like the recent Art Scroll series, fit into the same realm of Midrash, timebound, subjective understandings whose authority lies only in their ability to stimulate, inspire or trouble. The Rabbinic Bible, the *miqraot gedolot*, with its commentaries spanning the centuries ranged around the biblical text, is a celebration of, and indeed a warning about, the relativity of exegesis and the enduring, elusive nature of the debate about meaning.

With this preface let me come to the points I want to make based on the experience of thirty years of the Jewish–Christian Bible Week in Bendorf, Germany. The very title of the conference makes a point. The Hedwig-Dransfeld Haus where it takes place was founded by Catholic women, and after the war, under the leadership of Anneliese Debray, embarked on a series of programmes of reconciliation, including the attempt to work with Israel and Jews. But whereas all other contexts I know of where such dialogue takes place in Germany the title of such a dialogue project is 'Christian–Jewish', reflecting the nature of the host organization and the demographic reality of the Jewish community of Germany, the Bendorf Jewish–Christian Bible Week owes its form and development to the very specific Jewish input, and the significance accorded to this, from the beginning.

Three separate but interrelated aspects underpinned the Bible Week from its inception: the Jewish–German encounter, the Jewish–Christian dialogue and the study of the Hebrew Bible itself. The three aspects remain, though their relative significance varies from year to year, with the biblical study itself increasingly coming to dominate the Week. By working systematically through the Hebrew Bible from Genesis, we have allowed the particular text to determine the themes to be explored in the morning study sessions, guided by Jewish and Christian 'resource people', and the lectures.

The particular circumstance that made it possible to start the Week was obviously the sense of responsibility of some German Christians about the *Shoah* and the need for reconciliation. However, it soon became evident that although the Christian participants came to sit at the feet of rabbis out of a mixture of emotions, they stayed to listen because of the insights they came to gain into the Hebrew Bible and ways of studying it that were both disturbing and attractive at the same time. Perhaps it belongs to this particular German Christian culture, but they found the Jewish willingness to see a multitude of different possible meanings in a text as in marked contrast to the single 'authentic' meaning, backed by clerical or scholarly authority, that they were used to. When this plurality of meanings was illustrated by indicating the multidimensionality of the Hebrew text, and experiencing the richness of rabbinic and medieval Jewish commentary, they found themselves challenged and attracted all over again.[3]

For several years this was the situation as ever-new people attended the conference, but at some point an inevitable reaction occurred with the demand for 'authentic Christian interpretation' to be offered as well. And here difficulties arose. Because the findings of the Historical-Critical school, the dominant approach in their theological training, despite the theologizing of the 'sources', did little to nourish the spirit. Attempts to find a medieval Christian equivalent to rabbinic Midrash or the medieval Jewish commentators were not particularly successful. Too much of the material was concerned with allegorization, typology or foretelling the coming of Jesus rather than concentrating on the plain meaning of the text itself. That is to say, there did not seem to be a living tradition in continuity with the past as was available to the Jewish participants. We instituted in more recent years a shared study session of a New Testament text as a way of opening up a different dimension to the dialogue, but the issue of a sense of spiritual emptiness at the heart of contemporary Christian biblical scholarship, not to mention a certain dryness of presentation, still dominates.[4] I would add that my personal experience of lecturing at the Kirchentag in recent years to large and enthusiastic audiences is a further reflection of a hunger of some sort that a Jewish approach to textual study seems to satisfy.[5]

The quality and richness of the Jewish exegetical tradition offers a useful introduction to a second theme that we have been invited to discuss, namely, how we deal with texts which appear to run contrary to what we regard as the fundamental values of our tradition or which may be read as a licence for violence or bigotry. It is precisely here that the Jewish exegetical tradition comes into its own because of its breadth, containing often a plurality of views on any given subject necessitated by the traditional Jewish understanding of the Hebrew Bible as the revealed word of God.

In the school of Rabbi Ishmael it is taught: 'See, My word is like fire, an oracle of the Eternal, and like a hammer that shatters a rock (Jeremiah 23.29). Just as a hammer divides into several shivers (or sparks), so too every Scriptural verse yields several meanings' (*Sanh.* 34a).

Since God's word could not conceivably run contrary to the very highest contemporary values at any given period, and since the sealing of the canon required the opening of the doors of interpretation, legitimized through the concept of the 'Oral Torah', also given at Sinai, anything that might seem problematic must be 're-interpreted' so as to conform with those values. Perhaps in the past the rabbis were less self-conscious about what they were doing when they radically re-read problematic texts.

To give some illustrations: the law about the 'stubborn and rebellious son', in Deuteronomy 21.18–21, who is to be stoned to death, was turned into a purely hypothetical exercise in how to so hedge a law with conditions that it could never be applied. The notorious 'eye for an eye', even in its biblical context, might not have been intended to be understood literally. Just as the biblical 'goring ox' was a common Near Eastern artificial construct for addressing the legal problem of damages, so the 'eye for an eye' would have been similarly used for discussing 'compensation'.[6] That is certainly how the Rabbis saw it, whether based on a known tradition or applying their own legal principles. Issues like the commands to exterminate the Canaanites were addressed by the Rabbis by assuming that since the Assyrians had deported and re-imported populations, the original peoples intended by the legislation could no longer be identified. That is to say, rabbinic ingenuity, combined with their own sense of justice, ensured that whatever appeared to be problematic in their own time could be satisfactorily interpreted and hence effectively abolished.

To justify such a process, even when it meant going against earlier tradition, they could even cite biblical authority. Deuteronomy 17.9 instructs the people in case of a difficult legal decision: 'you shall go to the priests, the Levites and to the judge that shall be in those days'. Since the phrase 'that shall be in those days' is seemingly redundant, the Rabbis understood it to mean that the judge in your day is the one to consult and his judgment is to be accepted, even if he is less eminent than those of previous generations (*b. Rosh Hash.* 25b).

None of which is to say that there are no problems, nor that the Rabbis in their time were not limited by their own conventions and understandings of the world. Obvious examples of problematic areas are those concerning the legal status of women as it affects their opportunity to institute divorce proceedings, or the tragic case of a woman whose husband is missing and who cannot remarry. Such gender-based issues are rooted in the patriarchal biblical culture. Whereas the Rabbis did much to alleviate such injustices against women, they had limitations that we might identify today in terms of the psychology of patriarchy and issues of power and control.

Any number of questions must inevitably arise over time that challenge traditional conventions, problems that the concept of the Oral Torah was able to resolve. Today, in our post-emancipation society where rabbinic authority has been all but relinquished to the state, once a problem has been brought to our attention (and we are not always good at acknowledging problems) we are often stymied in attempting to resolve it. Orthodox authorities are notoriously unwilling to address certain issues because of internal disagreements that ultimately relate to a deep insecurity within the system itself

Conversely the solutions offered by Conservative and Reform rabbis are inevitably ruled out of order by Orthodoxy precisely because of their source, irrespective of the merits of the solution on offer. The threat held above everyone's head is the risk of somehow dividing the Jewish world in such a way that the breaches can never be repaired.[7]

Nevertheless, however difficult it may prove to be to address any given issue, there are innumerable mechanisms available, with or without the manipulation of biblical texts, for taking action that would satisfy at least some part of the Jewish world. After all we have 2,000 years of familiarity with such techniques and enough ingenuity and proficiency to address issues, more or less within the parameters of classical Jewish religious norms. What is more problematic today with regard to the use of the Hebrew Bible, our sacred scripture, is something very different, which by its nature is not so readily susceptible to classical scholastic or 'progressive' solutions. Rachel Adler[8] points to a radical change in our perception of the book of Esther following Purim 1994 when Baruch Goldstein entered the Mosque in Hebron and murdered Muslims at prayer. The choice of the date, occurring during a festival that celebrates the successful defence of the Jews against the attempted genocide by Haman, was no coincidence. Goldstein was acting out what he saw as a divinely ordained task. This horrifying example is one end of a spectrum of possibilities raised by our radically altered Jewish situation today. It is already evident that since the beginning of the Zionist movement, and more particularly the successful founding of the State of Israel, biblical materials, long relegated to a marginal place, have suddenly come alive again. The quest to locate place names that match biblical descriptions, the debate about the exact parameters of the borders of the land during different biblical regimes and hence the extent of the territory promised by God, the popular obsession with archaeology, the seemingly endless cycle of wars, secret negotiations and uneasy peace with surrounding neighbours, the internal struggle between religious and secular authorities about the nature of the State and which power should control it, all of such issues have precipitated us back over 2,000 years into the everyday preoccupations of the biblical world. Even the assassination of Yitzhak Rabin has haunting echoes of the assassination of Gedaliah, the last governor of the nation put in place by the Babylonians, at the hands of nationalist loyalists. The former marked the end of national sovereignty, the latter sets a kind of seal upon the political challenges that underlie its re-establishment.

In sum, we are in a radically new historical situation, the consequences and logic of which we are only slowly coming to terms with. Within a single lifetime, we have reversed 2,000 years of centrifugal forces sending us into ever-recurring exiles.

The entire rabbinic corpus of interpretation was created either in the lands of exile or under the psychological experience of exile. It was an adaptation to living under someone else's authority, and all its refinements, subtleties, compromises and adjustments have been done on the basis of a relative, even at times absolute, powerlessness. The beliefs, principles and practices of rabbinic Judaism now have to earn their place all over again amidst the radically different priorities and perceptions of a modern, Western-orientated, secular, democratic state. Moreover, the best qualities of Jewish tradition often take second place to the horse-trading and power politics of self-interest and coalition building of those who claim outright ownership of this tradition. Add to this the psychological ballast of the *Shoah* and a siege mentality that has inevitably determined priorities for several generations. Two thousand years of Jewish biblical exegesis, with all its refinements, may simply not get a look-in when Israelis confront the day-to-day problems of survival as a newly emergent nation, particularly one that must confront the challenge of holding power over another population.

Moreover, the Hebrew Bible, and not the *'chumash* and Rashi', the Bible read through the prism of rabbinic exegesis, is a school text-book and thus a directly available source of 'the word of God', unquestioned and uninterpreted. If 'fundamentalism' is a kind of 'selective literalism', there are fundamentalists galore, amongst secular Israelis no less than religious ones, who will make their selection from biblical passages to suit their private or public agenda.

Clearly the situation is not quite so grim or black and white as the above might suggest, the richness of rabbinic tradition being eminently available, even with its own time-bound limitations. But effectively we are seeing, and will increasingly see, a radically new hermeneutic emerge, one determined by the reality of Jewish sovereignty as predicted and promised in the Hebrew Bible. The effects of geography, geopolitical realities and internal adjustments amongst the ingathered Jewish 'tribes' that make up the new sovereign nation will determine how scripture is read, and, more importantly, acted out in the public arena with or without the refinements offered by Jewish tradition.

In such circumstances what of the dialogue with Christianity, and particularly the Catholic Church. Oddly enough there may be a new task of 'witness' that the Church can undertake. It is precisely because the Jewish people have not had to address the challenge of power and must now come to terms with this that the experience of the Church could be particularly relevant. If the Church can step back from its history, can evaluate the degree to which its own hermeneutics were a reflection of the power it has held over almost two millennium, and acknowledge the traps into which it was led, and not just with regards to the treatment of the Jewish people, then it might offer a model of self-criticism and a warning that may prove helpful within the frame-work of a new kind of partnership.

Let me end with a paradox that brings us again to the book of Esther. In his challenging book *The Jewish Bible after the Holocaust: A re-reading*,[9] Emil Fackenheim calls for a radical re-evaluation of scripture after the *Shoah,* by Christians and Jews alike. One of the points he makes is that the significance of Esther needs to be reconsidered because of the truth of its portrayal of the nature of the exilic situation. The threat of a Haman/Hitler, so wondrously resolved in the book, had a very different result in our time. The absence of God throughout the book also seems most accurately to portray the experience of that time when God did not appear miraculously to answer our prayers.

During the Holocaust there were thousands of nameless Esthers, less hesitant than the biblical one in risking their lives for their people: not one had the chance. The much-maligned *Judenraete* included countless would-be Mordechais: to none came the help from another place that would have made him an actual Mordechai. A heroism dwarfing the biblical – but, unlike the biblical, doomed to be unsung – was shown by a people, itself doomed to extermination. Yet not one of the saving 'what ifs' (of the book of Esther) occurred.[10]

The same biblical book can instruct a Goldstein to murder in the name of God and a Fackenheim to reflect on the implications for faith of the absence of God. Both address a challenge to a present Jewish world and a Judaism undergoing radical change. Will the Jewish people address such difficult questions alone, or are they willing, and indeed invited, to share them with Christian companions on their own parallel journey through sacred and secular time?

Notes

1. 'How do Jews Interpret the Bible Today? The Sixteenth Montefiore Lecture (17 Feb 1994), University of Southampton' *JSOT* 66, 1995, pp. 3–27, 15–17.
2. According to Rabbi Jacob Kranz, the 'Maggid of Dubno', no less an authority than the Vilna Gaon could locate the book of Deuteronomy outside the designation of unmediated divine revelation, seeing it as Moses' own retelling and reflection on what he learnt from God, exactly as in the case of the subsequent prophets. (Quoted in *Otzar hayyim* on Deuteronomy, edited by Hayyim Ya'aqov Zukkerman, Tel Aviv, date unknown).
3. The argument that is sometimes put forward that Christians in this way are simply exploring the Jewish roots of their own tradition may well apply to studying the Hebrew Bible itself, but hardly relates to the Jewish exegetical tradition that developed in the centuries after the beginnings of Christianity. Conversely, Jews are sometimes shocked to discover the influence on key Jewish commentators like Rashi of methods being developed in the contemporary Christian world. Understandably given the history of Christian treatment of Jews and of the Hebrew Bible, Jews have no such difficulties acknowledging the even more obvious influence of Islamic culture in creating new genres of biblical scholarship from philology to astronomy to philosophy by figures like

Abraham Ibn Ezra. This 'two-way' traffic at some periods in the Middle Ages needs to be more widely known.

4. One of the issues we have been asked to address at this conference is how we read each other's scriptures. The Bendorf experience shows the limitations of Jews studying the New Testament without access to Greek and a good background in rabbinic literature but at the same time the fascinating perspectives that are thrown up when Jewish understandings, even from a limited knowledge base, are brought to bear. Moreover, reading such texts without the ballast of a particular set of beliefs, if occasionally disturbing, seems to be quite refreshing and challenging to our Christian partners, but that is also a product of the mutual trust and respect engendered by the Week itself.

5. I have explored this subject further in 'Wenn Ich sehe, was Christen mit der Jüdischen Bibel machen', *Abraham-Jesus-Mohammed: Interreligiöser Dialog aus jüdischer Perspektive* ed. Jonathan Magonet, Gütersloh: Gütersloher Verlagshaus, 2000, pp. 79–94.

6. See David Daube, *Biblical Law*, Cambridge: Cambridge University Press, 1947, pp. 102–53.

7. The extent of such breaches and the need for radically new ways of addressing them would be the subject of a different kind of paper.

8. Rachel Adler, *Engendering Judaism: An Inclusive Theology and Ethics*, Philadelphia and Jerusalem: Jewish Publication Society, 1998, p. 18.

9. Emil L. Fackenheim, *The Jewish Bible after the Holocaust*, Sherman Studies of Judaism in Modern Times, Manchester: Manchester University Press, 1990.

10. Ibid. p. 62.

Discussant

– Robert Murray

I am in general agreement with Rabbi Professor Magonet's stance in exegesis, due to long friendship and shared experiences (at Leo Baeck College, Bendorf Bible Weeks and appreciation of each other's writings).

Rabbi Professor Magonet has rightly observed disappointment with Christian exegesis of our shared scriptures, in contrast with Christians' pleasure in learning something of Jewish approaches and tradition. The 'sense of spiritual emptiness' is partly due to the sterility of a predominantly 'historical-critical' method, but also to ignorance of many of the real treasures of Christian exegesis.

Among these I would emphasize the patristic exegesis that was developed by the chief heirs of early Jewish Christianity, those writing in Greek (the Antiochenes) and especially those in Syriac Aramaic. Ignorance of these in the Catholic and Protestant world has sadly impoverished Western tradition, especially as too few texts are yet known in modern translations. Though Antiochene and Syriac writers have passages of ugly anti-Jewish rhetoric, these are rare in their biblical exegesis, which is based on the intrinsic and lasting value of the shared scriptures in their own contexts and meaning. Syriac exegetes follow methods still akin to Midrash, and quite often reveal actual shared traditions. Their messianic interpretations are comparatively restricted, and their typology is not 'supersessionist', but rather expresses belief in the continuity of God's revealing action, in which they find significant similarities repeated. *Sanhedrin* 34a (several meanings in a text) has a beautiful parallel in St Ephrem (see appendix below).

The possibility of multiple meanings or implications has been controlled in both Jewish and Catholic traditions by similar sets of 'four senses'. I believe these really reduce to two: the 'plain sense' controlled by the context and the possible developments of this by imaginative application to other contexts, within the limits accepted by the interpreter's adherence to the essentials of Jewish or Christian faith. But Catholic theology has been shy of admitting imagination and the methods of poetic insight, even though the Bible is full of poetry and paradox, and Jesus' own parabolic method appealed primarily to imagination to bring about a response.

So I can welcome Jonathan Magonet's invitation to self-critical reflection. Official Catholic directives (mainly in the twentieth century) have insisted on control of exegesis by the 'Magisterium', but (except for a series of unfortunate interventions early in the twentieth century) acts of control have been rare, because bishops mostly rely on trusted teachers. Of course, we cannot but strongly approve of Pope John Paul II's insistent calls for radical changes in interpreting New Testament passages about Judaism. However, I believe it remains generally true that it is not authoritative direction but listening to the biblical text in humility, and listening to each other, that will make our listening most fruitful in our respective communities and for the faithful maintenance of our respective traditions.

Appendix

St Ephrem the Syrian (c.306–73) on how to read Scripture: *Saint Ephrem's Commentary on Tatian's Diatessaron*, tr. by Carmel McCarthy, *JSS Supplement* 2, Oxford: Oxford University Press for the University of Manchester, 1993, pp. 49–50.

§18. Who is capable of comprehending the immensity of possibilities of one of your utterances? What we leave behind us in [your utterance] is far greater than what we take from it, like those who are thirsting, [when they imbibe] from a fountain. Many are the perspectives of his word, just as many are the perspectives of those who study it. [God] has fashioned his word with many beautiful forms, so that each one who studies it may consider what he likes. He has hidden in his word all kinds of treasures so that each one of us, wherever we meditate, may be enriched by it. His utterance is a tree of life, which offers you blessed fruit from every side. It is like that rock which burst forth in the desert, becoming spiritual drink to everyone from all places. [They ate] spiritual food and drank spiritual drink (I Cor. 10:3–4).

§19. Therefore, whoever encounters one of its riches must not think that that alone which he has found is all that is in it, but [rather] that it is this alone that he is capable of finding from the many things in it. Enriched by it, let him not think that he has impoverished it. But rather let him give thanks for its greatness, he that is unequal to it.

Rejoice that you have been satiated, and do not be upset that it is richer than you. The thirsty one rejoices because he can drink, but is not upset because he is unable to render the source dry. The well can conquer your thirst, but your thirst cannot conquer the fountain. If your thirst is satiated, without the fountain running short, whenever you are thirsty, you can drink again. But if, through your being satiated, the fountain were rendered dry, your victory would be unto your misfortune. Give thanks for what you have taken away, and do not murmur over what remains and is in excess. That which you have taken and gone away with is your portion and that which is left over is also your heritage. That which you were not able to receive there and then because of your weakness, receive it at another time by means of your perseverance. And do not, in your impudence, attempt either to obtain in one moment that which cannot be taken up in one moment, or to desist from that which you are able to take up little by little.

Reading Our Sacred Texts Today

– John Pawlikowski

Introduction

Both Judaism and Christianity (and other 'religions of book' as well) must deal from time to time with the challenge of sacred texts which in part support outlooks no longer deemed acceptable. Textual obsolescence can result from fundamental changes in scientific outlook, gender relationships, or social philosophy, to name but three. Such obsolescence has sometimes led to calls for a total elimination of certain texts. Some Catholic scholars deeply involved in ecological issues, such as Thomas Barry, CP, have called for a total rewrite of the texts of creation. And the institutional Catholic Church has acknowledged the problem by allowing for the elimination of certain passages in the liturgy (especially in the Pauline corpus) which appear to countenance male domination of women. There is also the call by feminist scholars such as Phyllis Trible for a new reading of biblical 'texts of terror' in which the focus of understanding is placed much more on the exploitation of women in a particular story.

In the light of the above reality this essay could take several turns. Certainly there are texts that Jews and Catholics could profitably study together in the light of new understandings about creational, gender and social relationships as well as sexual orientation. Given that this book is centred on the Jewish–Christian relationship and the obstacles past and present that may impede the emergence of a true theology of partnership for our time, I will limit my analysis to three points: (1) the question of the proper appropriation of the first section of the Christian Bible which Catholics share in some measure with Jews; (2) approaches to New Testament texts that have historically provided a supposed biblical basis for a theology of Jewish covenantal displacement; and (3) how Jewish interpretation of certain texts might aid a better understanding of their significance for today. Section 2 will contain the heart of my analysis, an attempt to provide a viable interpretative framework for using or omitting such texts in theology and liturgy.

The Hewbrew Scriptures or First Testament

Throughout Christian history there has been a major difficulty in defining the role of the first part of the biblical canon used by the church. Some of this is highlighted in the recent debates over the proper name for this section of the Bible. Traditionally we have termed it the 'Old Testament'. That term is now under challenge from a number of scholars who would prefer *Tanach*, 'First Testament', or 'Primal Testament'. Others have argued for the retention of 'Old Testament' on the grounds that the Catholic canon is somewhat different in length and arrangement, and the arrangement in particular is due to a differing theological approach to these books on the part of Catholicism.[1] I do not wish to enter into a discussion of the 'naming' issue as such in this paper. I have done that elsewhere.[2] I could even settle for 'Old Testament' so long as the Catholic approach to the first part of the Bible was on the right track.

Historically we have seen three somewhat interrelated responses to the question, what role do the Hebrew scriptures play in the expression of Christian faith? The most radically negative was that proposed by Marcion who argued for their exclusion from the canon on the grounds that they had been totally supplanted by the New Testament. While the church as a whole rejected this radical surgery, Marcion's response left an imprint on Christian consciousness that continues into the present day. We can see its echoes in major twentieth-century biblical scholars who have exercised a tremendous impact on the modern Christian understanding of the Hebrew scriptures. Gerhard Kittel, the original editor of the highly influential *Theological Dictionary of the New Testament*, exemplifies the continuing impact of the Marcionite theology which had its roots in the 'Adversos Judaeos' theology developed in the patristic era. 'Authentic Judaism', he wrote, 'abides by the symbol of the stranger wandering restless and homeless on the face of the earth.'[3] And the prominent exegete Martin Noth, whose *History of Israel* became a standard reference for students and professors alike, described Israel as a strictly 'religious community' which died a slow, agonizing death in the first century AD. For Noth, Jewish history reached its culmination in the arrival of Jesus. His words are concise and to the point in this regard:

Jesus himself . . . no longer formed part of the history of Israel. In him the history of Israel had come, rather, to its real end. What did belong to the history of Israel was the rejection and condemnation by the Jerusalem religious community . . . Hereafter the history of Israel moved quickly to its end.[4]

A third example is Rudolf Bultmann who exercised a decisive influence over Christian biblical interpretation for decades. Unlike Kittel, Bultmann's exegesis did not carry over into politics, that is, joining the Nazi party. But, theologically speaking, his understanding of Christology also left Jews and Judaism bereft of meaning after the coming of Jesus. In his *Theology of the New Testament*, he held to the view that a Jewish people cannot be said to exist with the emergence of Christianity. For Bultmann, Jewish law, ritual and piety removed God to a distant realm while through the continued presence of Jesus in prayer and worship each individual is brought ever closer to God.

While Kittel, Noth and Bultmann may not go as far as Marcion in wanting the 'Old Testament' removed from the canon, their outlooks basically render it of little or no value for the church except as a 'foil' for Christian belief. The 'Old Testament' is to be retained in the canon, but only to show the superiority of Christianity. Such a perspective has in fact somewhat dictated the selection of readings from the Hebrew scriptures in the Catholic liturgy. There is little or nothing that Christians can learn from the 'Old Testament' so it rarely becomes the focus of liturgical preaching, except by way of negative contrast with the New Testament. This attitude likely contributed to the virtual omission of readings from the Hebrew scriptures in the Sunday Catholic liturgy until a few decades ago. And even on the rare occasions they were used (readings from the prophets in Advent and Lent and the Psalm texts) there was often a negative underside to their use. The prophets, for example, were seen as useful for understanding the birth and death of Christ, nothing more. And some approaches to the Psalms argued that their true meaning could be understood only by Christians. I recall an Advent Vespers service at Holy Name Cathedral in Chicago several years ago organized by the Office of Divine Worship of the Archdiocese and its companion unit Liturgy Training Publications. One of the readings during the service came from a major American liturgical publishers (The Liturgical Press). In that reading the author stated that the Psalms could be understood only in and through Jesus Christ. The sponsors I must say were quite red-faced over the selected text because they were in the forefront of promoting Catholic–Jewish understanding in the spirit of Vatican II.

This incident, however, is but one illustration of how deep-seated this 'foil' or the slightly better 'prelude' approach remains within the Church. Two recent examples of this mindset are to be found in commentaries on the readings for the Third Sunday of Lent 2000. The distributor of one of the most widely used parish bulletin sheets (J. S. Paluch) has in its introduction to the scripture readings for this particular Sunday the following statement:

> Throughout John's gospel, Jesus consistently transcends those things central to the Jewish tradition. Central to their tradition was the temple, so for Jesus to offer himself as a 'new' temple at the beginning of the gospel leads very naturally into the rest of the gospel.[5]

An even worse example is the commentary on the same texts found in the quarterly publication of another major American liturgical publisher, GIA Publications of Chicago. It reads:

> Jesus is determined to replace the tables of legalism tended by the merchants of hypocrisy. These tables, like the Temple, will be replaced by him, the new Temple of the New Covenant whereby he provides the passage to the Holy One. As assured as his replacing the wedding water at Cana with superlative wine, the replacement of the old temple with the new one would be just as earth shattering.[6]

While guidelines have been issued for preaching on such texts by the United States Catholic Bishops[7] and more recently by the episcopal conference of England and Wales[8], these have yet to penetrate the world of preaching and bulletin commentaries.

Another reality which adds to the problem of a deep-seated view within Christianity that the Hebrew scriptures have been 'transcended' by the New Testament, as the Paluch commentary puts it, is their absence from the lectionary during the Easter season. The message that is being conveyed, whether influenced by the classical attitude towards the 'Old Testament' which we have seen in exegetes such as Kittel and Noth or not, is that the first part of the Bible has no important role in the shaping of early Christian identity. As the Church retells the story of its origins during the Christian season the Catholic worshipper hears nothing from the Hebrew scriptures while at the same time being subjected to some harsh texts from Acts and the letters of Peter relative to the Jews. Thus it is still easy for the contemporary Catholic Christian to conclude that the Hebrew scriptures played no constructive role in the initial formulation of the faith tradition and hence there is no real reason to take them all that seriously today. There is a series of beautiful stained glass-windows at Princeton University chapel in New Jersey. All depict scenes from the Bible, both the 'Old' and the 'New' Testaments. A brochure explains that the designer so placed the windows that sunlight never shines through the windows depicting 'Old Testament' scenes, only those with 'New Testament' themes. While the brochure also includes a disclaimer that the Chapel no longer accepts the designer's approach to the 'Old Testament', we have yet another example of how pervasive the Kittel/Noth/Bultmann approach has been.

Finally, we need to be aware of the point that the late biblical scholar Fr Raymond Brown made on several occasions. Brown insisted that when Christians do in fact turn to the Hebrew scriptures they tend to focus on texts dealing with Israel's 'unfaithfulness' rather than its 'faithfulness'. Yet there are many poignant texts in the Hebrew scriptures that illustrate the Jewish people's faithfulness. Such a focus on texts of 'unfaithfulness' further contributes to the notion that the Hebrew scriptures have no substantial part in shaping Christian faith identity.

Jesus himself used the Jewish biblical texts in a central way in forging his spirituality and his sense of ministry. There was no 'Old Testament' for Jesus, and in my judgement there should be none for us today. I think Jesus would give us a quizzical look if we were to ask him about the 'Old Testament'. If Jesus did not call these texts 'Old Testament', but rather 'the scriptures', I ask should we? I am not denying the validity of the discussion about the 'unity' of the Bible from the Christian perspective. Such a discussion needs to be pursued and it may take Christians in an interpretive direction at times that will be quite different from the Jewish approach. This question has been addressed at some length in the 1985 document on presenting Jews in Catholic catechesis and preaching issued by the Vatican Commission for Religious Relations with Jews. While some of us in the Jewish–Catholic dialogue do not feel the question is handled there in a fully adequate manner, we also see an opening in the document for an enhanced appreciation of the Hebrew scriptures in Christianity and for the valid use of Jewish exegesis on these texts in framing Christian understanding of them. In his official commentary on the 1985 Vatican document now Bishop Jorge Mejia, then Secretary of the Pontifical Commission for Religious Relations with Jews, offered the following viewpoint on the document's treatment of the 'Old Testament–New Testament' relationship:

It is not always an easy matter to present the relations between both Testaments in a way that fully respects the validity of the Old Testament and shows its permanent usefulness for the Church. At this point, an effort is made to explain the meaning of what is called 'typology,' since on this a large part of our liturgical use of the Old Testament is grounded. In no way is 'typological' usage a devaluation of the validity proper to the Old Testament. Rather to the contrary. One can see this from another angle, since it has always been taught in the Catholic tradition that there is also a 'typological' use of the New Testament with respect to the 'last things' or eschatological realities (cf. no. 16). The importance of the Old Testament for Judaism is underlined. So, too, is the importance of Jews and Christians hearing the Old Testament together, so that together, in a path opened by the prophetic tradition, we may become more deeply engaged as fellow partisans for humanity today (no. 18, 19) . . . It should also be noted that limits of 'typological' usage are acknowledged, and other possible ways of reading the Old Testament in relation to the New are not excluded (cf. no. 11).[9]

We have seen some progress in recapturing the Hebrew scriptures as a living resource for Christian faith, not just as a 'foil' or a 'prelude'. Two examples come to mind. When the US Catholic Bishops were preparing their Pastoral Letter on the Economy and wished to develop a theology of human responsibility for creation they turned almost exclusively to the texts of Genesis. And the liberation theologian Gustavo Gutiérrez, faced with the increased recognition that poverty would likely continue for the foreseeable future among the people with whom he ministered in the barrios of Lima, turned to the book of Job for a fundamental resource for contemporary Christian faith expression in the midst of poverty. These are encouraging signs that Catholicism is taking a new look at the Hebrew scriptures but the lectionary commentaries which I cited earlier remind us we still have a long road to walk. Unless and until preaching and lectionary commentaries, retreats and other programmes in spiritual development, and theological reflection in the Catholic Church begin to draw from the well of the Hebrew scriptures far more deeply than they have, the 'Old Testament' will remain a barrier rather than an aid to improved Jewish–Christian understanding. We need to implement the words of the US Bishops' document God's Mercy Endures Forever far more extensively than we have to date. Speaking of the 'fulfilment' theme commonplace during Advent, the document insists:

This truth needs to be framed very carefully. Christians believe that Jesus is the promised Messiah who has come (Luke 4.22), but also know that his messianic kingdom is not yet fully realized ... While the biblical prophecies of an age of universal 'Shalom' are 'fulfilled' (i.e., irreversibly inaugurated) in Christ's coming, that fulfilment is not yet completely worked out in each person's life or perfected in the world at large. It is the mission of the Church to prepare the world for the full flowering of God's reign, which is, but is 'not yet.' Both the Christian 'Our Father' and the Jewish 'Kaddish' exemplify this message. Both Christianity and Judaism seal their worship with a common hope: 'Thy kingdom come!' With the Jewish people, we await the complete realization of the messianic age.[10]

The New Testament

The New Testament presents us with a fair number of challenging texts with respect to Christian–Jewish relations (as well as to gender and other issues). Focusing on the Christian–Jewish area, the statements which vilify the Pharisees, speak of 'the Jews' as responsible for the death of Christ or appear to abrogate the Jewish covenant are among the most prominent. I cannot go into an analysis of all the specific texts involved. Permit me to confine myself to some general observations that would apply to all of them. The first principle we need to apply to an interpretation of these troublesome texts I would term the 'principle of context'. The Gospels and letters of the New Testament were all composed in a specific geographical and theological context. While they certainly were intended to have broader application beyond their immediate setting, without a detailed understanding of that setting we can easily misconstrue their meaning. This has been a frequent occurrence in Christian biblical interpretation. Clemens Thoma, for example, has shown how many of the parables were understood by Christian exegetes as implying Jewish exclusion from the Covenant and the final divine reign when in fact they were based on Jewish parables rooted in internal Jewish religious conflict.[11]

The principle of context will help us tremendously with respect to some of the generalizations about 'the Jews' where it is clear that only Jewish leaders were involved or in locating texts in the late first century (rather than the time of Jesus himself) when there was evident conflict over converts and over the apparent expulsion of Christians from the synagogue. Knowing such a context certainly does not resolve all our difficulties with such texts. But it can aid considerably in taking the 'sting' out of them in terms of the Christian–Jewish relationship. The same can be said for the term 'the Pharisees'. Having become aware through recent scholarship on the Pharisaic movement by Ellis Rivkin, David Flusser and others that Pharisaism was a complex reality with considerable internal strife and recognizing considerable affinity between many core Pharisaic teachings and Jesus' religious perspective, a point highlighted by the 1985 Vatican *Notes on the Correct Presentation of Jews and Judaism in Preaching and Catechesis in the Roman Catholic Church*,[12] the principle of context allows us to defuse considerably the degree of hostility between Jesus and 'the Pharisees'. His conflict may in fact have been only with 'some Pharisees', as some recent New Testament translations now render the original Greek. Again, this application of the principle of context does not remove all problematical aspects of these texts. But it does help undercut generalized assertions about Jesus' inherent opposition to Pharisaism whose vision played a central role in generating post-biblical Judaism.

The principle of context also helps us resolve another source of tension in terms of key New Testament texts, especially when combined with the principle of 'authoritative interpretation'. I speak, for example, of the problem of deciding whether either Paul in Romans 9–11 or the letter to the Hebrews are to be taken as the definite starting point for a Christian theology of Judaism and the Jewish people today. In Romans 9–11 Paul definitely asserts that Jews remain in the covenantal relationship with God after the coming of Christ. While there remain some problematical aspects to his way of stating this, and while he cannot explain how this is so in light of the 'newness' in Christianity except by calling it a 'mystery', in the end his affirmation of continued Jewish covenantal inclusion is beyond question. The author of Hebrews, in contrast, leads us in an opposite direction. Employing the 'new' covenant text from Jeremiah (31.31–34), Hebrews argues that the old covenant is obsolete and about to disappear, to be replaced by 'laws' given directly into the minds of people and written upon their hearts (8.1–13).

How do we choose today between these two contradictory texts? Here again the principle of context can assist our choice. While the exact geographic and social setting of Paul's letter to the Romans is the subject of some disagreement among scholars, there is consensus that it comes rather late in Paul's ministry (perhaps very late if one attributes some of the late 'letters' to Paul's disciples rather than to Paul himself) and that it is the most theological of his letters. That Paul would devote three chapters to the Christian–Jewish relationship as he was ending his ministry and engaging in his most comprehensive theological analysis is especially significant. If these chapters had appeared in Thessalonians, for example, one could more easily downplay their significance. But located in Romans it becomes clear that Paul saw the Christian–Jewish relationship as remaining central in Christian faith understanding, and that the relationship was to be seen in a positive light. Alternatively, Hebrews is a rather ambiguous letter. Its authorship is uncertain. Virtually no one today attributes it to Paul as was the case in earlier times. Even the Catholic lectionary has dropped the notion of Pauline authorship. The social context is also rather fuzzy. One contemporary school of thought would place it in the period after the destruction of the Second Jewish Temple. In this view its immediate recipients were Jewish Christians who were devoted to the Temple and for whom its destruction was traumatic. What the author of Hebrews was trying to tell these distraught Christians was that the loss of the Temple should not be viewed so dramatically because Jesus had established a 'new' covenant not based in the Temple. Put another way, Hebrews is a pastoral response to the plight of suffering Christians, not a theological statement on the same level as Romans. Thus it has less theological authority.

This contextual understanding is critical for appreciating why the bishops assembled at the Second Vatican Council selected Romans over Hebrews as the scriptural basis of their new vision of the Christian–Jewish relationship which they articulated in chapter 4 of *Nostra Aetate*. Coming into play here is also the principle of authoritative interpretation. For Catholics scripture needs to be interpreted in the context of tradition. These are not two separate and distinct fonts of revelation, as the Second Vatican Council underlined. Rather they represent an integrated understanding of a biblical text. Behind this Catholic perspective on biblical interpretation stands the Pharisaic/rabbinic notion of written and oral Torah. For Catholic Christians scripture becomes the word of God through the authentic interpretation of the Church, especially as exercised through the teaching authority of the bishops. The bishops at Vatican II exercised that authority in selecting Romans 9–11 rather than Hebrews 8. And through the principle of context we see that their decision had firm footing. They opted for the more profoundly theological statement over the pastoral response.

Another aspect of the principle of authoritative interpretation which applies to the Romans/Hebrews conflict and to the many other troublesome texts as well is that the texts selected for use by the

Church for liturgy, preaching and theological reflection ought to be in sync with theological statements made by the popes and councils. In terms of the Catholic–Jewish relationship from Vatican II's *Nostra Aetate* onwards through the 1974 and 1985 Vatican statements and most especially in the writings of Pope John Paul II who has emphasized that Jews and Christians remain linked together in their very basic identities we see a strong affirmation of fundamental Jewish–Christian bonding and of the constructive Jewish influence on Jesus and early Christianity as well as a firm denial of collective Jewish guilt for the death of Jesus. Any scriptural texts that go contrary to such assertions, whether in John, Acts, Hebrews or elsewhere, no longer constitute the authentic catechesis of the Church, whether that catechesis is presented in the classroom or the liturgy. The late Cardinal Joseph Bernardin of Chicago, in his historic speech at the Hebrew University in Jerusalem, made this point quite forcefully, relying on the writings of the late Fr Raymond Brown. The Cardinal said:

> Father Brown maintains that this teaching of John about the Jews, which resulted from the historical conflict between church and synagogue in the latter part of the first century CE, can no longer be taught as authentic doctrine or used as catechesis by contemporary Christianity. This is a key pastoral point. Christians today must come to see that such teachings, while an acknowledged part of their biblical heritage, can no longer be regarded as definite teaching in light of our improved understanding of developments in the relationship between early Christianity and the Jewish community of the time. As Brown says in his book, *The Community of the Beloved Disciple*, 'It would be incredible for a twentieth-century Christian to share or justify the Johannine contention that "the Jews are the children of the Devil," an affirmation which is placed on the lips of Jesus' (John 8.44).[13]

The above contention by Cardinal Bernardin and Fr Brown presents a special challenge for the use of New Testament passages in the liturgy where the principle of context is difficult to apply. The US Bishops' Committee on Liturgy issued important guidelines for preaching on the texts in the current lectionary[14] as also have more recently the Bishops' Conference of England and Wales. These are helpful steps, but in my judgement they still remain inadequate for the task confronting us in light of the fundamental theological about-face undertaken by Vatican II in chapter 4 of *Nostra Aetate* where the council replaced the classical Christian theology of Jewish displacement from the Covenant with a theology of covenantal inclusion.[15] As I see it, we need a comprehensive look at the current lectionary as well as the very structure of the Catholic liturgy, especially during the major periods of Advent, Lent and Eastertime. Some of the most problematic New Testament texts from Acts and the letters of Peter occur, for example, during the Easter season.[16] While the principle of context can locate these in the conflict between Jews and Christians in the first century CE and hence somewhat ameliorate their negative impact in a classroom, they present a special challenge in the liturgy. Hence there is need for a total review of texts used in the current lectionary to see if some of the more problematical ones can be eliminated from liturgical use (not from the New Testament as such). Soon after the Second Vatican Council Fr Edward Flannery, then Secretary of the US Bishops' Secretariat for Catholic–Jewish Relations, convened a group of scripture and other scholars to do precisely that. We eventually completed a report which recommended some particular changes by way of elimination and substitution. Unfortuately hostile elements within the leadership of the Catholic Biblical Association blocked this report from reaching the American Bishops even though the then President of the CBA, my late colleague Fr Carroll Stuhlmueller, CP, was a member of this commission and enthusiastically supported its recommendations. I believe it is time to try this process anew. Also liturgists, experts in the Catholic–Jewish dialogue and scripture scholars need to engage in a long-term process of examining the very structure of Catholic liturgy. Does it convey to the faithful the truths underlined so forcefully in *Nostra Aetate* and the many statements from Pope John Paul II? Do Catholics leave worship during the central liturgical seasons convinced of Jewish–Christian bonding, of basic Roman responsibility for the death of Jesus and of the positive influence of Second Temple Judaism? If not, then we are failing to implement fully the constructive vision of the Jewish–Christian relationship offered us by Vatican II and John Paul II.

The Christian Bible and Jewish Interpretation

I would like to end my essay with some words on the importance of the principle of Jewish–Christian bonding, as I would term it. This principle grows out of the theological assertions of John Paul II in this regard.[17] The theology of Jewish–Christian bonding present in the writings of the Pope make continued Jewish interpretation of biblical texts in the First Testament as well as Jewish interpretations of the

New Testament by scholars such as Alan Segal, Michael Cook and Sarah Tanzer mandatory for Christian scholars. Beyond simply being helpful to the understanding of particular texts, such Jewish interpretations ought to be regarded now as 'in-house' material and not merely as interesting extrinsic data. In other words, if we take the principle of Jewish–Christian bonding seriously, as I believe we must in light of Vatican II and the teachings of John Paul II, consulting evolving Jewish interpretation of biblical texts should now be regarded as routine by Christian scholars. Incidentally, I would say the same for Jewish scholarship, but that is not my topic here.

Let me give just one example of how such consultation of Jewish interpretation can prove helpful. My Catholic Theological Union, Chicago, colleague Hayim Perelmuter has shown how the extremely controversial (in the context of contemporary ecological concerns) Genesis creation texts can in fact be understood in a manner that answers some of the objections raised by ecologists such as Lynn White and Thomas Berry. Perelmuter shows how later rabbinic interpretation clearly and consistently associated these creation texts with the human obligation to preserve rather than exploit what God has given humankind and what ultimately belongs to God alone. In the face of subsequent rabbinic interpretation of Genesis and Deuteronomy, Perelmuter concludes that

> It is a misreading of Scripture to suggest that the Bible is person centred, that the human bestrides the world like a colossus and can do anything with nature. The 'image of God' in us does not make us God. It does make us God's agent or steward, and God wants God's world hallowed and preserved. That is what '*mitzvah*' (divine commands to humans) is about, and doing ecology is a supreme *mitzvah*![18]

Yet few Christian scholars bother to consult the rabbinic interpretations of texts.

This principle is also helpful in Christian interpretation of the parables, to refer back to the point of Clemens Thoma, where the failure to understand Jesus' parables in their Jewish context has frequently led scripture scholars such as Bultmann, Perin and Crossan to interpretations which imply Jewish removal from the reign of God. Christians, in such 'reversal' parabolic interpretation, are seen as replacing Jews in the covenant since Jews have failed to recognize the 'light of Christ'.

The various principles explained and applied above certainly do not solve all the problems with difficult scripture texts. I would never make that strong a claim. But, if applied on a consistent basis, they can move Catholicism to a more comprehensive and in-depth appropriation of Vatican II and John Paul II's teachings on Jews and Judaism and begin to foment a more profound consciousness of inherent Christian–Jewish bonding. May we have the courage and resolve to commit ourselves as Christians wholeheartedly to this task.

Notes

1. Cf. Roger Brooks and John J. Collins (eds), *Hebrew Bible or Old Testament: Studying the Bible in Judaism and Christianity*, Notre Dame, IN: University of Notre Dame Press, 1990.
2. Cf. John T. Pawlikowski, 'Jews and Christians: The Contemporary Dialogue', *Quarterly Review*, 4:4, Winter 1984, pp. 23–36.
3. Gerhard Kittel, *Die Judenfrage*, Stuttgart: Kohlhammer, 1933, p. 73.
4. Martin Noth, *The Laws in the Pentateuch and Other Studies*, Edinburgh: Oliver and Boyd, 1966, p. 63.
5. Bulletin for March 26, 2000. Chiller Park, IL: J. S. Paluch, 1.
6. Commentary on Readings for Sunday, 26 March 2000 (Third Sunday of Lent), *GIA Quarterly* 11:2, Winter 2000, p. 22.
7. Bishops' Committee on the Liturgy, National Conference of Catholic Bishops, *God's Mercy Endures Forever: Guidelines on the Presentation of Jews and Judaism in Catholic Preaching*, Washington: United States Catholic Conference, 1988.
8. Committee for Catholic/Jewish Relations, Bishops' Conference of England and Wales, *Guidelines for Catholic–Jewish Relations*, Sparrows Herne, Bushey Heath, Herts, UK: The Secretariat, Committee for Catholic/Jewish Relations of the Roman Catholic Bishops' Conference of England and Wales, 1999, pp. 10–20.
9. Jorge Mejia, 'A Note for the Presentation of the Document of the Commission for Religious Relations with the Jews', in Eugene J. Fisher and Leon Klenicki (eds), *In Our Time: The Flowering of the Jewish–Catholic Dialogue*, New York/ Mahwah, NJ: Paulist Press, 1990, p. 55.
10. Bishops' Committee on the Liturgy, *God's Mercy*, pp. 7–8.
11. Cf. Clemens Thoma, 'Differences with the Church in the Rabbinic Parables', in John Pawlikowski, OSM, and Hayim Goren Perelmuter (eds), *Reinterpreting Revelation and Tradition: Jews and Christians in Conversation*, Ashland, OH: Sheed and Ward, 2000, pp. 51–62.
12. Cf. Fisher and Klenicki (eds), *In Our Time*, p. 45.
13. Cardinal Joseph L. Bernardin, *A Blessing to Each Other*, Chicago: Liturgy Training Publications, 1996, p. 155.
14. Cf. nn. 7.and 8.
15. Cf. John T. Pawlikowski, 'Vatican II's Theological About-Face on the Jews: Not Yet Fully Recognized, *The Ecumenist* 37:1, Winter 2000, pp. 4–6.
16. Cf. John T. Pawlikowski and James A. Wilde, *When Catholics Speak about Jews*, Chicago: Liturgy Training Publications, 1987.

17. Cf. Eugene J. Fisher and Leon Klenicki (eds), *Pope John Paul II on Jews and Judaism*, Washington: United States Catholic Conference, 1987, and *Spiritual Pilgrimage: Texts on Jews and Judaism 1979–1995 – Pope John Paul II*, New York: Crossroad, 1995.

18. Hayim G. Perelmuter, ' "Do Not Destroy" – Ecology in the Fabric of Judaism', ed. Richard N. Fragomeni and John T. Pawlikowski, *The Ecological Challenge: Ethical, Liturgical, and Spiritual Responses*, Collegeville, MN: The Liturgical Press, 1994, pp. 129–38.

Discussant

– Alexandra Wright

What constitutes the sacred texts of the Jewish community today? Perhaps that is where we should start before addressing the challenging and provocative questions raised by Dr Pawlikowski's paper. The Torah, indeed the totality of the Hebrew Bible, constitutes the principal textual cannon for an observant Jewish community. I see *Tanakh* through the twin lens of critical-historical scholarship on the one hand and on the other within an organic, cohesive, compelling and declamatory liturgical context. Let me spell out this schizophrenic approach. Reason demands that I bring to my reading of *Tanakh* a degree of scepticism conditioned by my knowledge of what Dr Pawlikowski has termed the principle of context. When I am reading or explaining a text I am anxious to reveal its contextual origins and to expose the composite nature of the Torah but at the same time, at the very moment of declaiming a text from the Torah within a liturgical setting such as a *Shabbat* morning service, the Torah must live, it must be unitary, it must be eloquent, it must compel from us a response that goes beyond critical scholarship, that awakens our moral faculties and our religious sensibilities. Ki hamitzvah hazot asher anochi mitzav'cha hayom lo nifleit himimcha velo rechoka hi.

> For this commandment that I command you this day is not too hard for you nor too remote; it is not in heaven that you should say: 'who will go up to heaven for us and fetch it for us so that we may hear it and do it?' (Deut. 30.11–12)

The nobility of this language, the dramatic effect of calling us to raise our eyes heavenward then across the sea, only to find that the word is very near to you, it is in your mouth and in your heart for you to do it, serve to bind us to the authority of the text and its meaning. It speaks to the heart of the people. Not so another a text, this time from Numbers, placed in God's mouth – the ordeal of the waters of bitterness. Is this too a sacred text, that when a spirit of jealousy comes upon a husband, whether his wife has defiled herself or not, she must be brought before the priest who shall humiliate her and force her to drink the waters of bitterness, with its grotesque consequences if she is guilty? Shall I select what shall be a sacred text for my people or shall I wrestle with its distorted misogyny and name the abhorrent holy? The *Siddur*, the Jewish prayer book, is to the text book of my faith, not a catechism, though it is perhaps the nearest one will get to an expression of belief in Judaism, but an organic and human expression of yearning for knowledge of the unseen God whose universal sovereignty has yet to be fulfilled. More diffuse, unsystematic yet profoundly influential is the oral Torah, the body of text that determines the sacred passage of time, the Talmud and its successive commentaries, codes and interpretations. All of these texts determine the pattern of observant and even not so observant Jewish life today. To read these texts is to engage profoundly with the past, to discern not simply one meaning but a multi-textured meaning. It is to engage in a dialogue with a text. When you read God's word, says Kierkegaard, you must constantly be saying to yourself, 'it is talking to me and about me'.

So much then for my own personal response to the reading of our sacred text today. To turn now to the context and questions that Dr Pawlikowski's paper raised, I will limit myself to just a few points. Dr Pawlikowski says that in 1985 the Vatican Commission for Religious Relations with Jews issued a document on presenting Jews in Catholic catechesis and preaching. What does this say to us as Jews? Yes, we know that there has always been a place for the Jews in Christian liturgy. It has been an uncomfortable and deeply painful place. But the very fact that the Vatican is thinking, is considering the place of Jews in Catholic liturgy is extraordinary. Consider it in the reverse. The names of Jesus and Jew have sat uneasily together. I speak not so much of the realm of scholarship but of liturgy and preaching. How will Jews find a place for the Christian scriptures or the figure of Jesus of Nazareth in their liturgical life? Put more impertinently, does the Greek Testament have anything to offer the Jew in their religious life? Is there a place for Jesus in contemporary Jewish theology? Rabbi Dr Ignaz Maybaum, one of British Jewry's few theologians and himself a refugee from the *Shoah*, drew on the imagery of the New Testament to place into context the sufferings caused by the Holocaust. 'The Golgotha of modern mankind', he wrote, 'is Auschwitz. The Cross, the Roman gallows, was replaced by the gas chamber.'[1] The crucifixion of Jesus becomes a paradigm for

Jewish suffering in the concentration camps of Europe – not the suffering caused by the destruction of the Temples, nor by the expulsion of the Jews from Spain, nor even by countless martyrs, burned by Hadrian or later by the Crusaders. However the Jew may choose to respond to this powerful imagery, it is clear that the Jesus of the Christian scriptures, as perceived by Maybaum, does not transcend his suffering but is the tragic human embodiment of it.

I find that imagery both tragic in the extreme but also profoundly moving. Dr Pawlikowski asks whether Catholic liturgy, and I quote,

> conveys to the faithful the truths underlined so forcefully in *Nostra Aetate* and the many statements from Pope John Paul II. Do Catholics leave worship during the central liturgical seasons convinced of Jewish–Christian bonding, of basic Roman responsibility for the death of Jesus and of the positive influence of Second Temple Judaism? (p. 132, above)

These questions are addressed to the Christian but they challenge too the questions of my own liturgy. There is no overt underlying theology in Judaism that guides us in the relationship we have with Christians. It has been a theology of rejection and blindness, mirroring undoubtedly the rejection and blindness attributed to Jews in the Christian liturgy. Indeed when my ten-year old son came home from his state primary school a few weeks ago clutching his hymn book in order to show me a verse in a hymn that referred to God's holy people rejecting Christ, stripping him and putting him on the cross, that theology was reinforced and it was a painful introduction for him to an antiquated Christian theology about Jews.

I would conclude by saying that while the Jew is becoming increasingly comfortable with the role played by Jewish scholars in examining the sacred texts of Christianity, there is an inevitable imbalance in the way the Christian can transform his or her perception of the Hebrew Bible or the place of the Jew within Christianity on the one hand and the way in which Jews can regard the place of the Christian in their world and the role of the Christian scriptures. Yet despite this imbalance, there is surely a certain stiff-necked stubbornness that refuses to allow us to move on from this rejection theology on our part to a theology of wrestling with our Christian sister. In Genesis 30, Rachel the matriarch finds herself unable to conceive, while her sister Leah is the mother to four sons and her handmaid Bilhah bears two sons. As the second of these boys is born, Rachel explains, 'Naftulei elohim niftalti im achoti, gam yacholti', which literally can be translated as 'with the wrestlings of God I have wrestled with my sister and have prevailed' (Gen. 20.8). This is the explanation she gives to the naming of Bilhah's second son Naftali. But what is actually meant by this phrase? Nachum Sarna, in his commentary to the verse, suggests that the phrase 'naftulei elohim' might mean a contest for God, that is for divine favour. Despite Rachel's triumphant 'gam yacholti', 'yet I have prevailed' – the same verb, by the way, which is used of Jacob who prevails over the man with whom he wrestles at the ford of Jabbok two chapters later – I believe the theological paradigm of wrestling is an appropriate, if somewhat physical, one. It reflects the visceral encounter that is the next stage in our relationship as Jews and Christians, sisters wrestling still for divine favour, still believing in the prevailing nobility of their own text, but touching, moving, forcing each other to recognize the voice and body of the other.

Notes

1. Ignaz Maybaum, *The Face of God after Auschwitz*, Amsterdam: Polak and Van Gennep, 1965, p. 36. Maybaum adds '. . . in Auschwitz the Jewish people had their Golgotha; six million Jews were crucified in Auschwitz' (p. 78). He goes on to say: 'We appreciate the warm fellowship in which this phrase is directed towards us, but we cannot help wondering whether the reference to Golgotha is appropriate to our martyrdom.' He then proceeds to – as it were dechristianize the symbolism of Golgotha: 'Auschwitz as a modern Golgotha was a place of cruel paganism . . . Golgotha with Christianity absenting itself is a "place of skulls". Auschwitz is the pagan Golgotha of our times' (p. 80).

Discussion recorder

– Elizabeth Tikvah Sarah

Following the remarks made by the speakers on their papers, and the responses of the discussants, eleven people contributed to the discussion. The first contribution came from Professor Elliot Dorff. He outlined four dimensions of the experience of dialogue: developments in scriptural understanding; developments in tradition; liturgy and moral values (education, religious services, etc.) which provide the context for scriptural interpretation; and the fact that dialogue is an on-going process, involving leaving behind 'repugnant interpretations', and choosing which texts we want to focus on to develop our awareness of one another today. According to Professor Dorff, this process leads to a situation where we produce new bases for Jewish–Catholic dialogue, retell our stories and select which tales we want to tell.

The next contributor was Professor Guy Stroumsa. He argued that it is necessary to resolve theological problems between Jews and Christians in the context of culture and history. As an example, he cited the cases of the biblical scholars Kittel and Bultmann of the 'Liberal Protestant' school in Germany and their attitudes to Nazism.

Father Michael McGarry pointed out that while 'past Catholic attitudes could be nourished fully without reference to the Hebrew Bible', since the Second Vatican Council, the Hebrew scriptures are now incorporated into the Lectionary (although not for the Easter season).

However, these texts are read for their Christian meanings. Dialogue today makes possible the exciting prospect of Catholics finding out the Jewish meanings of texts such as Isaiah 53. Father McGarry then drew attention to the fact that developments in inclusive language (with reference to people) and expansionist language (with reference to God) sometimes lead to problematic changes in the texts – such as Palestinians omitting references to 'Israel' and 'Zion', or the removal of 'violent' language. He suggested that 'we need to come to a place where we don't read literally'.

Sister Mary Kelly argued that in reading our sacred texts today, the most important question for all levels of the Church – scholarship, education and preaching – is the relationship of the first part of the Bible to the New Testament. She felt that this is so crucial that 'until we get it right, we can't get Covenant and Election right', adding that fundamentalism within Christian preaching rarely takes account of the historical context of the Gospel texts.

Professor Susannah Heschel pointed out – referring back to Professor Guy Stroumsa's remarks – that the German Protestant scholar, Bultmann, was a pivotal figure in the development of Christian exegesis, and that the more conservative Christology of Catholicism prevented the 'perversions' which led Protestants to embrace Nazism.

Dr Lynne Scholefield commented that Rabbi Alexandra Wright's treatment of the sisters Leah and Rachel 'wrestling' together, under-lines the different approaches of Jews and Christians to biblical texts. She argued that engagement with the language of the Bible enables Jews to draw on that language to speak about their own lives, and so connect themselves to their traditions and their scripture. She suggested that Catholics can learn from Jews and 'find from scripture the language of how to live our lives', adding that it is 'making connections between people's own experiences and the text which is enriching'.

Rabbi Dr Mark Winer acknowledged that as 'a self-confessed liberal' the session had reminded him 'to take texts seriously' so that 'we are able to deal with people who use/misuse them'.

Following on from the comments of Rabbi Professor Jonathan Magonet in his paper, Rabbi Winer raised the issue of the reading of the book of Esther at the Festival of Purim, and the variety of Jewish approaches: while one Reform tradition involves 'leaving out the nasty bits', in the Reform movement in Britain congregations read it all 'and choke on some of it'. He argued that the book of Esther is a source of 'anti-otherism', as is true of other texts within the Hebrew scriptures, and finished his remarks with a question: 'How do we handle texts which continue to be used in ways that are antithetical to our religious convictions?'

Professor Mary Boys commented that while the rabbinic way of reading texts involves beginning with questions, the Catholic approach emphasizes finding meanings. She pointed out that Catholic interpretation is not confined to allegory and typology, but also includes a contemplative approach, 'which helps us not to be so controlled by words in texts and to look deeper'. She suggested that the approach of Historical Criticism, which came late to Catholicism, has proved 'very enriching', in contrast with postcolonial-postmodern readings within the Church which are 'often anti-Semitic'.

Rabbi Sybil Sheridan drew attention to an important imbalance in Jewish–Catholic dialogue: Jews do not study the New Testament, while Catholics do study texts – the Hebrew scriptures – which are not central to Catholic teaching. She suggested that we need to redress the balance, and Jews should begin to read the New Testament. She argued that if we are to look together at texts like Isaiah 53, Jews will only be able to have a proper understanding of what such passages mean to Christians if they study the New Testament. Turning back to the issue of reading the book of Esther, Rabbi Dr Andrew Goldstein, said that he came from a Liberal synagogue 'where we don't read all of the Book of Esther', and pointed out that the late Rabbi Bernard Hooker did not read all the traditional *Haftaro,* the readings from the Prophets accompanying the Torah reading in services. Following on from Rabbi Sheridan, Rabbi Goldstein suggested that just as Catholics now read the Hebrew Bible in church, Jews should read the New Testament in synagogue.

The last contributor to the discussion was Father Peter Cullen, who pointed out that the texts which Catholic congregations hear when they go to mass are problematic and are at odds with the current stage of Catholic–Jewish dialogue. He closed with a request to his Jewish dialogue partners: 'In addition to helping us to read the Hebrew Bible, help us to read the New Testament through an understanding of Second Temple Judaism.'

How do we respond to the values of egalitarianism, autonomy, pluralism and democracy? How do we respond to the values of secularism and contemporary humanism?

C. The Challenge of Modernity and Postmodernity

– Susannah Heschel

Before beginning my formal presentation, I would like to note how deeply moved I am by the very existence of this conference, a dialogue between Jews and representatives of the Vatican. Although this sort of dialogue is one that is by now forty years old, and I myself grew up surrounded by discussions of the Second Vatican Council's *Nostra Aetate*, in which my father took part, I continue to be amazed at the extraordinary efforts that have been made by Catholic theologians to reach out in friendship with Jews. Indeed, we have been partners for some time, even though a theology of partnership may not have been articulated. I would also like to mention, on a personal note, how much strength and inspiration I have drawn as a Jew from Catholicism over the years. Since childhood, I have longed for the sort of intense religious community that Catholic Religious have created. Often, when Jewish demands seem particularly difficult, such as the extraordinary, laborious preparations required for Passover, I read Catholic writings on religious discipline and draw motivation from them. The work of Catholic feminists has helped me to understand the depth of the problems Jewish women face and through that understanding I have gained a sense of optimism. My exposure to Catholicism, in other words, has made me a better Jew, and I would like to acknowledge my gratitude.

My impression is that Jews throughout the world share my feeling of admiration for the extraordinary outreach of Pope John Paul II to the Jewish community. He has certainly made greater progress in Christian–Jewish relations than any other single figure of this century.

And I would quickly add my admiration not only for his statements concerning the Holocaust, but also for the respect he has shown Judaism, particularly in documents such as the 1998 statement concerning the Sabbath. Yet I must also articulate my concern about other aspects of Vatican teaching. As a speaker at the 1994 United Nations Conference on Population and Development, in Cairo, I was disturbed to see the inordinate and absolute opposition of the Vatican to women's right to control our fertility. My concern in that regard extends not only to the lives of individual women but also to the impact of uncurtailed population growth on the future of life on our planet. Thus, while I have unalloyed admiration for the Pope in certain areas, I am deeply troubled in other respects.

The title of this session is 'The Challenge of Modernity and Post-modernity Which Faces Us Alike', and the formulation for this session asks, 'How do we respond to the values of egalitarianism, autonomy, pluralism and democracy? How do we respond to the values of secularism and contemporary humanism?' Let me begin by noting that I am not a theologian, nor a rabbi, nor a representative in any way of a Jewish organization, but rather an academic with interests in the history of religious thought. Thus, my purpose will be not to respond to the challenges formulated in the questions posed to this session, but to outline in greater detail the nature and rubrics of those questions. I would first observe that the questions themselves are the questions of modernity, not of postmodernism, which are of a very different order, and that the questions are those of men, but not of feminists. My paper will begin by examining the differences between the challenges of modernity and postmodernism, and then look specifically at two of the central challenges to religion that have come to the fore in the postmodernist critique of religion: feminist theory and postcolonial theory.

The classic definition of modernity's challenge to theology has been formulated in a series of studies by the sociologist of religion Peter Berger. Berger's definitions have been widely influential, and yet their assumptions have been shattered by the rise of postmodernist criticism. Berger speaks of the pre-modern religious situation as occurring beneath a 'sacred canopy' of belief, a canopy shattered by modernity. The modern situation he defines, in *Rumor of Angels*, consists of a tension between what he calls 'value-free' social science and 'highly evaluative theological propositions'.[1] Modern secular thought, he argues, 'has sought to invalidate the reality of a religious view of the world,' using the sociology of knowledge 'to relativize the relativizers'.[2] The relativization of religion reached its crisis, he claims, in the challenge of religious pluralism, which undermines the authority of religious traditions and their claims to absolute truth. As a result, theology has been forced into three possible defensive positions, he argues in his book, *The Heretical Imperative*. These he characterizes as reaffirming the authority of the tradition in defiance of modernity's challenges; secularizing or modernizing the tradition; or uncovering and retrieving the experiences embodied in the tradition. He calls these three options those of deduction, reduction and induction, and concludes that only the inductive approach is a viable response to modernity and to the challenge of religious pluralism.

Let me note that Berger claims his analysis is equally applicable to all religious traditions, and that his concentration on Protestant theology is simply due to its own self-conscious response to modernity through theological liberalism, a tradition he sees beginning with Schleiermacher and culminating with Barth. Not only does Berger ignore Catholic and Jewish theological developments during the same period, he also ignores the representations of Catholicism and Judaism within Protestant theology. Yet it is precisely that valorization of Protestantism that requires reconsideration: how did German Protestantism manage so successfully to construct an image of itself as a mainstream, normative response to modernity, while constructing an image of Catholicism as a pre-modern backwater and Judaism as an avant-garde, even radical harbinger of the modern? Indeed, that image was dangerously successful; the association of the Jews with modernity, and the modern with the Jewish, was problematic enough during periods of economic and social stability in Germany, but once economic difficulties arose, such as the 1870s stock market problems, or the post-World War I economic collapse, Jews were blamed for forcing a destabilizing modernity on an unwilling Germany. Just as the Jew was modern, modernity was Jewish, and the association of the cultural flourishings of the Weimar era with Jews, as Peter Gay has delineated in several of his books, including *Freud, Jews and Other Germans*, contributed to Nazi anti-Semitism.[3]

Although Peter Berger's *The Heretical Imperative* was published only twenty years ago, in 1979, and remains a standard text in numerous courses on modernity and religion at universities and seminaries, its assumptions strike us today as remarkably naive and entirely out of touch with the methodological approaches to religious thought that have developed in the academy in the past ten or fifteen years. Our dissociation from Berger's work is a mark of how far behind we have left the agenda of modernity and entered the world of postmodernism.

There are numerous aspects to the dissociation we experience from Berger; I will address just several. There is, first, his insistence on German Liberal Protestantism as representative of religious thought; indeed, of exemplifying religion itself. No attention is paid by him to the historical context in which that theological tradition took shape, in Germany, concomittant with the rise of modern anti-Semitism, racism and German colonialism. With all of his insistence that religious pluralism is the central challenge to theology in the modern era, Berger ignores the presence of Jewish theologians in Germany, Jews who challenged Protestant theologians for their inaccurate depictions of Judaism, particularly in relation to the origins of Christianity. The Jewish challenge, briefly stated, was the demonstration by the *Wissenschaft des Judentums* that the teachings attributed to Jesus in the Gospels were common to the Pharisees of the first century. Jesus, Abraham Geiger wrote, in books and articles that were widely read by German Protestants, said nothing new, unique, or original, and Christianity could not consider itself to be the faith of Jesus, but the religion about Jesus.[4] Berger also ignores the important study of German Protestantism by Uriel Tal, which demonstrates the problem of the breakdown of boundaries between Liberal Judaism and Liberal Protestantism.[5] Once both theological traditions had accommodated modernity by eliminating belief in the supernatural – dogma as well as miracles – what remained was a set of moral platitudes shared by both communities, making the religion indistinguishable. Not only are non-Protestants ignored in Berger's definition of religion and modernity, women are absent as well, and I will turn to the role of the feminist movement in a moment.

The most significant way in which Berger's book seems dated, however, is the epistemological assumption of his arguments. Berger stands in a prior generation, as one of the last heirs to an Enlightenment understanding of knowledge as corresponding to reality, and reason to nature. By contrast, for our generation, deeply imbued with the work of Michel Foucault, concern with the relationship between power and religious thought constitutes the epistemological starting point. Ever since Foucault, we stand in a fully different intellectual context. No longer is it possible to speak, as Berger does, of a 'value-free' social science, in contrast to 'highly evaluative theological propositions'. Rather than standing in opposition, the social sciences and theology are both expressions of cultural and political values. That recognition constitutes one of the major signposts of postmodernism, and its challenge to religion centres on the four losses for theology that Mark Taylor has examined in his book, *Erring*: the death of God, the disappearance of the self, the end of history and the closure of the book, all of which are intertwined with the hermeneutical tradition associated with Nietzsche, Freud, Lacan and Foucault, among others.[6]

Under the influence of postmodernist thought, feminism is rooted in the assumption that knowledge and truth are embedded in political interests that impose their will through coercion and power. Religious thought is understood less as a matter of ontology, but a matter of politics. At stake is not discovering 'truth', but unmasking regimes of power that have succeeded in imposing themselves as if they were true and natural. Feminists have unmasked Western philosophy not as the mirror of nature, but of men's experience, ideas and power, and Jewish feminists have similarly unmasked the Bible, Talmud and even modern Jewish thought, as regimes preserving patriarchal power. There is no ontology of gender, but gender identities produced as the effect of cultural regimes. Judith Butler's highly influential work on feminist theory, based on Foucault, calls for a 'reconceptualization of identity as an effect, that is, as produced or generated . . . neither fatally determined nor fully artificial and arbitrary'.[7] Butler calls for a 'denaturalization of gender', viewing as political the variety of mechanisms, including language, that construct gender identity, and using techniques such as parody to reveal the absurdity and fantasy of such constructions.

If the theologians of the Enlightenment heritage faced the problem of religious pluralism, the challenge posed by postmodernism is the view of religion not as the product of metaphysics but of cultural and political commitments – sites of power that we try to unmask. Power, in Foucault's understanding, is both repressive and productive, and is concentrated not in one seat, whether text, person, or divinity, but is 'capillary', diffused throughout society. The manner in which power functions according to Foucault, as simultaneously repressive and productive, stands in sharp contrast to the modern understanding of power as concentrated at a centre or position above; power is not the Vatican or the rabbinate, but in a constructed regime of truth that convinces individual Catholics or Jews that it is in their best interest to follow the injunctions of popes and rabbis. At the same time, regimes that appear oppressive – for instance, Protestant evangelical groups that insist on women's subordination to men – may simultaneously promote women as vehicles for divine communications, with special relationships with Jesus that empower women in ways not possible in Liberal Protestant communities that have renounced divine–human exchanges. As a result of this realization, feminist scholars have come to recognize the greater complexity of delineating the nature and function of patriarchy within religious communities and within theology.

However difficult it may have been to establish some sort of exchange between Jewish and Christian theologians in the second half of the twentieth century, it has been nearly impossible to establish an exchange within each religion between liberals and reactionaries. For women theologians, the question of interreligious as well as intrareligious communication is laden with the problem of sexism within the tradition. How am I to engage in theological discussion if I believe my partner in dialogue is engaging in oppressive and immoral subjugation of women? Moreover, being a woman in the context of theological discussion automatically puts one in a position of alterity; how am I to represent a tradition which has failed to represent me? Who is the 'we' of the questions formulated for this session? Am I expected to speak in the name of a tradition that has excluded and oppressed me?

At the same time, an outspoken or activist woman does not necessarily prove that she is not serving patriarchal interests; indeed, precisely because contradictory gender images and roles are prevalent throughout the history of religious communities, it has become so difficult to recognize and overcome patriarchal power. Penelope Deutscher has recently argued that it is precisely the instability of gender, the constant flux in femininities and female roles, that is constitutive of phallocentrism and even an inherent aspect of its power.[8] Thus, what I may consider to be a liberated role today may turn out to be simply another covert aspect of patriarchy.

One of the major problems posed to women by modernity is its denial of women's subservience and substitution of a rhetoric of 'difference'. The shift did not affect only women; the transformation from a hierarchical society in pre-modern Europe, in which Jews occupied a position beneath that of Christians, to a nineteenth-century notion of citizenship, also spoke of Jewish difference, rather than subservience. As both women and men came to recognize that a belief in female inferiority was morally and politically unacceptable, an ideology of women's difference from men began to be developed, according to which women were in some ways actually superior to men, especially in the realms of religion and morality, a shift that began, as Marilyn Massey has delineated, in eighteenth-century Germany and became a central feature of nineteenth-century Romanticism.[9] Religion was domesticated as part of the ascendance of bourgeois culture in Europe and America, with Judaism practised far more at home than in public or in the synagogue, thus bringing Jewish identity increasingly under women's domain.[10] Indeed, Paula Hyman has argued that an ideology emerged by the second half of the nineteenth century that 'placed women at the heart of Jewish identity'.[11] The danger is that the veneration of the female, Maria Baader points out, also meant that women could be – and were – blamed for a weakened Jewish identity, for 'spreading materialism, empty synagogues, and declining domestic devotion'.[12] For middle-class women in Germany and America, the 'cult of true womanhood' kept them in a separate sphere of society that could be used to deny them access to power, while excluding working women (and, by extension, most African-American women) from the definition of womanhood.[13]

Placing women at the heart of Jewish identity fortified an ambivalence toward women and toward Jewish identity that was often expressed through the trope of nostalgia, a crucial component of modern experience that expresses a painful longing for an idealized, aestheticized and unrecoverable past. Richard I. Cohen explains the nostalgia for traditional Jewish life as compensating for the 'feelings of disorientation and emptiness' that Jews experienced as they moved from 'the relatively slow-moving Jewish community to the pulsating life of Europe's capitals and cities'.[14] For Arnold Eisen, a longer Jewish memory lies behind modern nostalgia: 'without Jewish nightmares there could be no Jewish nostalgia'.[15] Central to nostalgia is the gendered nature of its representations, in which the idealized object of longing is coded as female, while the one yearning for it is coded as male; the Judaism of old is feminine, while the modern, enlightened, progressive Jew is male.[16] The 'eclipse of patriarchal legitimacy', Trevor Hope writes, gave rise to 'the metaphorization of the feminine in its contemporarily hyperbolic intensity' in order to distract us from the dissolution of the traditional social bond.[17] In Freudian terms, the rivalry between son and father, based on the Oedipus myth, is for possession of the mother – which the son gains, at the cost of his self-destruction. Jewish nostalgia, expressed by modern men who had left piety for modern adventures, so often focuses on food, the classic commodity of women, and glorifies women's subservience by describing her in maternal terms, as the pillar of the family and home, the mythic point of Jewish origin untouched by modernity.[18] Within the nationalist movements of the nineteenth and twentieth centuries, nostalgia for the female played a particularly important role. Consider the early Zionist Moses Hess as he calls for a return to national identity:

Is it mere chance, that whenever I stand at a new turn in my life, there appears in my path an unhappy woman, who imparts to me daring and courage to travel the unknown road? Oh, how stupid are those who minimize the value of woman's influence upon the development of Judaism! Was it not said of the Jews, that they were redeemed from Egypt because of the merit of the pious women, and that the future redemption will be brought about through them?[19]

Despite the seeming centrality Hess gives to women in his effort to generate Jewish nationalist feeling, they inevitably remain sub-ordinate, functioning as 'an organic principle fixing a stable space to complement and thus guarantee the progress of male modernity'.[20] Within nationalist movements 'women seem to pay a special fee on behalf of the nation, even though it is traditionally represented as an honorarium given to them', as Jean Pickering and Suzanne Kehde write.[21] The very structure of nostalgia serves to undermine efforts at women's equality. 'A nostalgic structure both creates and obliterates a lost object,' writes Lynne Huffer.[22] The Jewish woman in her tradi-tional, homemaking glory was created as the image to emulate precisely at a time when pre-modern forms of Jewish life were no longer tenable and Jewish women were entering universities and embarking on careers.[23]

The question of power in relation to theology not only concerns internal religious matters, such as the treatment of women, but also the role of theology within global politics. As modern theology was taking shape, Europe was engaging in its project of colonizing the world's 'savages', a project that managed, by the 1930s, to place 84.6 per cent of the land surface of the earth under colonial domination.[24] Attention to the role of European scholarship (although not – yet – theological scholarship) in legitimating colonialism was stimulated by the publication in 1978 of Edward Said's by now classic study, *Orientalism*.[25] Said's own claim is that scholarly production of 'know-ledge' of the Orient was complicit in European overseas colonialist projects. He gives almost no attention to German scholarship, claim-ing that the German overseas colonial projects did not begin until late in the nineteenth century. What Said does not consider is that part of the German orientalist project included the scholarly investigation of Judaism, whose political ramifications entailed not an overseas colonization, but a domestic one. In Germany, as Sheldon Pollock has argued, orientalism was vectored not outward, toward the Orient, but inward, to Europe itself, to construct a historical German essence and to define Germany's place in Europe's destiny.[26] As Susanne Zantop writes in her analysis of German colonial fantasies,

> it was precisely the lack of actual colonialism that created a pervasive desire for colonial possessions and a sense of entitlement to such possessions in the minds of many Germans. Since a colonial discourse could develop without being challenged by colonized subjects or without being tested in a real colonial setting, it established itself not so much as 'intellectual authority' (Said) over distant terrains, than as mythological authority over the collective imagination.[27]

Indeed, the rise of scholarship on the history of the Jews and Judaism occurred coterminus with the struggle for Jewish emancipation in Germany, and Christian theologians were in no way disinterested in the political uses of their scholarship. On the contrary, from the eighteenth century onward, Christian historians of Judaism were active voices in the emancipation debate, the former carrying considerable political weight as self-declared experts on the nature of the Jews, based on their biblical scholarship.[28] Jonathan Hess has pointed out that Jewish emancipation functioned 'as a symbolic substitute for a foreign colony', and that 'fantasies of external colonial expansion are already inscribed into the project of internal colonization'.[29] Consideration of the linkage between Christian scholarship on Judaism and the emancipation of the Jews, in other words, was both symbolic of, and preparation for, the German colonialist ventures that began later in the nineteenth century. Extending Said's categories of discourse and representation as forms of colonialization, Christian theological denigration of Judaism, particularly of first-century Jewish religious movements, can be seen as similar to European orientalism: Christian studies of Judaism are also efforts 'to control, manipulate, even to incorporate, what is a manifestly different (or alternative and novel) world'.[30] Judaism came to function in Christian theology as the other whose negation confirms and even constitutes Christianity.

The projects of colonialism and the problem of patriarchy are not unrelated. One of the factors stimulating the modern glorification of Jewish women's domesticity was the gaze of Christian Europe. Many Jews were embarrassed at features of Judaism that seemed 'oriental', particularly certain ritual observances, yet felt a defiant pride about Judaism's monotheism, ethics and, especially, its freedom of thought, which they considered superior to Christianity's miracles and dogma.

Women were often the victims of that ambivalence, as reformers called for abolishing certain inequities, even while they insisted, along with traditionalists, that women actually held an elevated status in Judaism. The pressures of Christian anti-Semitism made Jewish criticisms of Judaism difficult, since they seemed to lend justifications to their enemies; one wonders how many Jewish feminists were suppressed by the implied or real threat of giving fodder to the enemy. In the end, both Reform and modern Orthodox rabbis agreed that Judaism placed women on a pedestal, in order to make it appear to be the religion of bourgeois gentlemen suited to full integration into Western society.

In addition, fantasies regarding gender have played a significant role in colonialism and its instruments of racism. Robert Young, in *Colonial Desire*, has pointed to the anxiety over hybridity that characterizes the colonial system, and is frequently expressed in fears over miscegenation.[31] Young notes the influence of Matthew Arnold's classic *Culture and Anarchy* (1869), which presents English culture as a combination of Hebraic and Hellenic cultures, the former characterized as strict and masculine, the latter as spontaneous and feminine. Within Germany, the search for cultural origins obsessed nineteenth-century scholars, who turned first to Greece, then to Rome, and finally to the so-called Indian Aryans as their spiritual ancestors. In all three cases, however, there was no purity of influence, but a hybridity that combined the Hebraic with, respectively, the Greek, Roman, or Aryan, to produce Christianity.

Nowhere within the field of theology was the anxiety over hybridity more forcefully expressed than in German Liberal Protestant New Testament studies. Liberal Protestantism had rejected all supernatural elements, including miracles and dogma, and called for a return to the faith of Jesus, which could be recovered through historical method. In the inaugural issue of the journal *Theologische Studien und Kritiken* in 1828, the editors declared that the vitality of theology depended upon the permeation of faith and knowledge. Faith, of course, was Christianity; knowledge meant historical scholarship, an objective analysis of sources that was often criticized by conservative opponents of historical theology as 'Jewish' for its lack of grounding in pre-determined spiritual commitments.

Liberal Protestant theology was to be dedicated to the study of Christian origins, and it was a topic that stood at the heart of the nineteenth-century theological enterprise. As Adolf Hilgenfeld, one of the founders of the Religionsgeschichtliche Schule, wrote as the foreword to the inaugural issue of the journal he founded in 1858,

Zeitschrift für wissenschaftliche Theologie, 'And the historical question regarding the original shape and development of Christianity still remains the real life question of our theology.'[32] This means an end to a representation of Christian origins as something outside of history or above history. By contrast the truth shows that 'the eternal and everlasting [elements] of Christianity and of Protestantism . . . is to be found in the kingdom of the spirit, in the eternal principles, which, in the earliest time of Christianity and of Protestantism appeared with the most powerful abundance'.[33]

The problem, these theologians soon discovered to their dismay, was that no clear, recognizably Christian principles guided the early Jesus movement. On the contrary, they discovered a hybridity that seemed impervious to surgical resection. Christianity was the product not of original teachings developed by Jesus, but of a miscegenation of Judaism and paganism, which had, in turn, generated Jesus. Responses to the discovery varied; the general paradigm of Protestant theology in the second half of the nineteenth century was the argument that Jesus himself, although a fully historical figure, possessed a unique religious consciousness that stood above historical analysis and that marked his extraordinary and unique significance. Religious consciousness replaced miracles and other discarded supernatural elements considered inappropriate to the self-proclaimed 'modern' theology of Liberal Protestants such as Daniel Schenkel, Karl von Hase and Theodor Keim, among others.

That response was only briefly sufficient. By the early twentieth century, racial thinking began to foment fantasies of 'uncontrollable, frenetic fornication producing the countless motley varieties of interbreeding', as Young describes it, that would bring about the degeneration of the pure, civilized, white, Christian, German Aryans.[34] One of the clearest targets of racial attack was Christianity, the hybrid religion produced by Judaism fornicating with Hellenism. Theologians quickly recognized the problem. How could Christianity be rescued? A thorough programme of de-Judaization was adopted, along with a shift from describing the 'Hellenic' to the 'Aryan' origins of Christianity. Whatever Jewishness could be found within the New Testament, they argued, was the result of Jewish falsifications of its text that required swift and thorough emendation.

The hegemony of Christianity over the German academy reproduced one of the central features of imperial powers: the control over its own representation, both of itself to others and of others to themselves. While Christianity has had relatively little interest in Islam over the centuries, its interest in Judaism has been profound and deeply intertwined with Christian self-interest. No narrative of Christian origins can be devised without consideration of Judaism; the explanation for the rise of Christianity cannot be formulated without a statement concerning the degenerate nature of first-century Judaism that necessitated God's sending forth of his only son to offer salvation. Given its significance to Christian self-understanding, Judaism's history and theology can only be narrated on Christian terms, to preserve the integrity of the Christian claim. With its scriptures taken over and read as prefigurations of Christ, its teachings declared superfluous after the life of Jesus, and its adherents labelled perfidious both for refusing to accept Jesus as the Messiah and then for killing him, Judaism became Christianity's first imperial conquest, its colonized religion. The emergence in the nineteenth century of Jewish historians who not only insisted upon their own self-representation, but went even further, writing histories of Christianity from the perspective of Judaism, was a rebellion of the colonized against the system of theological colonization.

In the course of articulating its critique of Christianity's colonization of Judaism, Jewish thinkers developed an understanding of the politics of knowledge that can be viewed as an early prototype for what Said later articulated in *Orientalism*. Jewish scholars in Europe were well aware of the politics of Christian theological scholarship, even as their own scholarship was shaped by the political interests of their own communities. Leopold Zunz, one of the towering figures of Jewish scholarship in nineteenth-century Germany, suggested that Christian scholars took on a 'demonic nature' when studying Judaism.[35] Judaism was being portrayed in a 'hateful light' by Christian theologians, asserted Immanuel Wolf, who published the first manifesto of Jewish Studies in 1823.[36] Ultimately, the most egregious step was taken by some leading Liberal Protestants of Germany just before and during the Nazi era who redefined Jesus as an anti-Semitic Aryan, befitting the politics of their day. The failure of German church leaders in the immediate post-war years to recognize and root out the political directions taken by so many theologians have left contemporary theologians with a large task. In this respect, at least, the more conservative theological traditions in Germany appear to have offered some benefit during the Third Reich, by rejecting the attempts made by theological liberals to alter the actual text of the New Testament, hymnal and catechism in accord with Nazi teachings. In that way, German Catholic theology, while erring in certain ways, turns out to have been far less anti-Jewish and pro-Hitler than German Protestantism.

This theology may not have originated as part of German racial theory, but it mirrored its assumptions and many of its intellectual structures. These began to become explicit by the early twentieth century, and reached full-blown status as racial theology after 1933. As Young writes, 'To suggest that culture and racism were complicit in the nineteenth century is not to say anything new. Yet the extent to which both the sciences and the arts were determined by assumptions about race is consistently underestimated.'[37] During the Nazi era, several Aryanized versions of the New Testament, Sermon on the Mount, hymnal and catechism were published, along with serious theological arguments 'proving' Jesus' Aryan identity.[38] Most of the Protestant theological faculties at German universities were dominated by the pro-Nazi faculty by the middle of the 1930s, and few were purged at the end of the war. Post-war Protestant theology in Germany thus retained many of the Nazi-era elements concerning the degeneracy of Judaism and Jesus' opposition to it, even if the term 'Aryan' fell into disuse.

I raise questions rooted in feminist theory and in postcolonial theory not because I expect answers from this group, but in order to demonstrate some of the scope of the problems that we both face, as Jews and Catholics. Neither community is exempt from the challenges of feminism, and while the problem of colonialism's impact on our theological teachings may affect Christians and Jews in somewhat different ways, we are both implicated in the need to respond effectively to the heritage of European colonialism on our thinking and on our religious institutions. Hopefully, our responses to these challenges can be formulated with mutual esteem and encouragement.

Notes

1. Peter L. Berger, *A Rumor of Angels: Modern Society and the Rediscovery of the Supernatural*, Garden City, NJ: Doubleday, 1969.
2. Peter L. Berger, *The Heretical Imperative: Contemporary Possibilities of Religious Affirmation*, Garden City, NJ: Doubleday, 1979.
3. Peter Gay, *Freud, Jews, and Other Germans: Master and Victims in Modernist Culture*, New York : Oxford University Press, 1978.
4. Susannah Heschel, *Abraham Geiger and the Jewish Jesus*, Chicago: University of Chicago Press, 1998.
5. Uriel Tal, *Christians and Jews in Germany: Religion, Politics, and Ideology in the Second Reich, 1870–1914*, translated by Noah Jonathan Jacobs, Ithaca: Cornell University Press, 1975. A more recent work on the topic is Christian Wiese, *Wissenschaft des Judentums und protestantische Theologie im wilhelminischen*

Deutschland: ein Schrei ins Leere?, Tübingen: Mohr Siebeck, 1999.

6. Mark C. Taylor, *Erring: A Postmodern Theology*, Chicago: University of Chicago Press, 1984.

7. Judith Butler, *Gender Trouble: Feminism and the Subversion of Identity*, New York: Routledge, 1990, p. 147.

8. Penelope Deutscher, *Yielding Gender: Feminism, Deconstruction and the History of Philosophy*, London and New York: Routledge, 1997.

9. Marilyn Massey, *Feminine Soul: Fate of an Ideal*, Boston: Beacon Press, 1985.

10. Marion Kaplan, *The Making of the Jewish Middle Class: Women, Family, and Identity in Imperial Germany*, New York: Oxford University Press, 1991, pp. 64–84.

11. Paula E. Hyman, 'The Modern Jewish Family: Image and Reality,' ed. David Kraemer, *The Jewish Family: Metaphor and Memory*, New York: Oxford University Press, 1989, p. 190.

12. Maria Baader, 'From "the Priestess of the Home" to "the Rabbi's Brilliant Daughter" Concepts of Jewish Womanhood and Progressive Germanness in *Die Deborah* and the *American Israelite*, 1854–1900', *Leo Baeck Institute Yearbook* 43, 1998, p. 61.

13. Cf. Nancy F. Cott, *The Bonds of Womanhood: 'Women's Sphere' in New England, 1780–1835*, New Haven: Yale University Press, 1977.

14. Richard I. Cohen, ' "Nostalgia" and "return to the ghetto": A Cultural Phenomenon in Western and Central Europe', *Assimilation and Community: The Jews in Nineteenth-Century Europe*, ed. Jonathan Frankel and Steven J. Zipperstein, Cambridge; Cambridge University Press, 1992, pp. 130–55; 131.

15. Arnold M. Eisen, *Rethinking Modern Judaism: Ritual, Commandment, Community*, Chicago Studies in the History of Judaism, Chicago, IL, and London: University of Chicago Press, 1998, p. 169.

16. See Jonathan Steinwand, 'The Future of Nostalgia in Friedrich Schlegel's Gender Theory: Casting German Aesthetics beyond Ancient Greece and Modern Europe,' ed. Jean Pickering and Suzanne Kehde, *Narratives of Nostalgia, Gender, and Nationalism*, New York: New York University Press, 1997, pp. 9–29.

17. Trevor Hope, 'Melancholic Modernity', *Feminism Meets Queer Theory*, ed. Elizabeth Weed and Naomi Schor, Bloomington, IN: Indiana University Press, 1997, p. 189.

18. On Jewish women's preparation of food as a religious activity and as a vehicle for transmission of Jewish identity, see Susan Starr Sered, *Women as Ritual Experts: The Religious Lives of Elderly Jewish Women in Jerusalem*, New York: Oxford University Press, 1992, pp. 87–102.

19. Moses Hess, *Rome and Jerusalem: A Study in Jewish Nationalism*, trans. Meyer Waxman, New York: Bloch Publishing Co., 1943, p. 44.

20. Pickering and Kehde, 'Introduction', *Narratives*, p. 6.

21. Pickering and Kehde, *Narratives*, p. 5.

22. Lynne Huffer, *Maternal Pasts, Feminist Futures: Nostalgia, Ethics, and the Question of Difference*, Stanford: Stanford University Press, 1998, p. 3.

23. Ute Frevert, *Women in German History: From Bourgeois Emancipation to Sexual Liberation*, trans. Stuart McKinnon-Evans in association with Terry Bond and Barbara Norden, Oxford and New York: Berg, 1989, pp. 107–30.

24. Ania Loomba, *Colonialism/Postcolonialism*, London and New York: Routledge, 1998, p. 15. See also Howard Eilbeg-Schwartz, *The Savage in Judaism: An Anthropology of Israelite Religion and Ancient Judaism*, Bloomington, IN: Indiana University Press, 1990.
25. Edward Said, *Orientalism*, New York : Pantheon Books, 1978.
26. Sheldon Pollock, 'Deep Orientalism? Notes on Sanskrit and Power beyond the Raj', *Orientalism and the Postcolonial Predicament: Perspectives on South Asia*, ed. Carol A. Breckenridge and Peter van der Veer, Philadelphia: University of Pennsylvania Press, pp. 76–133.
27. Susanne Zantop, *Colonial Fantasies: Conquest, Family, and Nation in Precolonial Germany, 1770–1870*, Durham, NC: Duke University Press, 1997, p. 7.
28. Among these figures were Johann David Michael and Johann Gottfried Eichhorn, both professors at Göttingen, Anton Theodor Hartmann, professor at Rostock, Christoph Friedrich von Ammon, professor at Erlangen, and Heinrich Paulus, professor at Heidelberg. For a discussion of their writings, see Heschel, *Abraham Geiger and the Jewish Jesus*, ch. 2.
29. Jonathan Hess, 'Sugar Island Jews? Jewish Colonialism and the Rhetoric of "Civic Improvement" in Eighteenth-Century Germany', *Eighteenth-Century Studies*, 32:1, Fall 1998, p. 98.
30. Said, *Orientalism*, p. 12.
31. Robert Young, *Colonial Desire: Hybridity in Theory, Culture, and Race*, London and New York: Routledge, 1995.
32. Adolf Hilgenfeld, 'Die wissenschaftliche Theologie und ihre gegenwärtige Aufgabe', *Zeitschrift für wissenschaftliche Theologie* 1, 1858, p. 17.
33. Ibid., p. 19.
34. Young, *Colonial Desire*, p. 181.
35. Alexander Altmann, 'Jewish Studies: Their Scope and Meaning Today', Hillel Foundation Annual Lectures, London: Hillel Foundation, 1958.
36. Immanuel Wolf, 'Über den Begriff einer Wissenschaft des Judenthums', *Zeitschrift für die Wissenschaft des Judenthums* 1, 1823, pp. 1–24.
37. Young, *Colonial Desire*, p. 90.
38. Susannah Heschel, 'When Jesus Was an Aryan: The Protestant Church and Antisemitic Propaganda', *Betrayal: The German Churches and the Holocaust*, ed. Robert Ericksen and Susannah Heschel, Minneapolis: Augsburg-Fortress Press, 1999, pp. 68–89.

Discussant

– Michael McGarry

I am very grateful to Professor Heschel for her insightful paper. While in substantial agreement with most of her paper, which seeks to respond to the 'Challenge of Modernity and Postmodernity' for both the Catholic and Jewish community, I wish to make four comments.

First, in today's world, we are all being asked to respond, as religious communities to the values of egalitarianism, autonomy, pluralism, democracy, secularism and contemporary humanism. The Roman Catholic Church has only recently and corporately addressed some of these issues, beginning with the Second Vatican Council (1963–5). In many ways, we continue to address them inasmuch as the Catholic Church is a multinational community which finds itself both in countries still in pre-modern conditions and in countries that are decidedly post-industrial and postmodern. It was the good Pope John XXIII who summoned the Second Vatican Council to engage modernity and, among other things, to rid the Church of its perennial position that 'error has not rights'. This fundamental view had stood in the way of both seeking for dialogue with Judaism and other world religions and embracing religious liberty not only as a value but also as a human right.

The challenge for us Catholics, then, is to deepen and continue the embrace of religious liberty as a positive value. Therefore I believe that we Jews and Christians must find ways, in dialogue and common ventures, to address the streams of pre-modern religion both within our respective traditions and outside them, as in, for instance, our dialogue with Islam. Sad to say, in Israel where I live, it is often the religious traditions who pose the biggest obstacles to religious liberty and the embrace of the other, the embrace of pluralism and diversity. And so we have the paradox of Western Christians supporting secularists within Judaism and Islam because it is they and not the traditionally observant who may provide the protection of religious liberty for Christians in the Holy Land.

Second, I am not qualified to assess Dr Heschel's assessment of Peter Berger's work, which epitomizes the view that there can be a non-perspectival, scientific approach to religion. But given her brief synopsis, I find rather persuasive his taxonomy of three ways religious groups approach modernity: in a defensive posture, they retrench and reaffirm the authority of the tradition; or they try to secularize the tradition; or they seek to uncover and retrieve the useful experiences embodied in their respective traditions. While it is true that Berger restricted his analysis to Western Protestant (especially German) theology, I believe that there is still something to be learned from looking at such an analysis.

Third, while I may be a bit in the next generation to Dr Heschel's, she notes that for 'our' generation 'the relation between power and religious thought constitutes the epistemological starting point' (p. 147). This is a very important insight and one which anyone approaching the modern world with some reflection must ponder. In particular, Dr Heschel notes the usefulness of feminism and post-colonial analysis in assessing the present situation. She notes that from a feminist perspective, knowledge and truth are embedded in political interest. Again, one must note that truth is never value free nor is the perspective of the speaker a neutral one – including Professor Heschel's. I understand Professor Heschel to argue that all truth statements are expressions of maintaining, or upsetting, power relationships. While I do not wish to suggest that feminist analysis is marginal or arbitrary, I would like to hear more about how the feminist analysis itself could be subject to its own razor; that is, is not the feminist insight itself muted by the charge that it is simply an 'expression of maintaining – or upsetting – power relationships'? Similarly, I would like to hear more from Dr Heschel about how religion is simply or more than the product of cultural and political commitments.

Similarly the suspicion of Western analysis in a postcolonial world (taking one's cue from Edward Said's *Orientalism*) needs to be addressed in at least two ways. First, it must be noted that almost all of us here at this conference are white, Western and beneficiaries of the colonial enterprise. Therefore, anyone from the Orient or the Southern Hemisphere should be wary of what we say and we should be rather humble, I suggest, in our analysis . . . which should make us suspicious of anything we say precisely because of where we come from – economically, socially, racially, educationally and geographically. I myself find the economic analysis, although unpopular in a post-Soviet world, nonetheless very persuasive. Secondly, as one who

lives in Israel (although not yet for very long), I am keenly aware
of how the postcolonial critique has been used to great effect to
delegitimize the Jewish state. I would like to hear more from Dr
Heschel on how one might effectively use this tool without its having
the deleterious effects that I have seen (e.g. Michael Prior's work on
Israel and the land; the regular comparison of Israeli settlement
policy and South Africa).

Finally, I think that Dr Heschel has been most insightful in her
description of Christian colonial efforts at portraying Judaism,
'Christianity's colonization of Judaism', as she puts it. This area
deserves much more attention from Christian scholars than it has
received. Dr Heschel's comments are a provocative and very helpful
beginning in this direction.

D. The Challenge of Modernity and Postmodernity

– Janet Martin Soskice

The Pope has shown in his recent visit to Israel that silence is often the most eloquent speaking, but this silence must be based upon what has been said, shared and understood if it is to be welcome silence, and not simply another failure to address difficult questions. It is this joint speaking, this conversation, that we further here at our meeting.

My own field is philosophy of religion and modern theology. The remarks that follow frame no grand thesis but hope to sketch some points of challenge and confluence. Some observations arise from my own current interest in the 'naming God'. Others bring current moves in critical theory to bear on understandings of Jewish–Christian relations past, present and future – thus I reflect, for instance, on the 'placed' nature of speaking and Western tendencies to 'binarism'. The paper has its focus on questions as to how we speak and who we are, and how we can speak of God and to each other.

The average Catholic

Let me begin with the Pope's visit to Israel and the coverage it received in the world's media as far as the average Catholic is concerned.

I was in the United States during this period reading the accounts in *The New York Times* which, as far as news coverage goes, were extensive and excellent. Who met whom, who said what, when and where, the public response – even the weather was described in some detail. What I missed, however, in both secular and religious press on my return to Britain, was reflection on the significance of the visit for the average Catholic. Why is this important?

Let me remind you that in crude demographic terms 'average Catholic' is an African woman, not wealthy and by Western standards not well educated. The majority of the world's Catholics live in the so-called 'Third World'.

Coverage of the papal visit in British and American papers was understandably Eurocentric and left untouched the assumption that all Catholics stand in roughly the same relationship to European history, apart from the blip across the waters that gives us the Americas. A moment's reflection reminds us that they do not. Most Catholics live in countries where there are few Jewish people. Many Catholics have never met a Jew, and most Catholics view European history or even the history of the European Catholicism as 'their' history in an important but distant way. It seems to me, that it is of the utmost importance that the Pope made this visit at this time – at this calendrical time – that is, the first months of the first year of the new millennium, and at this time in his pontificate, arguably its crowning moment. That the Pope at this time should apologize to the Jewish people for all Catholics is of great significance for, perhaps surprisingly, this apology comes symbolically as much from Catholics in Peru and Bolivia, Zambia and India, Sri Lanka and Barbados – people whose ancestors were in many cases the victims of European cruelty and intolerance – as also from Catholics in Europe and the Americas. The papal visit said to all Catholics that Catholic–Jewish relations are not negotiable or peripheral, even if you live in Bogota or Goa. This is an important point to make when a number of bodies in world Christianity are anxious to distance themselves from the history of the European church. It is also why I believe that the work done by dedicated scholars of early Christianity and early Judaism – people like Professor Stroumsa and his Christian colleagues – remote though this may seem from the lives of a Nigerian woman who is a market trader – is of greatest importance for the future of Jewish–Christian understanding – a point to which I shall return.

The tainting of words

I am writing a book about the Names of God and the Naming of God. A delightful and somewhat unexpected aspect of this project has been the extent to which it has drawn me into the Jewish literature – Philo and the Rabbis, Moses Maimonides and Moses Mendelssohn, Buber and Rosenzweig. And let me say what a pleasure it is to read hundreds and hundreds of pages which attest to the positive regard and shared wisdom between Jews, Christians and – on this issue – Muslims. One moves between Philo, Gregory of Nyssa and the

Rabbis not as through a seamless web, but through conversations importantly addressed to the same questions of God's holiness and our proper modesty and reverence. Let me share one fragment from this study which may serve to bring this paper to the stated topic of this session: the challenge of modernity and postmodernity.

Franz Rosenzweig wrote in 1929 an article entitled ' "The Eternal": Mendelssohn and the Name of God'.[1] Rosenzweig and Buber were translating the Bible into German. In this they had as a predecessor Mendelssohn's important commentary on the Pentateuch, the so-called *Biur*, published at the beginning of the nineteenth century, which, in Rosenzweig's terms,

> situated just at the threshold of our century of biblical criticism – already, that is, in the modern spirit and yet still naive, equally distant from biblical criticism and neo-orthodoxy – takes up once again the torch of the great medieval exegetes and kindles it anew.

It is Rosenzweig's view that, 'apart from its role in the shaping of German style', the most lasting effect of this *Biur* on German and world Judaism was 'its rendering of the divine name as "the Eternal" ', a translation which 'everywhere coloured . . . Jewish piety of the emancipation.'[2] From Rosenzweig's point of view this was an unfortunate translation, since 'the Eternal' seems metaphysical and remote, and loses the moment of presence and intimacy both he and Buber wished to emphasize. But why did Mendelssohn choose it?

Mendelssohn, like earlier Judeo-German translations to which he refers, avoids the apparently obvious rendering of 'the Lord'. Rosenzweig has this to say,

> We can presume that 'the Lord' seemed to him too freighted with Christian associations; it has after all through the diction of the Greek and so the German New Testament come to refer not to God but to the founder of Christianity – a reference that even today gives a Christian colouring to the Old Testament. When the devout Christian says, 'The Lord is my shepherd,' he thinks not of God but of 'the Good Shepherd'.[3]

Thus Rosenzweig, and by conjecture Mendelssohn, makes the point also important to George Steiner – that words carry histories, that shared languages and even shared terms do not indicate shared understandings and may even, in damaging ways, conceal real differences. The same point is made by Elliot Dorff in his discussion of 'covenant' which he suggests Jews before the Enlightenment found

too suggestive of assimilation, and after the Enlightenment too exclusive.[4] Words, even words for God – even biblical words – are not
always neutral but carry a freight of meaning and stand within structures of meanings and representations that are not shared by all who
use them. This insight of discourse theory was clearly known long
before Foucault – probably, if Rosenzweig is correct – long known by
Mendelssohn and other Jewish writers but, only recently, rising to
broader cultural consciousness.

But if I may continue with naming God. Where did Mendelssohn
get 'the Eternal' if, as seems to be the case, it was he who introduced it
into Judaism? Rosenzweig suggests this: it is a term of biblical origin,
but one whose origin 'lies in the Old Testament in the strictest sense,
i.e., in the part retained only in the Christian Bible as the Apocrypha'.
Baruch uses *ho Aionios* six times as a name of God. It is Calvin who
introduces this name into Western translation more broadly in the
French edition of his commentary on the Hexateuch in 1564. *L'Eternel*
then replaces *Seigneur* as found in the Geneva Bible of 1535 in editions
of the Genevan Bible after 1588. From this Bible the name influences
French and other European literatures and thus, Rosenzweig
surmises, influenced Mendelssohn, a citizen of Berlin which had a
strong Huguenot community.

'Placing' and power

And so a Greek name, which seems first to appear in a text not recognized as canonical by either Jews or Protestants, finds its way from a
French Reformer into Jewish translations of the Bible. Even if
Rosenzweig's reconstruction is not accurate in its entirety it is a testimony to the complicated borrowings and crossings in European
Christian and Jewish life over the past centuries – names that can be
used and cannot be used, texts that are read by different communities
in different ways. Our knowing and speaking and even our praying is
'placed'. It is not, relativistically, that there is 'no truth at all' but that
we need to ask who is speaking and on what basis. That 'Columbus
was the man who discovered America' was a commonplace of my
Canadian schooldays and (leaving aside the claims of some
Norsemen) it never occurred to us or our teachers to ask how this
dictum might have sounded to the Nootka or Shuswap tribes who
were the first dwellers in that land.

A rather different instance of 'placing' has to do with the inter-
confessional foundations of certain strands of Christian anti-Judaism.
It is well attested that the anti-Judaism often apparent in nineteenth-

century German theology and biblical criticism (for instance, the dismissal of the Law as a symbol of spiritual desiccation, etc.) indeed had a target but that the target was principally German Catholicism which was regarded as a religion of law and not of grace, infested by priests, etc. We can find similar polemical strategies right back to the sixteenth century. This does not mean that the authors were not also anti-Judaic and even anti-Semitic, but that Judaism suffered at the hands of what was *au fond* an interdenominational Christian dispute. In case it be thought that I am employing the old apologetic strategy of finding someone (Protestants) even worse than we (Catholics), I should say that Catholics didn't hesitate to play the same trick. An example internal to Catholicism would be those defamatory medieval paintings which depict, often in a series of panels, Jews insulting the consecrated host. The polemical intention was, in the first instance, not against Jews but rather against other Catholics at the time of heated theological debates concerning the real presence in the Eucharist. 'The Jew' is there as pictorial short-hand for someone who does not believe in this doctrine – a recognizable figurative shorthand for 'someone who is wrong', and thus indicating clearly 'the position that is right'. In postmodernist theory this logic is sometimes called 'binarist' – I'm good because you are bad, I'm right because you are wrong, you're female because I am male, etc. Of course these works are anti-Judaic and probably anti-Semitic as well and this reminds us that, by long tradition, it is perfectly possible to be anti-Judaic and even anti-Semitic, even in circumstances where those Christians concerned have little or no direct knowledge of actual Jews – which takes us back to our Nigerian market trader. For this is why we (Catholics and Jews) should have some care about how the theologies of our brothers and sisters in the Third World develop, even while they may in many respects rightly claim that the history of European anti-Semitism is not their history. To return to my theme of placing, it is perfectly possible that a Korean liberation theologian may write a work that has its place as part of a minority discourse (Korean rural poor) but also as part of a dominant discourse (Christian anti-Judaism). Indeed this is not only possible but actual. A recent piece of Asian feminist theology (thus doubly peripheral) which came my way spoke movingly of the sufferings of Asian women but the Christology, one would have to say, was recognizably the genre 'Christian feminist anti-Judaism' – that is, a picture of Jesus as revolutionary prophet of love, liberation and concern for women triumphing over the strictures and structures of a patriarchal religion.

Whether this is a 'postmodern condition' is hard to know – the term is so broad in current usage as to cover polar opposites. It is a feature of modernity and not just postmodernity to find oneself inhabiting different conversations and needing to negotiate between them. Moses Mendelssohn wrote as a Jew and a German, a reader of French literature and citizen of Berlin and man of the late eighteenth century. My feminist theologian writes as an Asian and a woman and a Christian. Our identities are almost always folded in upon each other in these ways.

Binarism and myths of origin

How does this bring me to the importance of studies in early Christianity and Judaism? Underlying the binarism which, I suggested, was an important feature of classical Christian anti-Judaism is a certain view of the origins of Christianity as from a pristine spring which is certainly a fiction. Roughly speaking this is the idea that within weeks, possibly days, of the death of Jesus – or even in his lifetime – we find amongst his followers a fully fledged 'new religion' called Christianity that was not only a radical departure from 'Judaism' but which represented a triumph of light over darkness. This picture will be so familiar to all of you here that I will spare you its development. There are Protestant and Catholic versions of this historical and improbable version of earliest Christianity – many, it seems to me, which are not so much concerned to establish Christian credentials over and against Judaism as to vindicate their own church order over against that of other contesting Christian parties.[5] One Catholic version suggests that Jesus, perhaps in his teaching during the resurrection appearances, put in place all the structures of the post-Constantinian church. One Protestant version leaps back over what it regards as the deforming centuries of papal Christianity to drink once again from the pure wells of the teachings of Jesus, with the implication that Christian self-definition was clear and obvious from its earliest days. It may be worth mentioning here that Christian anti-Judaism has many forms and that some of the most damaging recent ones have not been the products of 'conservative' but of liberal theologies (although I feel myself to be unhappy with these terms). For instance, the quest for the historical Jesus in nineteenth-century Protestant Liberalism was undoubtedly radical in its day, but the focus on the teaching of Jesus, rather than on claims made about him, lead in some cases to extravagant claims about the altogether radical and innovative nature of this teaching: Jesus as the outsider, the critic of the law, the prophet of love who transcends 'tribalism and particularism' at a time when the world is emerging from tribal cultures, and so on. It is this trajectory of Liberal Protestantism in which my Asian feminist theologian, albeit unwittingly, still stands. But it won't do.

It is now altogether clear, at the scholarly level, that we cannot possibly understand Christianity by seeing it as a radical and complete rupture with Judaism in the first century CE. And here the work of Jewish scholars is having enormous impact and will have more. There is, of course, the deepened understanding of Jesus, the Jew, and here one naturally thinks of Geza Vermes and others whose impact on Christian understandings of Jesus has been considerable. But I am thinking also of recent work by Jewish scholars which casts light on 'Christian origins' and has the potential to transform our understanding not just of the historical Jesus but also of the emergence of mainstream Christian doctrines such as those of Eucharist and Trinity. Here I mention by example Jon Levenson's *Death and Resurrection of the Beloved Son* which, through close analysis of the treatment of the binding of Isaac in Rabbinic and pre-Rabbinic Judaism, sheds important light on early Christian understandings of sacrifice and Eucharist. These last are not only inseparable from some understanding of then contemporary Judaism but are, Levinson argues, 'incomprehensible apart from the history of Jewish biblical interpretation'.[6] One might mention too Alan Segal's work on Gnosticism and early Christianity. Segal suggests that Paul's 'naming' of Jesus as the Lord who 'Let light shine out of darkness' (II Cor. 4.5–6) is an early seed of the Christian doctrine of the Trinity. His work on Gnosticism also gives a means of seeing how Christian claims about Jesus might have appeared to the rabbis as a recognizable 'two powers' heresy.[7] I am reluctant to expand upon such things with so eminent an authority as Professor Stroumsa in our group. I am not a biblical scholar or a historian, but mention these by way of saying that it is now impossible to see Christianity as springing, like Athena, fully-armed from the head of Zeus – however convenient such a binarist fiction might have been for forging Christian identities, and however disastrous in matters of religious tolerance.

Rather than this clean-cut profile it seems that we always already find a situation of overlapping discourses, Jewish and Hellenistic and Gnostic and Christian, and so on. Daniel Boyarin, in his *Dying for God* makes this observation:

Not long ago, everyone knew that Judaism came before Christianity. The story would go that Christianity developed out of the 'orthodox' Judaism of the first century, Rabbinic Judaism, and either deviated from the true path or superseded its ancestor. Interestingly, it was more or less the same story for both Christian and Jewish scholars.[8]

Boyarin also suggests that there has been 'a kind of general collusion between Jewish and Christian scholars (as early as the Rabbis and the Doctors of the Church) to insist on this total lack of contact and interaction, each group for its own reasons. For Christians the purpose was to show how their faith 'transcended' Judaism, and for the Jews to show Christianity as a deviation from the right path.[9] It may be a shock to some Christians to realize the extent to which Christian teaching is not novel but distinctly Jewish. It may be an offence to some Jews that many Christian doctrines, while richly dressed up in Hellenized categories, are nonetheless in continuity with recognizably Jewish, if sectarian, ideas.

On the one hand, I do not wish to suggest that Judaism and the history of Judaism should only be of interest to Catholics in an opportunistic way – as enhancing our own faith. On the other hand, it seems to me that from this shared seed of mutual understanding greater familiarity and love may grow – and this for all Catholics and not just those in countries with a significant Jewish presence. Realization that their own Christian scriptures and doctrines can only adequately be understood with reference to Jewish teaching and interpretations should also keep Christians from freezing Judaism in some forced, Christian construct based only on the biblical texts, and thus ignoring the nuanced rabbinic commentaries on these texts formative for modern Judaism.[10] It is important, that is, for Christans – not just theologians – to realize that the Jewish community, like the Christian, develops 'organically' (to use Dorff's term) responding and changing over time. At the moment it is all too common to find Christians comparing their twenty-first century moral intuitions to a 'Judaism' that is a Christian construct from the biblical literature and shows no acquaintance or regard for Jewish self-understanding.[11] It is my hope that, for the Catholic and even more broadly Christian side, we may return to these early centuries and rediscover the extent of similarity and indebtedness, and thus put in perspective the antagonistic rhetoric which has so frequently erupted where one group, in binarist mode, achieves self-definition by contrasting its own position over and against 'the other' (whether that be Christians/Jews, Protestants/ Catholics, third-world Christian/first-world Christian, women/men, etc.).

Moving beyond monologue

We need to find a view of faith and of religious truth that moves beyond monologue – even perhaps even beyond the false dialogue where so often two opposing sides state their position with little genuine hearing of the other.

How can we sing this sacred polyphony? How can we allow difference without losing truth? Some postmodern theorists have looked for help to the strategies of Rabbinic Judaism which seem to have found ways of 'housing' genuine disagreement without the tendencies to schism so apparent in Christian history. Often mentioned here is the jostling together of opposing positions in the Talmud, without apparent concern for a reconciliation or emergent party line. This polysemic aspect of rabbinic teaching is particularly prized by postmodern Jewish philosophers – and not by them alone – as facilitating dissent, heterogeneity and even contradiction in Jewish thought and practice, while preserving the unity of the whole.[12] Yet rabbinic Judaism was not, of course, infinitely elastic and here again there is much that Catholics can learn about the authority of the text and the importance of the living community in reading and appropriating that living word of God.

Also of interest for Catholics as well as Jews is the new, or at least renewed credibility of tradition and established wisdoms – the renewed acceptability, that is, of dialogue with one's past. Generally speaking for Enlightenment modernists 'tradition' was, as Peter Ochs put it, identified with 'someone's oppressive past', something in short that one wanted to escape to be free and wholly human.[13] Catholics and Jews have been uncomfortable with sweeping denunciations of tradition and now need to show how traditions can provide positive and creative placing, a 'relational pull' in Ochs's terms, which does not preclude new thinking or indeed obviate its necessity as we find ourselves in new times. Such reflections on diversity, dialogue and tradition suggest that postmodernity may prove fertile soil for our faith communities, but there is a dark side.

If, following Edith Wyschogrod, we take modern philosophy to describe Western thought from Descartes through Husserl and modernism 'to designate the spirit that characterises modern philosophy, principally its faith in reason',[14] we must admit that there was much in modernism that was good. Confidence in the human condition (if sometimes misplaced), respect for the individual (even if autonomy oversimplified) and the emphasis on the universal and ethical (if over-optimistic). As the rubrics of this session's session, these values were, if not discovered by Western modernity, then firmly set in place by it. After some initial reluctance these values are now accepted by most Christians and Jews.

Yet, whatever its value for inspiring optimism, activity and a bold vision of human possibility, the high modernist faith in reason fell in the trenches of the First World War and the death camps of the Holocaust. The 'Man of Reason' now appears largely a delusion, a Promethean charade.

So where are we now? The recent papal encyclical *Fides et Ratio* is in many ways a diagnosis of the 'postmodern condition'. In it the Pope sees our time as marked by a 'crisis of meaning'. We find ourselves with more and more information – a 'maelstrom of data and facts' – yet with less and less sense what to do with it. We are told constantly that our world is pluralistic and, by implication, that questions of meaning and truth – big questions about being and the meaning of life – can not only no longer be answered but indeed cannot even be asked. The result is scepticism, indifference and nihilism. If we have a shared notion of the 'common good' or the human good then it is a self-contradictory one – we aspire to be totally 'in control' while fearing that we are 'out of control'. If we have given up the fiction of the 'Man of Reason' then we have not given up the 'pious' hope that science will solve all our problems. We have visions of determining the sex, height and intelligence of our offspring, of defeating aging and cloning ourselves. Meanwhile a reductionist theory of human existence, fluently popularized in sociobiological tracts, tells us that we are no more than complicated mechanisms for the transmission of genetic information and suggests that it is 'species-ist' to put human life, especially 'deficient' human life, above that of other intelligent mammals. Paradoxically it may now fall to Judaism, Christianity and other faith traditions to speak up in defence of the dignity and distinctiveness of the human race and of each human person in an age which shows a worrying inclination to misanthropy. (Witness some 'deep green' rhetoric.)

But the defence of human dignity and even human glory which arises from the faith traditions is not the same confident Enlightenment anthropology in which man, his own master, casts off any need for a celestial pilot. What was lacking in high modernist humanism was the appropriate modesty that religions at their best allow. Hume seemed to believe that an exalted picture of God would produce an abased and servile humanity. It seems arguable that the opposite is the case – we can retain a highly positive anthropology only when this is kept in check by an ever strong conviction of the holiness and goodness of God whose wisdom infinitely surpasses our own. We cannot claim for ourselves, as modernist epistemology aspired to do, a 'God's eye view'. Like Moses and the people of Israel we move forward in the desert not because we drew the map, or can even aspire to do so, but because step by step we try to follow the maker.

There is something tender and moving in Moses' question to God at the burning bush – 'and if they ask me his name, what shall I tell them?' What did Moses expect or want? This has been the basis of much speculation. Perhaps he sought a means of invoking Israel's God in power. In response Moses receives as a gloss upon the Holy Name, 'ehyeh asher ehyeh', 'I Am Who I Am'. This is 'a name which is no name', according to Paul Ricoeur. Yes, and no. In a profound sense God cannot be named by us, if that implies in any way a capturing of essence and this the name itself suggests. But nonetheless when Moses asked for a name he was not met with silence. He was answered and did learn how to call upon his God. To capture the sense of the passage 'I Am Who I Am' is an unsatisfactory translation. As Rosenzweig constantly reminds his readers and correspondents,

> God calls himself not 'the-one-who-is' but 'the one-who-is-there,' i.e. there for you, there for you at this place, present to you, with you or rather coming toward you, toward you to help you. For the Hebrew *hayah* is not, unlike the Indo-Germanic 'to be,' of its nature a copula, not of its nature static, but a word of becoming, of entering, of happening.[15]

Despite its Hellenizing tendencies, I do not think the Christian tradition – not even the high mystical tradition – ever lost sight of the particularity of this moment. Christianity is, like Judaism, a deeply historical religion. Here is a notion impossible and offensive to the Greek philosophers who were in possession, let us remember, of sophisticated monotheistic visions: that God who is above all our human conceiving nonetheless is able and freely chose to make himself known in the history of Israel, not as the end product of a syllogism but as an irruption in her life. This claim is at the heart of both Judaism and Christianity. If this is an extravagant claim it may also be seen as a modest one. The burning bush is the beginning of a journey and not its end, and the way that is clear to Moses is the way of a follower. Gregory of Nyssa glosses this in his *Life of Moses*. Why was it that Moses is only allowed to see God's back? Because when you see someone's back you know that you are following them.

God cannot be captured, controlled or contained – and God does not need to be. This is one of the meanings of the names given from the burning bush. Martin Buber says, referring to the gloss on the name,

> The first *ehyeh* says simply, 'I shall be there' (with my host, with my people, with you) – so you do not need to conjure me up; and the next *asher ehyeh* can according to all parallel passages mean only, 'as the one I shall always be there as,' as who I shall on this or that occasion be there as, 'i.e., just as I shall on this or that occasion want to appear . . . Or, in summary: you do not need to invoke me; but neither are you able to invoke me. What is here reported is, in the context of the history of religion, the demagicalizing of belief – in the self-proclamation of the God present to his own, abiding with his own, accompanying his own.[16]

Whatever his deficiencies, Augustine never loses sight of this important distinction between who God is in himself (which we will never know) and who God is 'for us' which has been graciously disclosed in the history of Israel and, for Augustine, the life, death and resurrection of Christ. He confesses himself glad that after 'I am who I am' of Exodus 3.14 we hear in Exodus 3.15 'I am the God of Abraham, the God of Isaac and the God of Jacob'. 'What belongs to God alone' we will never fully understand, he says, and even Moses was frightened by hearing God's proper name – which makes it all the more important to know who God is for us.[17]

How shall we proceed then, with Moses, as followers of God? I would say that at this moment Catholics and Jews may play an important part in facilitating the broader culture in recovering what is good about our murky past, not by stripping or bowdlerizing it. Jews and Catholics especially have some idea that traditions can be freeing friends and not embarrassing strictures, and that the long dead have still much to teach us. We must move beyond agonistic or binarist strategies in which 'I am right' only if 'you are wrong'. Modesty about our limitations, such as our own sacred texts teach us, will be invaluable.

Rosenzweig's philosophy of 'speaking thinking' has much to teach us. This is thinking always done in genuine response to the other and always allowing of difference. It is modest in acknowledging that the other may have something to tell us, yet it is not fearful. In contrast to the Hegelian pattern where thesis and antithesis sublate one another to be mutually annihilated in synthesis, in dialogical thinking the one and the other one are not destroyed by their encounter but become more truly themselves.

Kissed Him and They Wept

It is unfortunate that the word 'dialogue' has been used and over-used for many ecumenical and interfaith encounters that were in fact little more than reciprocal monologues. It is hard to find synonym, yet we can try to be clear about what real dialogue is or might be. Rosenzweig is insistent that, in contrast with the pretensions of so much philosophy to speak from a timeless 'nowhere', speech is 'bound to time and nourished by time'. Because of this, dialogue 'does not know in advance just where it will end. It takes its cue from others.' Unlike the *faux* dialogues of Plato or of Hume, where the philosopher controls and brings it to a predetermined destiny, 'In actual conversation, something happens.' We are changed. 'Perhaps the other person will say the first word for in a true conversation this is usually the case; a glance at the Gospels and the Socratic dialogues will show the contrast.'[18]

I am warmed by Rosenzweig's suggestion that the Gospels, and he must mean their accounts of Jesus, show someone who is a 'speaking thinker', someone who is actually hearing and responding. The Church has not always shown such courtesy.

Dialogue, if it is true dialogue, will bring change. Indeed, I think we can see this is happening already between Christians and Jews in the scholarly encounters of the last thirty years to which I have referred. The transmission of these insights, in Catholic terms, from the researches of biblical scholars and historians to doctrinal theology, priestly formation and preaching will not be an overnight affair, but it will go on if those of us here and other like-minded people will hold, treasure and foster it. Speaking personally, I view the time before us with the greatest excitement, not simply because I am growing in my love for Judaism and, I hope, my understanding of Jewish people, but also because my own Catholic faith is being transformed into something richer, deeper and more authentic by this conversation too long overdue.

Notes

' "The Eternal": Moses Mendelssohn and the Name of God' (1929), *Scripture and Translation*, ed. Martin Buber and Franz Rosenzweig, trans. Lawrence Rosenwald with Everett Fox, Bloomington: Indiana University Press, 1994, pp. 98–9.
3. Ibid., p. 101.
4. Elliot N. Dorff, 'The Covenant as the Key: A Jewish Theology of Jewish–Christian Relations', *Toward a Theological Encounter: Jewish Understandings of Christianity*, ed. Leon Klenicki, New York: Paulist Press, 1991, p.43.
5. It is important to speak of Catholic and Protestant *accounts* (plural) just as one

must speak of many Jewish positions and not 'the Jewish position'.

6. Jon D. Levenson, *The Death and Resurrection of the Beloved Son*, New Haven and London: Yale University Press, 1993, p. 75

7. Daniel Boyarin, *Dying for God: Martyrdom and the Making of Christianity and Judaism*, Stanford: Stanford University Press, 1999, p. 1

8. Ibid., p. 7.

9. Boyarin adds, 'Indeed the very distinctness of Judaism has been articulated by Jews as its distance from a 'syncretistic' Christianity whose defining feature is that it is somehow a composite of Judaism and Hellenism, p . 7.

10. For instance, the passage that Elliot Dorff cites where God's 'rebuke' to the jubilant angels at the triumph of the Red Sea occurs, 'My children lie drowned in the sea, and you sing hymns of triumph?' (ibid., p. 46).

11. I would judge that most Christians are unaware of the fact Elliot Dorff draws our attention to, that for Jews it is 'the Rabbinic tradition which is the fulfilment of the Hebrew Bible, not the New Testament' (ibid. p. 58). Most would realize, one hopes, that the New Testament is not directive for Jews but what they would not usually think of, indeed will be predictably almost entirely ignorant of, is the rabbinic tradition or even the existence of the rabbinic tradition. To return to my earlier point, this situation is unlikely to improve without conscious Christian effort in a world where so many Christians have no contact with Jews whatsoever.

12. See Steven Kepnes in Steven Kepnes, Peter Ochs and Robert Gibbs (eds.) *Reasoning after Revelation: Dialogues in Postmodern Jewish Philosophy*, Boulder, CO: Westview Press, 1998, p. 27.

13. Ibid., p. 135.

14. E. Wyschogrod, 'Trends in Postmodern Jewish Philosophy: Contexts of a Conversation' in Kepnes, Ochs and Gibbs (eds), *Reasoning after Revelation*, p. 135.

15. 'A Letter to Martin Goldner', *Scripture and Translation*, Buber and Rosenzweig, p. 191.

16. Martin Buber, 'Kingship of God' (1920), *Scripture and Translation*, Buber and Rosenzweig, p. 195.

17. In *Enarratio in Psalmum CXXI*. This is discussed by T. J. von Bavel, OSA in 'God in between Affirmation and Negation according to Augustine', *Augustine: Prebyter Factus Sum*, ed. J. T. Leinhard, E. C. Muller and R. J. Teske, Collectanea Augustiniana, New York: Peter Lang, 1993, p. 79.

18. 'The New Thinking: Philosophy and Religion', *Franz Rosenzweig: His Life and Thought*, ed. Nahum N. Glatzer, Indianapolis and Cambridge: Hackett Publishing Company, 1998, pp. 198–9.

Discussant

– Guy Stroumsa

Professor Stroumsa had been unable to read the conference papers beforehand and could not contribute a written introduction. However, we want to recognize his contribution both because of his influence on other contributors and because of his brief, albeit off the cuff, remarks. Professor Stroumsa is a leading figure amongst Jewish scholars who is exploring that period in which both Rabbinic Judaism and Christianity emerged. He endorsed several important propositions advanced by others elsewhere in this book. He was clear that both were emerging out of a substantially common source at much the same time. He was emphatic in endorsing Dr Soskice's critique of the myth that Christianity was a radical and complete rupture with Judaism in the first century CE and of the picture of overlapping discourses. Guy Stroumsa is one of a significant band of Jewish scholars who gives reality to the proposition that not only do Christians need to know more about Judaism and understand Judaism within its own terms of reference but Jews need equally to understand Christianity from its very origins and the influence that it has had on Judaism as well as vice versa.

Dr Stroumsa goes further. His experience in Israel has shown him that Israel has to take note of the Christian presence there because that Christian presence is part of Israeli culture and even identity. This moves the dialogue, in part, from theology to culture. Stroumsa also argued for the need to move the dialogue from theology to education since little can be achieved unless both Jews and Catholics are educated about their theological, historical and cultural interrelationship.

Discussion recorder

– Clare Jardine

This session was different from any other during this conference firstly because the papers were delivered by two women and secondly because both the discussants work in an Israeli context. The contributions of the women gave rise to discussions on feminism and the presence of the two from Israel led to an exchange on the importance of the cultural milieu of dialogue.

Susannah Heschel's paper discussed postmodernity with respect to feminism and postcolonialism. The issue of feminism together with Michael McGarry's response sparked off some lively discussion. A number of people criticized Susannah Heschel for her use of the feminist and postcolonial critique, saying that there is a danger of reductionism in the use of these two particular critiques and that there are other critiques that could have been chosen. Some of the participants (both Catholic and Jewish) objected to this counter-challenge and went on to express how feminism can contribute to a methodology of interreligious dialogue. Dialogue means listening to others, acknowledging the experience of others and reading texts through the eyes of others. The 'other' who is to be listened to, whose experience is to be acknowledged, and through whose eyes texts are to be read obviously includes women. The fact that this often does not happen was voiced by one participant who spoke of 'the pain of alterity'. Another pointed to a felt importance of feminism in theology in general as she cannot read theology now without feminist writers. The women present were clearly making a particular contribution to the conference. A male participant noted that the two papers for this session had been delivered by women and that there was a relatively good proportion of women compared to other gatherings (although there were many more men than women taking part). In her summing up Susannah Heschel defended her position by stating that issues of feminism and postcolonialism cannot be dismissed. She added that feminism is not only for the benefit of women and asked what it can do for men as well as for women. Janet Martin Soskice said her position overlaps with Susannah's on this point and felt that feminism has much to offer.

The challenge of modernism/postmodernism prompted the participants to view the contribution of the cultural milieu of dialogue. This discussion was stimulated by Guy Stroumsa's response to Janet Martin Soskice's paper when he suggested that it may be useful to examine the move from theology to culture. Guy Stroumsa's experience in Israel showed him that Israel has to take note of the Christian presence there, not only because of interreligious dialogue but also because the Christian presence is part of the Israeli culture and identity. The interface between religion, society and culture challenges those in dialogue to adopt a more nuanced approach. Moreover, the differences in cultural context mean that there should be different kinds and different levels of dialogue according to each context. The example was given of the 'dialogue of life' referring to the everyday contact between people of different faiths which must be present alongside the dialogue between theologians.

The papers and responses stimulated a lively discussion on the distinction between pre-modernism, modernism and postmodernism and the question as to which level/s we are operating on. Are we operating at the moment on a modernist or a postmodernist level? Some participants felt we do operate at one or other level while others felt that people operate on all three levels at the same time. In her concluding remarks Susannah Heschel added that those who are pre-modern are also part of the modern and so on, showing that there is a fudging and overlap of boundaries. Janet Martin Soskice pointed out that the Vatican document *Fides et Ratio* is a critique of modernism in the Catholic Church.

Picking up Guy Stroumsa's point about moving the discussion from theology to education, some time was spent on this area. Its importance for the future of dialogue was stressed and several participants noted the great need for Jews to be educated about Chrstianity as the present teaching is based on pre-Vatican II perceptions. The recent visit of Pope John Paul II to Israel prompted a call from the Israeli government in the form of circulars and teaching materials to Israeli schools encouraging them to change the teaching of Christianity in line with the texts of the Pope. It was noted that there is a perception that we can change people through textbooks but in reality it will take time and effort to change attitudes and mentality. It was mentioned that one of the main areas where education is needed vis à vis the Christian–Jewish relationship is in the seminaries.

One of the other issues that was brought up during this session was the importance of Franz Rosenzweig's thought for Christian–Jewish dialogue today. One participant spoke of the importance of 'place' and the need for a relocation of Christian–Jewish dialogue which takes Judaism seriously. Rosenzweig's use of the image of the star to describe the dependence of Christianity (the rays) on a strong core (living Judaism) for its very existence can help formulate a new theology of the relationship. Janet Martin Soskice added that another factor of Rosenzweig's thought which could be helpful is his belief that in dialogue one partner does not annihilate the other but rather enhances the other.

The session may have seemed to end on a note of pessimism or perhaps realism when one participant spoke of the greatest challenge being a general lack of faith and lack of meaning of life in society. In her summing up Susannah Heschel said that for her the real problem is the death of faith itself.

The discussion following this session proved to be most lively if somewhat controversial in content. The reaction of some of the women had taken some of the men participants by surprise but it was clear that future dialogue has to take note of feminism and the contribution of women. The visit of Pope John Paul II to Israel had definitely made an impact there and some of the repercussions would be felt in the teaching about Christianity in Israeli schools, showing the importance of taking the cultural milieu into account in inter-religious dialogue. The issue of how to distinguish modernist/post-modernist thought does not seem to be at stake as the boundaries are blurred. What is clear is that Jewish and Christian thinkers both have a role in shaping the future attitudes of their respective communities with regard to dialogue and other issues affecting human society as a whole.

5

A Partnership for the Glory of God, the Good of Humanity and the Future of the Planet

What can we do together to enhance God's name and make a real contribution to the betterment of life? How can we make the third Christian Millennium an age in which religion is an unqualified source of peace and good and also a time of dynamic interfaith relations?

How do we tackle the issues of religious power and powerlessness? What role should religion seek in state and society?

A. Religion, Government and Society

– David Rosen

The Bible reflects a profound awareness of the problem of political power. The dangers of monarchy are eloquently described by Samuel in his efforts to dissuade the people from choosing a king.[1] Notwithstanding, the Pentateuchal model of governance is in fact monarchical.[2] However, the dangers are offset by the fact that the people as a whole play a key role in the monarch's election and authority. Moreover, in being subject to the law, the king is bound by a social contract that makes demands of him in relation to the people as well as to God, ensuring that no illusion of superhuman status gains sway.[3] Government is clearly not an end in itself, but has the purpose of serving the public. A special ceremony every seven years precisely to affirm the rule of law emphasized the status of the king as representative of the people.[4]

Indeed, the community at large, has a central role in Jewish historical religious life. The revelation at Mount Sinai is described as a communal experience taking the form of a covenant between a people and the sovereign of the world.[5] (The collective nature of the experience is even seen by some Jewish philosophers, notably Yehudah Halevi,[6] as serving as proof of its authenticity.) In fact, the significance of the concept of the collective in Jewish thought goes so far as to include the sinner as well, so that the community of the Covenant can never be conceived as an aristocratic, elitist structure, even in spiritual terms.[7]

The importance of consultation with the public before appointments are made, is confirmed in the Babylonian Talmud[8] on the basis of the biblical narrative.

Rabbi Isaac said one must not appoint a public leader without first consulting the community; for it is said 'Moses said to the children of Israel, see the Lord has nominated Bezalel'.[9] The Almighty said to Moses, 'Moses, do you think Bezalel is suitable?' Moses replied, 'Master of the universe if You think he is suitable, I certainly think so.' The Almighty said to him, 'Nevertheless, go and ask the children of Israel.' Moses went and asked the children of Israel, 'Do you think Bezalel is suitable?' They replied, 'If both the Almighty and you think he is suitable, we certainly think so.' The reason for seeking public approval is explained as follows by Rabbi Hayim Zundel,[10] principal commentator on the collation of the Aggadic sections of the Talmud, in reference to the above text. 'In the selection of the court of three judges to deal with a monetary quarrel, each side nominates one judge and the third judge is chosen jointly; we do this so as to ensure that the judgment will be acceptable. Likewise in the choice of a leader, we wish to ensure that his policies will be accepted and we therefore arrange that he should be chosen by the public.

In keeping with the above, the theme of public consultation recurs throughout the Bible and Talmud. Saul is selected by Samuel with the guidance of the Almighty, and is then brought to the people of Israel for their approval.[11] David is selected and anointed in a similar manner, but it takes seven years of his reign to secure the approval of all the tribes of Israel.[12] The sages Hillel and Shammai agree to introduce certain legislation, but the public does not accept it.[13] It is only a generation later that it gains public acceptance. These ideas are formally incorporated into the Code of Jewish Law[14] where the authority of communal leaders is discussed, clarifying that their authority derives from their acceptance by the people.

Thus the dangers of the abuse of power are offset by the weight of public authority. Yet the latter itself is rooted in the concept of the value of each and every individual who together make up the body politic.

The idea of the sacrosanct nature of the life and dignity of every person is enshrined at the very beginning of the Hebrew scriptures in the story of the creation of the human person, as it is stated: 'This is the book of the generations of Adam, in the likeness of God He created him. Male and female He created them and blessed them and called their name Adam on the day He created them.'[15]

This text serves for a very important discussion between two sages from the second century of the Common Era on what is the guiding principle, not simply conceptually but practically, in terms of moral conduct. But before addressing this text, I would like to refer to the Mishnah that deals with the formal caution given to witnesses in capital cases, warning them of the dire consequences of false testimony.[16] The admonition continues:

> Therefore the first human being was created singly, to teach you that he who destroys one life, it is as if he destroyed the whole world. And he who preserves one life, it is as if he has preserved the whole world.

The very question as to why the first human being was created singly arises, of course, from the fact that in the biblical story of creation, all creatures are created in couples and ultimately Adam is separated into both male and female. If Adam is going to be separated into male and female anyway, then why didn't God save himself the trouble and create them to begin with as separate individuals, just as he did with all other creatures? Accordingly the sages conclude that the reason for the creation of one human person singly is to convey a moral message. There is of course an essential moral message in the text itself in the very union of male and female together, establishing the fullness of Adam, and therefore the Talmud states[17] that he who does not have a spouse is not a complete human being, emphasizing the Jewish perspective of marriage as the ideal state for human fulfilment. But the Mishnah does not focus on that particular message.

It focuses upon what it sees to be the most basic moral message of the idea of the creation of the single human person. Namely, the supreme sanctity of human life, to the extent that each person is seen as a whole world. But the moral message goes further. The text of the Mishnah continues: 'And (also) a single human being was first created for the sake of peace amongst mankind, so that no person can say to another, my father was greater than yours.' In other words, the purpose is also to emphasize our common humanity. The text continues:

> And (another reason why) a single person was created first (was in order) to proclaim the greatness of the Holy One, Blessed Be He. For when a human being (mints coins, he) uses one mould (and) all the coins are identical. But the King of Kings coined every man out of the mould of the first human being and not one is like the other [i.e., each person is unique]. Therefore every person is obliged to say, the world was created for me.

(Of course, the Talmud goes on to say we should keep our sense of proportion and remember that the mosquito was created before the human and that moreover a person should always acknowledge that in addition to the fact that he or she is a world in himself or herself, we are but dust and ashes. In other words, there has to be a creative tension between avoiding arrogance and at the same time appreciating one's worth and value as a human being created in the Image of God.) Thus the Mishnah not only seeks to impress upon us the supreme value of human life and dignity, but also to direct our moral conduct accordingly.

This fundamental moral imperative is further explicated in the famous Midrashic text to which I have already alluded, namely the discussion between Rabbi Akiva and his contemporary Ben Azzai, on what is the principle moral rule of the Torah, of Judaism. The text appears in two different forms and chronology in *Genesis Rabba* and in the *Sifra*.[18] However, the sixteenth-century author of the very important Midrashic commentary, the *Matnot Kehuna*,[19] explains how these two fragmentary texts need to be put together as originally intended, in order to understand the fullness of the discussion between these two sages and the deeper implication of the text. In the *Sifra*, it simply appears to be a discussion without any explanation. Rabbi Akiva declares that the central guiding principle for moral conduct is the commandment in Leviticus 19.18 to love one's neighbour as oneself, whereas his contemporary Ben Azzai says that the guiding principle is that every human being is created in the image of God. A cursory

view of this discussion would suggest perhaps that it is a debate
between a more particularist world-view and a more universalist
weltanschauung. According to such an interpretation Ben Azzai is saying to Akiva that, while the commandment to love your neighbour as
yourself is most important, people might nevertheless become selective in their interpretation of who is their neighbour. Therefore we
should emphasize that every human being is created in the image of
God, so that the universal moral responsibility that God demands of
us is clear to each and every person. As important as this message is
(resonating with the teaching of Jesus of Nazareth), it is a questionable
interpretation of this debate. To begin with, there is no Mishnaic sage
who uses the phrase that the human being is created in the image of
God more than Rabbi Akiva himself. It is Akiva who says: 'Beloved is
the human being that is created in the Image of God.'[20] Moreover
when Akiva wants to impress upon us how serious murder is as the
greatest offence of all, he says: 'He who sheds blood diminishes the
Divine Image [i.e., it is as if he destroys a piece of God himself]. For it
is written "in the Image of God He created him".'[21] The principle that
all persons are created in the divine image is clearly central to Akiva's
moral value system. So the issue here is not that Rabbi Akiva is somehow more particularist or insular than Ben Azzai. Exactly why Akiva
prefers the golden rule here is a subject for further deliberation. But I
wish to clarify here what Ben Azzai's concern is. Why does he think
that the golden rule is inadequate? With the benefit of the elucidation
of the *Matnot Kehuna*, who explains that the subsequent phrase that
appears in *Genesis Rabbah* belongs to Ben Azzai, we can understand
exactly what is his fear. 'So that you do not say "in as much as I have
been despised, so let my fellow be despised with me, in as much as I
have been cursed let my fellow be cursed with me".' Ben Azzai is
warning against the danger of making one's subjective experiences
the basis for one's moral conduct, with the possibility that one might
interpret Leviticus 19.18 to mean love your neighbour as you have
been loved. He is concerned not only with the immorality of tit-for-tat
but also with the danger that an individual's lack of self-respect will
mean lack of respect for others' dignity: Ben Azzai is above all warning against the danger of relativizing one's moral responsibilities to
all other human beings. For regardless of how one may be treated and
no matter how badly others may have dealt with one or one's people,
we are all still obliged to behave toward others with respect for their
lives and dignity, simply by virtue of the fact that each and every
person is a human being – created in the divine image. And here
comes the punch line of the Midrashic text: 'Said Rabbi Tanhuma, "if

you do so" [i.e., if you say because I have been despised let my fellow be despised], know whom you despise, "for in the image of God, He made the human person" '.[22] In other words, any act of disrespect to another human person is an act of disrespect towards God himself and it is not possible to be truly God-fearing unless one behaves with respect towards all human beings.

It is commitment to this *weltanschauung* that countervails any tendency to lord it over another and abuse any position of power.

While political power remained a theoretical problem for most of the last 2,000 years of Jewish history, there were a number of medieval philosophers who addressed the question of Judaism's preferred political system. Happily to my mind, there was not uniformity on the question. However, one of the most interesting approaches is that of Rabbi Nissim of Gerondi[23] who envisions the parallel functioning of two frames of authority even in a Jewish polity – a broad civil moral structure and a non-coercive religious framework – arguably laying down one of the earliest philosophical arguments of separation of religion and state.

The establishment of the State of Israel led to renewed discussion of the matter, but I would imagine that most of us would happily endorse Gerondi's approach if on no other basis than the wisdom of historical hindsight, which seems to prove conclusively that religion is far healthier when it is in creative tension with political authority than when it is bolstering, let alone being part of, political authority.

However, the primary problem that the Jewish community faced in the course of most of the last two millennia was not the problem of power, but that of the lack of it.

One of the most fascinating discussions that reveals the way the rabbinic mind coped with this challenge, is the following text in the Babylonian Talmud.[24]

R. Joshua b. Levi said: Why were they called men of the Great Synod? Because they restored the crown of the divine attributes to its ancient glory. (For) Moses had come and said: 'The great God, the mighty, and the awesome'.[25] Then Jeremiah came and said: aliens are destroying His Temple. Where are, then, His awesome deeds? Hence he omitted (the attribute) the 'awesome'.[26] Daniel came and said: aliens are enslaving his sons. Where are His mighty deeds? Hence he omitted (the attribute) 'mighty'.[27] But they came and said: on the contrary! therein lies His mighty deeds; that He suppresses His wrath, that He extends long-suffering to the wicked. Therein lies His awesome powers: for but for the fear of

Him, how could one (single) nation persist among the (many) nations! But how could the (earlier) teachers abolish something established by Moses? R. Eleazar said: Since they knew that the Holy One, blessed be He, insists on truth, they would not ascribe false (things) to Him.

What we see here is a moralization of the concept of power, in which not only is the latter given a new and spiritually positive interpretation, but the powerless are accorded the moral high ground.

Presenting the vulnerable not only as occupying the moral high ground but also as actually preferred by the almighty is powerfully expressed in the Midrashic passage[28] on the phrase in Ecclesiastes.[29]

'And God shall make requirement for the persecuted (lit. pursued).' Rabbi Yehuda, the son of Rabbi Simon, said in the name of Rabbi Yehuda, the son of Rabbi Nehorai:

'The Holy One blessed be He demands the blood of the persecuted from the persecutors. Know that it is so, for Abel was persecuted by Cain, and the Holy One blessed be He chose Abel.[30] Noah was persecuted by his generation and the Holy One blessed be He only chose Noah[31]. Abraham was persecuted by Nimrod and the Holy One blessed be He chose Abraham.[32] Isaac was persecuted by the Philistines and the Holy One blessed be He chose Isaac.[33] Jacob was persecuted by Esau and the Holy One blessed be He chose Jacob.[34] Joseph was persecuted by his brothers and the Holy One blessed be He chose Joseph.[35] Moses was persecuted by Pharaoh and the Holy One blessed be He chose Moses.[36] David was persecuted by Saul and the Holy blessed be He chose David.[37] Saul was persecuted by the Philistines and the Holy One blessed be he chose Saul.[38] The people of Israel is persecuted by the nations of the world and the Holy One blessed be He has chosen the people of Israel as it is said: The Lord has chosen you to be his specially treasured people.[39]

The implications of this moralization of power are further expressively articulated in the Midrash[40] on the verse.

'Let the Lord arise and scatter His enemies and may those who hate Him flee from before Him.'[41] Says the Midrash: '(in the book of Psalms we find that) on five occasions (King) David calls on God to 'arise and scatter His enemies' and yet there is no mention (in Psalms) that God arises (in response). When *do* we find (mention of)

God arising? 'For the oppression of the poor and the cry of the needy, then will I arise, saith the Lord'.[42]

This Midrash brings to mind the comment attributed to Abraham Lincoln when asked on the eve of battle whether God was on their side. 'The question is', Lincoln is reported to have replied, 'whether we are on God's side'!

What the Midrash is saying in effect is that even if you are God's anointed himself, even if you are King David, you may not assume that God is on your side. When is God on your side? When you are on his. And what is his side? It is above all, the side of the needy and vulnerable; and the extent to which a nation addresses itself to these is the extent to which it is godly.

Accordingly, while Judaism seeks to countervail the possible abuse of power by emphasizing the value of every individual and necessitating public legitimization of authority, the problem of powerlessness was addressed by presenting the vulnerable not just as the litmus test of moral conduct, but as the authentic representatives of divine authority itself.

Notes

1. I Sam. 8.11–18.
2. Deut. 17.15.
3. Deut. 17.20.
4. *m. Sot.* 7.8 (cf. Deut. 31.11–12).
5. Ex. 19.5 and 6.
6. The *Kuzari*, Sect. 1.
7. See S. Schechter, *Studies in Judaism*, Philadelphia: Jewish Publication Society of America, 1915, pp. 18–23.
8. *Ber.* 55a.
9. Ex. 35.30.
10. Etz Yossef on Ein Yaacov, *Berakot*.
11. I Sam. 8.22.
12. II Sam. 21.11.
13. *b. Sab*, 17a.
14. Shulchan Aruch, *Choshen Mishpat*, ch. 2.
15. Gen. 5.1 and 2.
16. *Sanh.* 4.5.
17. *Yeb.* 62a.
18. *Sifra Kedoshim* (Lev. 19.18), 4.12 *Genesis Rabba* 1.24.
19. Rabbi Yissachar Ber Katz a.k.a. Berman Ashkenazy.
20. *m. Ab.* 3.14.
21. *t. Yeb.* 8.
22. *Genesis Rabba* 1.24.

23. *Drashot HaRan*, Feldman edition, Jerusalem 1974, pp. 189–92.
24. *Yom.* 69b.
25. Deut. 10.17.
26. Jer. 32.18.
27. Dan. 9.4.
28. *Leviticus Rabbah* 27.
29. Eccles. 3.15.
30. Gen. 4.4.
31. Gen. 7.1.
32. Neh. 9.
33. Gen. 26.3.
34. Ps. 135.4.
35. Ps. 81.6.
36. Ps. 106.23.
37. Ps. 78.70.
38. I Sam.12.13.
39. Deut. 14.2.
40. *Shochar Tov*.
41. Ps. 62.1.
42. Ps. 12.6.

Discussant

– Mary Boys

I consider the just and wise use of power on both the structural and personal levels to be of immense significance in our religious communities. Power, however, is not easily defined. Rollo May's typology of five kinds of power offers language helpful for specifying the sorts of power we are talking about:

- Exploitative power (power that uses the other for the service of self)
- Competitive power (power directed against others in order to defeat them)
- Manipulative power (power using indirect control through propaganda, ideology and tokenism)
- Nurturant power (power that educates and advocates for the sake of the other)
- Integrative power (power that is devoted to mutual concerns, working with others for the sake of developing both parties).[1]

One would hope that the power exercised by the church and synagogue should be nurturant and integrative. Nonetheless, I suspect we have all witnessed power that is exploitative, competitive or manipulative within our communities of faith.

Rabbi Rosen speaks especially to the nurturant type of power when he writes: 'Accordingly, while Judaism seeks to countervail the possible abuse of power by emphasizing the value of every individual and necessitating public legitimization of authority, the problem of powerlessness was addressed by presenting the vulnerable not just as the litmus test of moral conduct, but as the authentic representatives of divine authority itself' (p. 187). It is this claim that I wish to emphasize in my response.

The Gospels portray Jesus as an eschatological prophet who summons Israel to live more justly in view of the judgement at hand.

He proclaims a God who reverses the order of things. In the eschato-logical language of Second Temple Judaism, the advent of the divine rule did not necessarily mean a catastrophic end to all earthly realities, but could instead refer to a 'revolutionary transformation of the world itself, whereby the righteous and beneficent will of God comes to reign'.[2] This revolutionary transformation meant reversals: the powerful dethroned and the lowly raised, the hungry receiving their fill and the rich sent away empty (Luke 1.52–53). The meek will inherit the earth, not the self-aggrandizers; those who hunger for righteousness will be filled, not those who manipulate the system (see Matt. 5.5–6).

We see this mirrored in German biblical scholar Gerd Theissen's work of 'narrative exegesis', *The Shadow of the Galilean*. He constructs a dialogue between Chuza, an official in the court of Herod Antipas, and his wife Joanna. Joanna says to her husband: 'What irritates you about this Jesus is precisely the opposite of the limited morality of little people. He gives little people attitudes which previously were your privilege.' Chuza protests, 'But why does he present his teaching only to the little people? Why doesn't he come to Tiberias? Why doesn't he teach Antipas? I can think of only one answer. He dreams the dreams of little people.' In response, Joanna says:

> Of course he dreams the dreams of little people. He's not address-ing the rich and powerful. But what does he want to do? These little people are bent double by their toil. He wants them to walk upright. They're bowed down by cares. He wants them to be free from cares. They're people who feel insignificant. He gives them the feeling that their life has meaning. And you're all worried about that. All of you and Herod Antipas, you're worried that the little people might come to feel that they're not little people. So you've spread the rumour that you want to kill Jesus. So that he disappears over the frontier. So that he leaves you in peace. So that the little people don't hit on rebellious notions and become a danger to you.[3]

This advocacy for the vulnerable seems to have given the disciples a keen sense of going over against certain Greco-Roman mores. We see texts in which the 'Followers of the Way' are engaged in battle with the 'principalities [*archai*] and powers [*dynameis*]'. To be 'in Christ' meant to be dead to the 'elemental spirits of the universe' (Col. 2.20).

Yet this sense of clash with the powers of the culture diminished in the post-Constantinian era. If at one juncture we might have had the church vs. the empire, it all too soon became the church allied with the empire – and then, tragically, the church as empire in which exploitative, competitive and manipulative forms of power were all too readily exercised – and consistently against Jews.

All this leads to several questions today. For whom and how does the church exercise its power? In a powerful passage, the world's bishops write:

> Action on behalf of justice and participation in the transformation of the world appear to us as a constitutive dimension of the preaching of the Gospel, or, in other words, of the Church's mission for the redemption of the human race and its liberation from every oppressive situation.[4]

It has become increasingly common to speak of the 'preferential option for the poor'. Yet within the Church itself, forms of power are exercised that deny due process and exclude non-ordained theologians – especially women – from formulating ecclesiastical documents and policy, leading many to wonder whether the official Church exercises its power in ways conducive to nurturance and integration.

I end with an aphorism from Jesus: 'Like sheep in the midst of wolves, be wise as serpents and innocent as doves' (Matt. 10.16). Sage advice for dealing with power and powerlessness.

Notes

1. See Rollo May, *Power and Innocence: A Search for the Sources of Violence*, New York: W. W. Norton, 1972.
2. See A. Roy Eckardt, *Reclaiming the Jesus of History: Christology Today*, Minneapolis: Fortress, 1992, p. 66.
3. Gerd Theissen, *The Shadow of the Galilean*, Philadelphia: Fortress, 1987, pp. 123–4.
4. The 1971 Synod of Bishops, 'Justice in the World' (*Convenientes ex universo*), *Vatican Council II*, vol. 2, ed. Austin Flannery, Northport, NY: Costello, 1982, p. 696.

B. Religion, Government and Society

– Adrian van Luyn

The question 'what role should religion seek in state and society' can only be answered fruitfully when we also ask 'what role can religion seek in state and society'. I think here above all of the thoroughgoing changes to which both our society and our institutional religions are subject at present.

Our society is changing at a tempo that is perhaps only comparable to the first industrial revolution. As for the Church – and I limit myself with this observation to the Roman Catholic Church – its social and political meaning has changed greatly in this part of the world over the last fifty years. In addition, the Roman Catholic Church is, of course, undergoing a fundamental change with regard to its attitude to Judaism. It would not be an exaggeration to state that *Nostra Aetate* No. 4 (1965) has lead to a silent revolution. After the long night of separation and misjudgement, in which Christianity was unable to free itself from a sense of superiority, the Church is seeking a position marked by increasing repentance and conversion and by respect for Judaism as 'elder brother' in faith (John Paul II in the synagogue in Rome, 1986). This development, unfortunately, does not always prove to be a steady motion forward. At times we encounter regression or painful misunderstandings. Nevertheless, the dawn of a new reality is unmistakably breaking in the Church.

We witnessed this recently in a very special way: Pope John Paul II's historic visit to Israel. The image of a fragile man in Yad Vashem, the conversation with survivors of the *Shoah*, his gesture at the Western Wall of the Temple, a gesture that witnesses to Christian failure toward the Jewish people: here something of this new reality became visible.

With these three dimensions – society, Church and society, and Church and Judaism – we have circumscribed the three parameters of our question 'what role should religion seek in state and society'. They merit individual analysis.

Yet the topic of Church and society is interwoven in a special way with the Church's relation to Judaism. This goes for the past, as we shall see. This applies to the present as well. As religions descended from Abraham, we face a new challenge: can we as religions bear witness to modern society in a credible and comprehensible way? A positive answer is only possible to the extent that we succeed in divesting our relationship, as Jews and Christians, of intolerance and a sense of superiority. Too much energy has been wasted: in the meantime, society is no longer waiting for religion. Religion's authority can no longer be taken for granted. Yet religion's new position does offer fresh opportunities to communicate without having recourse to power.

If such communication is to be credible, it will have to satisfy several conditions. Since these conditions are related to the above-mentioned analysis of the three parameters: society, Church and Judaism, I would like to go further into them first. In the second part of my essay, I would like to present some outlines of a theological framework within which the common task of Judaism and Christianity can take shapes so as to establish signs of God's kingship. That theological framework includes messianic hope and a biblical anthropology of humanity as the image of God. Finally, I would like to present in that context a few specific questions to which our respective traditions can make an authentic contribution, preferably in shared reflection.

First, I should like to pause with you over several observations derived from the history of the past century and a half – but not without placing an important 'caveat'. Christians and Jews have to take into account the great difference in their history over the past centuries. Although this analysis has an unavoidably fragmentary character, I will still try to highlight some aspects of this divergent history.

First and second modernization

At the end of the nineteenth century, Europe underwent a first modernization, which changed the face of all society: technical revolution and industrialization, a developing world market and modern rationalism. It is clear that with these developments people's pre-modern attitude to life began to drift. 'Modern times' were felt to be both a vision and a threat. Optimism about progress and fear of degeneration went hand in hand. The sociologist Max Weber spoke of a profound process of demystification of the world (*Entzauberung der*

Welt): the shared sense of meaning and ethics founded on religion were destroyed by modern civilization.[1] Christians and Jews hesitated at that time between assimilation and opposition, although Christians then had little appreciation for the tradition they shared with Judaism.

Around the year 2000 people speak of a second modernization. The sociologist Manuel Castells wrote in a monumental three-part work *The Information Age* about 'The Rise of the Network Society'. Based on a new 'Information Technology Revolution' the West and the rest of the world are undergoing a revolution (globalization) with unheard of ramifications in economic, political and cultural fields. In the place of the old industrial class society and the post-war welfare state, there is a completely new type of society, a 'network society', without the old social movements and, important for our question, without the classical 'great narratives'. Castells put it like this:

> A new world is taking shape in this end of millennium. It originated in the historical coincidence, around the late 1960s and mid-1970s, of three **independent** processes: the information technology revolution; the economic crisis of both capitalism and statism [Eastern Europe] and their subsequent restructuring; and the blooming of cultural social movements, such as libertarianism, human rights, feminism, and environmentalism. The interaction between these processes, and the reactions they triggered, brought into being a new dominant social structure, the network society; a new economy, the informational/global economy; and a new culture, the culture of virtual reality.[2]

Like the Industrial Revolution, this network society also has an ambiguous character. In themselves, these developments are neither good nor evil. Decisive is how people can and will use them. This revolution calls to life a dream of uninterrupted progress, wealth and knowledge for all, but at the same time it creates new divisions, within one country and on a world scale. New forms of exclusion directed toward individuals, groups and countries, for example, the 'Poor Side' in the Rich West or large parts of Africa, are being developed. Castells speaks of an increase in social inequality and polarization. The 'poor' have not disappeared, only their place and nature have changed. The exploited of the earth are no longer the 'labourers' from the period of heavy industry, but rather people and countries without education and cultural baggage. Global migration and forced flight strengthen this division. They lose contact with the swift changes that, like an 'invisible hand', change the shape of the world. In this way important values, such as the involvement of the human person and solidarity within the community, come under pressure. A third phenomenon of our time is the technological 'can-do' ideology. Communication technology and opportunities in medical technology have been greatly expanded. Does not the inherent good in these developments also contain the risk that we will lose our awareness that the person lives in a fundamental relationship to a Transcendence and can experience him/herself and reality as a gift?

With this last point we note that, just as in modernity, present social and technological changes coincide with a shift in attitude to life. The second modernization at the end of the twentieth century has major consequences on cultural, ethical and philosophical levels. We could almost say that the 'demystification of the world' of which Weber spoke is only now reaching full development. There is no question of great social movements that represent a shared world-view and a common ethical sense: there are no longer any 'great narratives' recognized by all. Society is becoming multicultural and religions are losing more and more of their grass-roots support in the classical sense of the word.

In what is called a 'postmodern' period, sociologists and philosophers are drawing attention more emphatically to the ambiguity of the first modernization. The sociologist Giddens says that modernity was not only a grand project for progress but also a 'riding the Juggernaut', while Bauman speaks of a 'Life in Fragments'.[3] At the end of a century of modernization and in the midst of a new wave, society also has a great hunger for meaning and shared hope, a hunger for spirituality in an increasingly shallow world, a hunger for collective solidarity. Fundamentalist currents and new religious movements (New Age) are only the external signs of this. Civil society, moreover, shows a new tendency toward conservatism. It sees in the second modernization primarily a threat to 'law and order', to family and morality, to its own culture and own ethnic group.

In brief: this new world, with its global dynamic and its new division, its demystification and at the same time mystifyingly fantastic technology and virtual reality, is the new challenge for both Judaism and Christianity. At the same time, Judaism and Christianity are part of this society, with its opportunities and ambiguities. How are we to react to this challenge?

Separate history and divergent perception of modernity

Judaism and Christianity, despite their shared hope – about which I will speak later, have different starting points for approaching this new challenge. Their histories in the past one hundred and fifty years, during the reaction to the first modernization, differ considerably from one another. It is important, as I said before, to keep this difference in mind.

The greatest difference lies in the history of the Jews as a persecuted minority in Europe. Here we meet the question of anti-Semitism and Christian anti-Judaism. At the end of the nineteenth century, the Jewish minorities in various European countries were involved in a difficult process of weighing the need for integration on one side and the importance of preserving their own identity within the new modern states and societies on the other: between assimilation and preserving their own cultural and/or religious identity. Although there were Jewish social organizations operating within Jewish circles, there was never any single Jewish socio-political pillar.[4] As a minority they tried to find their way within, not in contrast to, modernity. This led some to abandon their Jewish faith, while others were strengthened in their orthodoxy.

At the same time a new form of political and racial anti-Semitism developed in the surrounding society of Western and, later, Eastern Europe. The Jewish minorities were held increasingly responsible for the paradoxes and asocial consequences of modernization. In Eastern Europe, this resulted in pogroms and mass emigration, for example, to the USA. In Western Europe, it led in the twentieth century to the *Shoah*, the destruction of the Jewish minorities in most European countries, by the racist and atheist ideology of Nazism.

At the end of the nineteenth century a new political movement, Zionism, arose in Jewish circles in reaction to ecclesiastical anti-Judaism, political anti-Semitism and persecution. This was based initially on secular messianism, although a religious form of Zionism arose later. This Zionism resulted in the establishment of the State of Israel in 1948. This special history is and remains the frame of reference for every search for the role of Judaism and Christianity in our new century.[5]

Anti-Judaism and anti-Semitism

It is fitting here to go briefly into Christian anti-Judaism. It seems clear that from the perspective of Judaism, the centuries-long experience with Christian anti-Judaism was closely related to the political and racial anti-Semitism that had developed since the nineteenth century. Christian anti-Judaism was certainly one of the breeding grounds for anti-Semitism, although there remains a qualitative and fundamental distinction that cannot be denied. This was also apparent from the fact that the churches were also the object of National Socialism's political actions during the 1930s and 1940s. In 1995, in the framework of the fiftieth anniversary of liberation from Nazi Germany, the Dutch bishops reflected on this connection. In what we call a 'Word', a pastoral declaration, on our relationship to Judaism, entitled *Sustained by One Root: Our Relationship to Judaism* (1995), the bishops spoke as follows:

> A tradition of theological and ecclesiastical anti-Judaism contributed to the rise of a climate in which the *Shoah* could take place. A so-called 'catechesis of contempt' (Jules Isaac) taught that Judaism, as people, was rejected after the death of Christ. Due in part to such traditions, Catholics in our country adopted a reserved stance toward Jews, sometimes they were indifferent, sometimes averse. Directly after the war this was still visible when those who had been hidden and those who survived the extermination camps returned. We reject this tradition of ecclesiastical anti-Judaism and deplore the terrible consequences of it. With our pope and other bishops' conferences, we condemn every form of anti-Semitism as sinful before God and humanity.[6]

By way of footnote to this quotation: of course these words of recognition, however necessary, are not sufficient. With the establishment of an episcopal commission for relations with Judaism and a practical Church policy we try to add deed to the word of this recognition in pastoral work in our Church communities, especially in our academic theological programmes. Only by taking consistent practical initiatives can we contribute to the success of the intended change of course. Meetings and discussions with the Jewish community in The Netherlands, such as took place in 1998 during the first so-called 'Conference of Church Leaders' in Amsterdam, are indispensable for this.

To return to our question – how did Christians react to modernity? This reaction was rather different from that of the Jewish minorities in Europe. There, Christians were not a persecuted minority, although some groups of Christians, such as Catholics in The Netherlands, were for some time a disadvantaged minority. Many countries had (or previously had) state or official churches that could take for granted a broad support by the majority of the population. Many Christians, and certainly the churches, often experienced the first wave of modernization at the end of the nineteenth century as a threat to faith and morals. Historians speak of an anti-modern sentiment, of a revolt against the spirit of the times. However, they also emphasized that this resistance against the spirit of the time took on a modern shape. Christian socio-political pillars or networks arose in several countries. The Christian Labour Movement and Christian-Democracy are examples of this. Where necessary, these groups struggled for their own emancipation and everywhere provoked confrontation with modernity and modern socialism, especially communism. These groups thought of themselves as the third way. Although after the war the direct link between churches and Christian organizations became looser, in many countries a link was assumed to exist between the majority of church members and this infrastructure of 'confessional' organizations.[7]

Social teaching

This confrontation with the first wave of modernization in Europe produced, in the twentieth-century Catholic world, a Christian 'social teaching' that wanted to correct both liberalism and Marxism. Reaching back with scholasticism to Aristotle as well as to the Church Fathers and biblical views, a Christian answer was developed to the challenge of modern society, in particular to the modern market economy. In 1891, Pope Leo XIII published the first social encyclical *Rerum novarum* (of new things). This marked the start of a long series of encyclicals that extends via, among others, *Quadragesimo anno* (1931), *Mater et magistra* (1961) and *Populorum progressio* (1967) to the social encyclicals of Pope John Paul II. The major encyclical *Centesimus annus* was published in 1991, a century after the first encyclical. Its key themes include: the precedence of the right to life over all, world solidarity, the social use of private property, the guiding and protecting role of government, the right to a social minimum for the poor, ('choosing for the poor') the primacy of labour, the subsidiarity principle (the principle that civil society has its own responsibility), the dignity of the human person (*imago Dei*), tolerance. Seen historically, the first phase of Catholic social teaching emphasized primarily a solidarity between the classes and estates. In the interbellum crisis period, it argued for a corporate reorganization of the market and society. After the Second World War, personalistic philosophy and biblical theology exerted greater influence on

Catholic social teaching. This latter stressed both the unique value of the human person (*imago Dei*) and the biblical tradition of prophetic criticism and messianic hope. This provided a first opening in our times for a dialogue with Judaism on a philosophical level (Buber, Levinas) and in theology.[8] Given the background of the social teaching, religious ethics on property and possession and the unique dignity of the human person can be fruitful subjects in a dialogue with Judaism, as we shall see further on.

Let us summarize and evaluate what we have said. At the end of the twentieth century, we are compelled to note that secularization has eroded many of the historical forms of Christian presence in the modern world: the churches are no longer broad-based churches, but volunteer-churches; the Christian framework of organizations has crumbled; mission has taken on the character of a dialogue; the Christian nature of culture can no longer be taken for granted; the churches' framework has weakened. This loss of social influence and power can, however, be explained theologically as a fortuitous emancipation from a closed social fortress, as a new opportunity for an original, messianic prophetism. In addition, a strong individualization is accompanied by a network society in which we see new forms of exclusion. Within Catholic social teaching we can find fruitful contact points for a dialogue with Judaism, especially the value of the human person in an economy dominated by interchangeability and an ethic of possession. Christians and Jews face the same challenge here, but their starting points, and certainly their most recent history, are different. Experiences with Christian anti-Judaism and with twentieth-century anti-Semitism add an extra taxing feature. A deeply rooted distrust of Christians and a shocked trust in the non-Jewish environment are but two of the deep wounds in the soul of the Jewish community. Only when Christians become aware of this will there be space to shape together a shared hope within our network society.

Preconditions for an ethical presence

As has become clear, a church's views can no longer presuppose the same political and social effect that they once had, or at least believed that they had. We have recognized this sufficiently in our analysis of postmodern society. This also contains a positive moment, namely, the personal responsibility and the critical consciousness of the modern person. These starting points compel us to a reflection on the way in which our involvement in social and ethical questions can be

fruitful. If religious discourse is to be authentic and fruitful in a postmodern society, then certain communicative preconditions must be
respected.

As the first, I would like to mention humility in current questions.
The modern person no longer wants to take orders on matters of good
and evil, and no longer accepts directions based purely on authority.
Whether we regret or appreciate this, we will in any case have to consider it. That we must also be self-aware when speaking on behalf of
religion fits in well with this. The modern person puts great emphasis
on skills born of experience. This means in practice that insights on
vital questions should be presented in dialogue with people who have
learned from experience. To mention one example: the religious
perspective on medical-ethical questions is still very important for the
current discussion, but is no longer imaginable without close contact
with medical specialists, health care workers and nursing staff.
Moreover, religious discourse will retain its own power of conviction
above all when it makes no attempt to interfere in the practical ins and
outs of medical specialization.

Second: religious discourse is not primarily oriented toward the
defence of its own institutional interests or dogmatic convictions, but
seeks to defend threatened humanity, in society, in health care, in life.
Only then will the witness be credible. Here we touch upon a biblical
truth that finds expression in action rather than verbal declaration
(Ex. 24.7 and John 3.21).

Third: whatever we bring forward in the name of religion, the individual responsibility of the modern person cannot be removed. A
religious institute or religious discourse cannot replace the responsibility of the human person.

It will not seem strange to you that these basic rules of communication for religious speech presuppose a basic attitude. It is characteristic of this attitude that in a postmodern society an authentic
spiritual presence is more convincing than a strict political institu-
tionalizing of religious discourse.

Shared hope, an openness to transcendence

In which religious concepts is an authentic presence of Judaism and
Christianity rooted? At the start of my presentation, I referred to the
new Catholic teaching on the relationship with Judaism since *Nostra
Aetate* No. 4 (1965). This took shape in Vatican (1974 and 1985) and
national declarations and in addresses by Pope John Paul II. With
Nostra Aetate No. 4 the Church states, with the words of the apostle

Paul, that the continuation of the Jewish people after Christ is a divine mystery. Moreover, it recognizes that this continuation is related in a special way with the mystery of the Church's own existence.[9] This new vision of our relationship to Judaism assigns theology two tasks.

The first is to think through a theology of the difference, by this I mean the positive acceptance of the uniqueness of Judaism's otherness. The Church faces a challenge here to rejoice honestly in the Jewish tradition as sign of the Eternal One's faithfulness to a never rescinded covenant. The second is to rediscover Christianity's Jewish roots and spread awareness of this rediscovery throughout the life of the Church.

Given the value of both the agreements and the differences between Judaism and Christianity, what is the source of our common effort in this new world? What links Judaism and Christianity with a view to this world? At least two aspects can be mentioned: shared hope and an awareness of transcendence.

First shared hope: On 1 November 1999, the Dutch bishops published a second 'Word' on the relationship to Judaism, this time focusing on the meaning of our relationship to Judaism for Catholic identity. I would like to quote a central passage, on messianic hope. I need add nothing to these words:

Judaism and Christianity differ in the expression of the messianic hope. Judaism sees the arrival of messianic time as future. For Christians, looking forward to God's dominion has become an immediate reality in the person and teaching of Jesus Christ. The joyful cry on Christmas Eve: 'today a Saviour is born to you, Christ the Lord' (Luke 2.11), is the starting point of Christian identity. These differences need not be disguised. They are one reason why early Christianity was seen as a separate sect and they lay at the basis of the schism between Judaism and Christendom. Rather, it is important to recognize that these differences in the past were for many Christians a reason to see Judaism only as negative and superseded. Thanks to dialogue, we Catholics have come increasingly to realize that we share a common messianic mission to make the earth inhabitable; that we live in an incomplete reality. In this we are linked to Judaism, Judaism keeps us mindful of this. The *Tanach*, the Jewish Bible, ends with the call to set out for Jerusalem: 'Whoever is among you of all his people – the **Lord** his **God** be with him and let him go up!' (2 Chron. 36.23). The New Testament ends with the desire for the ultimate completion: '*maranatha*, come, Lord!' (Rev. 22.20). Both Jews and Christians bear a messianic perspective, witness to God's Kingship, to His *Shalom*. That not slavery and death have the last word but liberation and life in God's presence, is our common conviction. Here more than anywhere else we meet the only element that really convinces, acts of humanity and loving-kindness.[10]

Beside this shared hope for justice, another awareness characterizes both traditions: the awareness that the person is 'the image of God'. His or her destination reaches to eternity. The creation narratives in the *Tanach* and their explanation in the rich Midrashic and patristic traditions are a valuable treasure house. This core experience of Jews and Christians, which Jews articulate as waiting for the Messiah and Christians see as faith in the 'resurrection' of Jesus, expresses the fundamental conviction that the person does not come and go, like some mundane element of nature, but that he/she has an awareness of transcendence. This tradition can be a source of energy for a critical statement regarding modern culture and modern secularism. This is not so much a new cultural pessimism or conservatism. Rather, it is the special critical function of Judaism and Christianity when faced with daily delusion, materialism and the dominance of the economy, the tendency of modern culture to relativize, the fragmentation of the modern attitude to life, and the illusion that everything can somehow be 'fixed'.

Shared reflection and common effort

Finally, there comes the question: what specific points can Judaism and Christianity profitably discuss when the theme is social commitment? And also, what can they do together without this necessarily implying an identical standpoint? In a general sense we have seen that both traditions are confronted in modern society with new forms of exclusion and social injustice. It seems to me, however, that some areas here are barely explored yet. Surprisingly, these areas lie at the heart of both religious traditions, namely in what Catholics generally call spirituality and Jews put under the heading *Halakhah*. These two share a common concept: the sanctification of life.

I think here of the tangible daily use of earthly goods: property, food and drink, consumption and enjoyment. The biblical foundation for our use of creation is marked by the awareness that God is the source of all that is good. The blessing, the *berakhah*, is the human answer to God's gift. A person blesses God and, at least in the Catholic tradition, the gift he/she receives. But here we are concerned with more than just individual piety that is, so to say, added to a person's possession: what we must do is rethink the very meaning itself of possession and property. The recognition that God is the owner of all goods, means that man is no longer a sovereign owner. He may enjoy these goods with God's blessing, but because he enjoys them he also learns to become conscious of the need to allow others to share in his enjoyment. As theologians we have thought too little about the fundamental meaning of 'enjoyment' in the Bible and about the opportunity for community and solidarity that this enjoyment creates. Here we see that something that is highly spiritual can also be political.[11]

Moreover, starting from the tradition of Catholic social teaching we can point to the absolute primacy of the person in the economy, even in the new economy of the year 2000. Ultimately, the individual person, as *imago Dei*, has precedence over all other priorities. The economic and social consequences can be discussed on the basis of expertise and political analysis, but the principle cannot. Perhaps I could call on a recent event in The Netherlands to illustrate this connection between religious spirituality and Catholic social teaching.

Bishop Muskens of Breda stated in the media that according to Catholic teaching a person who has nothing at all from which to live is allowed to steal bread. This statement caused an uproar, and the first reaction was indignation. Was this the way to respect the possessions of people, of shopkeepers and others? The heart of the question was the conflict between two basic values: the right to ownership and the right to life. The higher value of life has precedence over the lower value of ownership and this sheds new light on our human responsibility with regard to our possessions. Only gradually did people come to understand that here the question of justice and ownership was being addressed from a religious perspective and that this question did indeed have a political meaning. The Church did not assume political responsibility, but it did point out to politicians where their responsibility lies in the framework of human values and authentic biblical foundations.

That what a believer says cannot be separated from self-criticism and self-examination is inevitable. During the 1999 European Bishops' Synod in Rome, I argued for Western society's and the Western Church's need of such a self-examination. I argued then as follows:

As bishop of one of the richest countries in Europe and one of the

largest port cities in the world, I suggest that this Synod issue an
urgent call to reach a substantial reduction in the First World of
consumption, comfort and egoistic and arbitrary use of the goods of
the earth. It is urgently necessary to stress the cardinal virtue
of moderation and austerity. When the logic of consumption
penetrates the whole life of individuals, it smothers their full
human development. It inhibits the relationships that are essential
for their growth as people: that with God, their Creator and
Redeemer, and with others their brothers and sisters, who are sons
and daughters of this same Father. The virtue of moderation is an
indispensable condition for fulfilling the only thing that is required:
loving God with all one's heart and one's neighbour as oneself.

This perspective, I argued then, reaches further than the individual or
local community. I said that

We must invite the bearers of responsibility and the whole community to make genuine and meaningful sacrifices in solidarity
with the outcasts in our own country, with other countries on our
continent, with other continents of the world and with future
generations who have the same right to the resources of the earth as
we do.[12]

A second subject concerns the transition moments in life: birth and
death. Judaism and Christianity share a concern for a humane
existence, including where these transitions come into view. As
religions we must be cautious here that we do not become trapped in
a defensive position, that we do not give the impression of not being
abreast of the times. Without knowledge of the latest technical
insights (which can themselves be blessings) and without consultation with medical specialists, anything we say will lack the power to
convince. Perhaps Judaism is better able than Catholicism to fulfil this
condition because the great scholars of the past and present were able
to combine the medical profession with knowledge of Jewish law. The
first that comes to mind is Maimonides. Catholicism will have to work
to bring religious knowledge and the medical profession into
renewed contact. The bishops' 1999 text on the relations with Judaism
that I cited earlier said the following on this subject:

The sanctity of human life – from its earliest beginning to its last
moment – is for Jews and Christians a common concern. The
fundamental approach manifest in Jewish ethical reflection is very

meaningful for us. Medical expertise must, of course, be fully respected and used. But it is the conviction of Judaism and Christianity that medical-ethical questions ultimately touch the heart of human existence and cannot be answered only from the point of view of medical science and technology. We believe that here the voice of religion is indispensable for society. A joint ethical reflection, preferably in cooperation with medical experts, seems very meaningful to us.[13]

Taking technical-medical insights seriously must not tempt us to think that the major questions in this area have been answered.[14] Medical skill alone can never answer the existential question that Kant posed: what must a person do? The place where people are most impressed by technical abilities is just the place where they run the greatest risk of overlooking ethical dilemmas. Even though, for example, a pre-natal diagnosis is possible, this does not mean that people must opt for it. A pragmatic approach is not enough where the great questions of life are concerned. It is this awareness that religions must humbly but confidently keep vibrant.

Third: we have already noted the place and importance of communication in our society. Worldwide communication draws to our attention the inhuman situation of peoples in other parts of the world. However, there is a danger here that the media produce the opposite of what they intend. All the suffering that we see makes us immune and can even lead to a dangerous form of cultural relativism. War is seen as just another part of life; other cultures are not advanced enough to know how to control their conflicts. At such moments we need the voice of the biblical prophets: peace is a perspective involving all people and to which every person has a right. Messianic peace is the hope of humanity. By careful education in responsibility religions can point out that increased communication does not relativize our responsibility but rather increases it. This requires an education in hope against defeatism. Our ability to shape this education in hope convincingly depends on our own inspiration.[15] We should not hesitate to point to the small strengths of people who help shape this hope through their unselfish effort. We Catholics speak in that regard of saints, Judaism speaks of the *tsaddik*, the just one, whether hidden or open. It is a beautiful and profound conviction in our traditions that saints or the just are unaware that they are holy. The invisible holy, or hidden just, the famous thirty-six needed to preserve the world: these are the stories that we hear as a personal call.[16] Perhaps you are one of these hidden just. Here Jewish wisdom and imitation of Christ, which both appeal to personal, inalienable responsibility, agree. Both Judaism and Christianity know that this hidden power underpins hope and gives people the courage to continue when despair seems to have the upper hand.

On this hope the Dutch bishops commented:

> Jews and Christians live from one and the same hope. With this hope as a solid basis, modern man does not necessarily have to experience the future as an ominous void. Rather, at every moment the loving invitation of the living God to do full justice to all his creatures resounds. Judaism and Christianity each answer this invitation in their own unique way. In this way they each help shape His Kingdom on earth, looking forward to the day of which it is said: 'And the LORD shall be king over all the earth: on that day the LORD shall be one, and his name One' (Zech. 14.9).

Respected listeners, good friends. At this point in time, marked by memory of the *Shoah* but also by the revival of the Jewish people in Israel, we may follow the example of events that contain something of a messianic power and so contribute to the restoration of the world (*tikkun olam*). I refer here to events that help history along because they are a gesture of reconciliation that surpass calculation and political opportunism. One such gesture was the Pope's visit to the State of Israel, to the Chief Rabbi of Israel, to President Weizman, this gesture was above all the letter in the Western Wall. Such gestures have great consequences for the whole Catholic world, such as recognition of the suffering caused to the Jewish people, recognition, too, of the theological errors that have contributed to a climate in which anti-Semitism could flourish. Recognition, finally, of the special meaning of Judaism within God's Covenant with humanity. This recognition creates a new reality for Catholics, not because it wipes out the past, but because it preserves it as a dangerous memory. The Pope's visit was a sign of hope. Catholic theology does not yet have the words to explain what these gestures mean. They may therefore be considered 'messianic': they bring people to a new reality. May our meeting, our shared learning process and, ultimately, our common effort in the world make something of this reality visible.

Notes

1. Patrick Dassen, *De onttovering van de wereld: Max Weber en het probleem van de moderniteit in Duitsland 1890–1920*, Amsterdam: Van Oorschot, 1999.

2. Manuel Castells, *The Information Age: Economy, Society and Culture. Volume III: End of Millenium*, Malden, MA, and Oxford: Blackwell, 1998, p. 336.

3. Anthony Giddens, *The Consequences of Modernity*, Cambridge, UK: Polity, 1991, p. 151; Zygmunt Bauman, *Life in Fragments: Essays in Postmodern Morality*, Oxford, UK, and Cambridge, MA, Blackwell, 1995.

4. See the comparative study by Karin Hofmeester, *Van Talmoed tot statuut: Joodse arbeiders en arbeidersbewegingen in Amsterdam, London en Parijs 1880–1914*, Amsterdam: Stichting Beheer IISG, 1990.

5. G. Kressel e.a., *Zionism*, Jerusalem 1973; L. Giebels, *De zionistische beweging in Nederland 1899–1941*, Assen 1975.

6. *Sustained by One Root: Our Relationship to Judaism*, Message from the Dutch Bishops to their Faithful in the Fifteenth Year since the Liberation and the Thirtieth Year after the Promulgation of *Nostra Aetate*, Ocober 1995, Utrecht.

7. See: Staf Hellemans, *Strijd om de moderniteit in Europa sinds 1800*, Leuven 1990; Urs Altermatt, *Katholizismus und Moderne: Zur Sozial- und Mentalitätsgeschichte der Schweizer Katholiken im 19. und 20. Jahrhundert*, Zurich: Benzinger, 1989; Hans Righart, *De katholieke zuil in Europa: Een vergelijkend onderzoek naar het onstaan van verzuiling onder katholieken in Oostenrijk, Zwitserland, België en Nederland*, Meppel and Amsterdam: Boom, 1986; Michael P. Fogarty, *Christelijke democratie in West-Europa, 2 dl.*, Hilversum 1965. Olaf von Blaschke, *Katholizismus und Antisemitismus im Deutschen Kaiserreich*, Göttingen: Vandenhoeck & Ruprecht, 1997, has pointed out the role of anti-Judaism and anti-Semitism in nineteenth-century Germany in the process of establishing a Christian identity within the turmoils of modernity, both within the pillar and within the church.

8. D. Dorr, *Option for the Poor: A Hundred Years of Vatican Social Teaching*, Dublin: Gill and Macmillan, and Maryknoll, NY: Orbis, 1983; Th. Salemink, *Katholieke kritiek op het kapitalisme 1891–1991: Honderd jaar debat over vrije markt en verzorgingsstaat*, Amersfoort en Leuven: Acco, 1991.

9. Pope John Paul II articulated the connection between both dimensions in an address in Mainz (1980): 'The first dimension of this dialogue, that is, the meeting between the people of God of the Old Covenant, never revoked by God (cf. Rom. 11.29) and that of the New Covenant, is at the same time a dialogue within our Church, that is to say, between the first and the second part of the Bible.' See also the studies of F. Mussner, most recently 'Was macht das Mysterium Israel aus?' '*Nun steht aber diese Sache im Evangelium . . .': Zur Frage nach den Anfängen des christlichen Antijudaismus*, hrsg. Rainer Kampling, Paderborn: F. Schöningh, 1999, pp. 15–30.

10. *Living with One and the Same Hope: On the Meaning of the Meeting with Judaism for Catholics*, Message from the Roman Catholic Bishops of the Netherlands, November 1999, Utrecht.

11. The French-Jewish philosopher Emmanuel Levinas has given a large place to enjoyment in his philosophy doubtless inspired by the Jewish notion of Sabbath rest. See *Zie Totalité et Infini*, Den Haag 1974, pp. 81–160.

12. See *Kerkelijke Documentatie*, 28:3 (March 2000), esp. pp. 96–9.

13. *Living with One and the Same Hope*.

14. I think here of the noteworthy comment by Chief Rabbi Immanuel Jakobovits in his well-known book *Jewish Medical Ethics: A Comparative and Historical Study*

of the Jewish Religious Attitude to Medicine and Its Practice, New York: Philosophical Library, 1959.

15. The need for this was argued in the oration by the educationist L. Dasberg, currently working in Israel. See: L. Dasberg , *Pedagogie in de schaduw van het jaar 2000 of Hulde aan de hoop*, Meppel and Amsterdam: Boom, 1980.

16. See Gershom Scholem, 'Die 36 verborgenenen Gerechten in der jüdischen Tradition', *Judaica*, Frankfurt am Main, 1963, pp. 216–25.

Discussant

– Richard Block

It is my privilege to respond to the stimulating and inspiring paper of Bishop van Luyn, 'Signs of a New Reality'. I join enthusiastically in his assertion that Catholics and Jews, despite the painful dimensions of our history and significant differences of theology, can nevertheless 'share hope in a divided world'. That vibrant hope is grounded in our common aspiration to experience God's presence and do God's will, in our common affirmation that every human person is created in God's image, and in our common commitment to reflect God's presence and human worth in our individual and communal conduct. The existence of that hope, though not yet realized, is cause for rejoicing. Though our understanding of that hope will sometimes find expression in different or even opposing positions on matters of social policy, it will also, more often I think, provide a basis for a shared critique of state and society and a common agenda of advocacy, action and efforts to bring about change.

Among the many substantive issues the paper considers, I wish to respond principally to those that concern the challenge of modernity. As Bishop van Luyn indicates, modernity brought about a profound transformation in religious authority, in the relationship of the individual and society, and in Christian–Jewish relations.

Perhaps the primary impact of modernity on religious authority was to render religion a voluntary enterprise. The normative modern state is a secular state, whose coercive power is generally unavailable to enforce religious doctrine or reinforce religious norms of behaviour. For some in both the Catholic Church and the Jewish world, this change constituted a monumental threat and an unmitigated disaster. They understood that in a truly free society, religion would have to compete for the allegiance of the individual and the soul of the state itself. It could no longer take them for granted.

For others, of course, the freedom of conscience and conduct offered by modernity was a profound, long-sought blessing. Blessing or curse or more likely both, I would argue that modernity affected Jews and Christians quite differently. For nearly 2,000 years, Jews were forbidden to own land, attend university, or enter most trades and professions, to become citizens, serve in the armed forces, or live outside ghetto walls. Therefore, for Jews, modernity represented not merely the decline of religious authority, but our entry into Western civilization, culture and society.

It is also critical to note that Progressive Judaism, the Jewish dialogue partner in the present conference, was, as Professor Michael Meyer points out, a response to modernity. It was a product of the Enlightenment and emancipation, and its fundamental premise is that wholehearted Jewish commitment and full participation in civil society are complementary and compatible aspirations. Progressive Judaism accords to the informed individual conscience a central role in the shaping of one's Jewish life and recognizes in Judaism a dynamic character that allows it, indeed, that compels it, to adapt to contemporary needs and our evolving understanding of God's will.

Thus, I would regard it as something of a false dichotomy to describe modernity as presenting Jews the choice between abandonment of Judaism or 'assimilation' on the one hand and strengthened orthodoxy on the other. Progressive or 'Reform' Judaism sought the middle way of acculturation and Jewish renewal. From its inception, Progressive Judaism placed particular emphasis on the prophetic message, the imperative of social justice, and of partnership with those of other faiths in the pursuit of 'tikkun olam b'malchut Shaddai', repairing the world under God's sovereignty. We take seriously the Midrashic admonition that we are God's partners in the ongoing work of completing and perfecting creation. This emphasis offers a most fruitful point of contact between the social agendas of the Church and of Progressive Judaism.

Despite its debt to modernity, Judaism in general, and Progressive Judaism in particular, are necessarily ambivalent toward it. First, throughout history, Judaism has always offered a trenchant critique of society and its ills. Despite all that has changed in the intervening millennia, I know of no more compelling religious challenge to state and society than that of Isaiah, whose words we read in the synagogue on Yom Kippur, the Day of Atonement:

Is this the fast that I have chosen? The day for a man to afflict his soul? To bow his head like a reed and spread out sackcloth and ashes? Will you call this a fast? A day acceptable to the Lord? Is not *this* the fast that I have chosen? To loose the fetters of wickedness, to undo the fetters of bondage, to let the oppressed go free, to break every cruel yoke? Is it not to share your bread with the hungry, and to bring the poor and outcast into your house? When you see the naked to clothe him and not to hide yourself from your own kin? Then shall your light break forth as the dawn and your healing spring forth speedily. Your righteousness shall go before you, and the glory of the Lord shall be your rearguard. Then shall you call and the Lord will answer. You will cry out and God will say, 'Here am I.' (Isa. 58.5–9)

Clearly, we have our work cut out for us.

An ambivalent religious response to modernity derives from its inner contradictions. Consider technology. Technology enables us to eradicate diseases, dramatically increase agricultural productivity, and to reverse at least some of the environmental offences we have committed. Yet it was advanced technology harnessed to the power of human evil that produced the *Shoah*, the Holocaust. Contemporary communications technology offers a new version of the Cartesian formula: I email, therefore I am. Yet those who use it with ill intent can now disrupt communications and commerce worldwide. Cellular phones, pagers and handheld computers provide instant access to the world, twenty-four hours a day. Yet they can also be tremendously intrusive and threaten to eradicate the protective barrier between work and personal life. The Internet is a powerful medium for the teaching of Torah and the transmission of the religious message. Yet it also offers unrestricted, universal and unprecedented access to purveyors of hatred, racism, pornography and anti-Semitism.

A central defining feature of modernity has been the liberation of the individual. Never in human history have we had such unfettered freedom of choice and such manifest opportunities for self-expression and self-realization. And yet, like any other good taken to extreme, freedom can be destructive of the individual and of society itself. I wonder if we can really say that 'the individual person, as *imago Dei*, has precedence over all other priorities'. It seems to me that here, too, we must seek a middle way between the exaltation of the individual, which is idolatry, and the degradation of the individual, which is slavery. A Midrash, already quoted, teaches that we should carry two notes in our pockets. One says, 'The world was created for my sake.' The other says, 'I am only dust and ashes.' We live in the tension between these two incompatible truths.

Before closing, I'd like to comment on a few of the bishop's beautifully expressed observations about Catholic–Jewish relations. He is certainly right that we have divergent histories and most sensitive to observe that experiences with Christian anti-Judaism and twentieth-century anti-Semitism continue to affect the Jewish response to Christians and Christianity. Still, I am happy to say that I do not perceive 'a deeply rooted distrust of Christians' as the predominant feeling among contemporary Jews. I would add that the asymmetry between Jewish and Christian perceptions is not limited to the realm of history. We are also theologically asymmetrical. As the Bishop observes, an understanding of Judaism is essential for Christian self-understanding. The reverse is not true. There are many important reasons for Jews to get to know Christianity, but Jewish self-understanding is not among them.

I have long been puzzled by the seeming contradiction between *Nostra Aetate*'s endorsement of Paul's belief that 'the continuation of the Jewish people after Christ is a divine mystery' and the affirmation that God's covenant with the Jewish people was 'never rescinded'. If our Covenant is enduring, where is the mystery in our endurance?

I am moved by the bishop's emphasis on humility as the starting point for understanding. Claims to an exclusive understanding of religious truth and that one's own faith offers the only means of obtaining God's grace strike me as arrogant and ultimately dangerous. I believe that one of our common challenges as Catholics and Jews is to cleanse our theologies and our liturgies of such claims, while maintaining our cherished, and essential, particularities. If we fail to do so, our affirmation of each other's covenant with God will be hollow. If we succeed, we will not regard each other's continued existence as a mystery, but as a profound blessing.

I conclude with a statement of gratitude to the bishop for sharing, among other wise insights, the statement of the Dutch bishops that 'the only element that really convinces [is] acts of humanity and lovingkindness'. This echoes the teaching of Jewish tradition, 'Ein hamidrash ikkar, elah hama'aseh.' ('Words are not primary. Deeds are.'). Let us do deeds of goodness together.

Discussion recorder

– Michael Hilton

David Rosen – first speaker – spoke of being the odd man out in the Jewish team, as an Orthodox rabbi, but nevertheless grateful for the warmth of his reception. He was, at first, surprised and a little disappointed with his topic on power and powerlessness, specifically as the sole Orthodox representative. Maybe, he suggested, this was the only topic left!

He put together a paper based on traditional Jewish sources, and then received a polite note back asking if he had read various books, as if his paper was rather weak!

He then realized that it might well be because he lives in Israel that he had been asked to speak about power and powerlessness. [This is correct! eds.]

He is proud to be one of the founders of 'Rabbis for Human Rights', which has 12 Orthodox rabbis, half the conservative and nearly all the Reform rabbis in Israel – about 100 in all – as members. The organization is born out of the concern about the *hillul ha-shem* (desecration of the name of God) in the way religion is abused when it takes power – it causes a condition of blindness, and allows a sacred means (land) to become an end in itself. The divisions today among religion are no longer horizontal but vertical, and thus it is possible for Rabbi Rosen often to feel closer to his Catholic colleagues with whom he can share a teleology, than to some of his fellow-Jews.

Adrian van Luyn – second speaker – told the conference that after ten years in Rome he had become secretary of the Bishops' Conference of the Netherlands, and soon noticed that there was no commission there for relations with Jews. After discussions, Dutch Jews were found to be in favour of the idea, and he then convinced the bishops, and became chairman himself when appointed Bishop of Rotterdam. From their 1995 conference on the *Shoah*, they produced a public declaration *Living from One Root: Our Relationship with Judaism*, and later a second publication *Living from the Same Hope*. These are published declarations, based on Vatican guidelines. Now they are discussing 'The future as messianic hope.'

His paper develops ethical and social questions and the perspective of messianic hope. His dialogue is not with Jews alone but together with government and political parties on social and ethical issues. He posed the question: is there any such collaboration on the European level? Catholics have a representative body which meets twice a year to discuss European issues. Is there such a Jewish group? If not, would it not be a good idea for Jews to start such a group for the future of the Union?

Mark Winer said that he wanted to pay tribute to David Rosen who had the audacity to infuriate Jews at a conference by inviting the Pope to Israel! That which appears powerless is the most powerful, as we find in our *haftarah* (reading from the prophets) for Chanukah – ' "Not by might, not by power, but My spirit", says God' (Zech. 4.6). This text exemplified David Rosen's career. He had no power but was the most powerful rabbi in Israel, if not in the world, because others recognized his influence. The critical divide was not between Jews and Christians, but between fundamentalists and pluralists.

Elliot Dorff said that lacking in David Rosen's paper was a discussion of the role of law. From David and Batsheva, to Clinton and Monica, the law applied to kings and presidents as much as to ordinary individuals.

Many think Israel should separate religion and state, but how would it then be distinctively Jewish? Israel is still officially at war and this changes the way one is able to worry about individual rights. How does the duty of self-defence balance with the rights of self and others? Both individualism and modernity have been seen as threats against Catholicism. How should we act when conscience has to be maintained?

Professor Susannah Heschel observed that Adrian's paper touched on serious issues when he said:

> Bishop Muskens of Breda stated in the media that according to Catholic teaching a person who has nothing at all from which to live is allowed to steal bread. This statement caused an uproar. (p. 203)

Could we steal a medicine to save a life? Not everyone has always agreed on the primacy of human life. What do you do when the moral consensus of society differs from religious values? When you discuss the sanctity of human life, Jews and Catholics disagree, for example, on abortion. Should the Catholic teaching become national law in a country, or Jewish teaching?

Elizabeth Tikvah Sarah said that feminist theory taught the importance of empowerment as being not over others but in relation to others, and one of the tragedies of Israel was the devastating macho-powerfulness and the new image it gave of Jewish men, with tragic consequences. That dimension was missing from our discussion.

We are made in the image of God (*b'tzelem elohim*) – and God here is grammatically plural – we have many images, therefore. Is the God of creation superpowerful and dominating only? We have to find other and new ways of being in the world, a new attitude to power.

John Pawlikowski commented that there were two competing trends in the Second Vatican Council, the primacy of conscience was endorsed, even the right not to believe. But in the document on 'The Church and the Modern World' they talked of vandalized culture. How do you promote culture and still allow individual conscience? We could pursue the second task only because we had renounced the desire to control society

In response to Susanna Heschel, Pawlinkowski said that Cardinal Bernadien wrote on this subject and said the Church no longer had to have state power to enhance its own moral positions – a Catholic politician could therefore vote for legislation which only partly supported the Catholic position.

Guy Stroumsa commented that Israeli Jews could learn a lot from the long experience of the Christian relationship to state and power. The Constantinian revolution had theological repercussions: most intellectuals in ancient society got pushed out of power. When you have no relationship to power, you may develop eschatological ideas which may not have a direct political influence. But when power returns these ideas become problematic. Jews had been out of power and now suddenly had it, and this might lead them to take their ideas formulated in times of powerlessness seriously, which would be a mistake. It was better to express religion in the personal realm, not the political.

Rabbi Tovia Ben-Chorin observed that Israel after the *Shoah* was an example of power arising out of powerlessness, from people who came out of the ashes. The week's *sidrah* (Torah reading in the synagogue) began: 'If you follow my laws' (Lev. 26.3). In this statement 'you' is plural, representing the group together. Now the fundamentalists understood this well, but liberals did not. They try to understand the other but forget the 'we' as a group. The power of the word must be rediscovered especially in this era after the *Shoah*.

Sidney Brichto said that we were dealing with a powerless God as well. There was a Midrash in which God meets Jeremiah after the destruction and says 'Woe to a king who has lost his strength in old age'. We had no means of influencing God's power as we should. This was a theological problem as well as a social one.

Jacqueline Tabick stated that her comment, by chance, was diametrically opposed to Sidney Brichto's. There was a stained-glass window at West London Synagogue, her favourite, which quoted the verse 'The fear of God is the beginning of knowledge' (Prov. 1.7). Though God may seem powerless, ultimate power rests with God, and we as a religious grouping should remember that.

Robert Murray commented that Elizabeth Tikvah Sarah mentioned the 'image' of God in which we are created. But 'image' and 'likeness' were not identical. The text said 'let them rule over'. We had not talked at all in this conference about our responsibility for the rest of creation. Power given was power to act in a godlike way, and that was what it must be. Power in that passage had been attacked again and again, but the passage was misunderstood. It meant responsible power.

Concluding remarks

Adrian van Luyn summarized his experience at the conference. As a diocesan bishop he had to act as a generalist, and so welcomed the opportunity to participate. He expressed gratitude to the organizers, and called the conference 'an inspiration to continue – may we unite our efforts for a better humanity'.

David Rosen specifically wanted to respond to Elliot Dorff and to express gratitude to Mark Winer for his 'eulogy'. Dorff had made a very important point, which really should have been tackled in his paper with an excursus about Judaism and democracy and religion and state.

It was not clear-cut what a 'Jewish democratic state' meant. The term did not enter Israeli law until the Law on Human Dignity and Freedom of 1992. Herzl used the term 'State of the Jews' not ' Jewish State'. Now Barak the Chief Justice had recently been offering his interpretation of this new phrase. He made a ruling that the Jewish Agency was no longer entitled to claim that it was exclusively qualified to distribute land to Jews in Israel. Precisely because of Zionism there must be equal rights, because Israel was now defined as a 'Jewish' democratic state. The term 'Jewish', ruled Barak, was adjectival not ethnic. This must be our principle, that 'Jewish' equalled 'morally responsible'.

We must be careful not to confuse the state as a legitimate entity and the role of religion and religious language and institutions. The way it had been bound to the state had even been destructive for religion. Rabbis for Human Rights was showing us today that there was an important way for religion to be expressed. Members of the organization still did their reserve duty as soldiers, even while saying there was a moral imperative.

As President of the Jewish Vegetarian Ecological Society, David Rosen expressed thanks to Elizabeth Tikvah Sarah and to Robert Murray for their contributions to the debate and acknowledged his omissions in this area. He continued: 'Perhaps my Jewish colleagues are uncomfortable at my self-castigation but in this conference we do not need to have these fears. The spirit of self-criticism is more important than our fears.' There was power in the Jewish–Christian relationship. Leon Klenicki had written of 'The triumphalism of pain'. We needed an essential humility but also a historical humility. In the debate between the rabbi and the king in Yehuda Halevi's *Kuzari*, only twice does the rabbi say he has no answer. At one point the rabbi say, 'Look at how Christians and Muslims abuse power', and the King replies, 'Of course you don't. You have no power to abuse.' And the rabbi has no answer.

What can each of us contribute and how – are there shared values and are there particular insights and skills which may be regarded as a *specialité de la maison*? What do we do with values which reflect our particularism? What do we do with values over which we differ, or which may promote conflict with other faiths or society at large?

C. The Values We Bring to the Partnership

– Sidney Brichto

As a member of the organizing committee of this conference, I have seen it primarily as an opportunity to explore the theological differences between Catholicism and Judaism. My participation in the conference is due to the meeting with Cardinal Cassidy at the Vatican on 12 January 1999. It was then that a symposium of Catholic and Jewish religious leaders was proposed and agreed. It was there that Cardinal Cassidy welcomed the opportunity for us to explore these differences. He said, in so many words, 'Unless I know how you differ from me, I cannot really understand you.'

My intention in this paper is to address the briefing of my topic put in these questions. What can each of us contribute and how – are there shared values and are there particular insights and skills which may be regarded as a *specialité de la maison*? What do we do with values which reflect our particularism? What do we do with values over which we differ, or which may promote conflict with other faiths or society at large?

Before I put pen to paper, I was fortunate to receive the paper of Dr Eugene Fisher, my Catholic partner in the session we are both addressing. Because I feel the challenge of this conference is to boldly confront our differences, I begin my excursions by referring to Dr Fisher's reporting of the absence of Orthodox Jewish participation in a theological conference in January 1965 in Latrobe, Pennsylvania. Based on an *obiter dictum* of Rabbi Soloveitchik, the Jewish Orthodox had chosen to steer clear of attending the conference. Rabbi Arthur Gilbert, who was present, explained their motivation to be based on 'an understandable defensiveness and fear, that conversations on matters of faith are futile and that Jews must, of necessity, be disadvantaged in such encounters'. To a limited extent I would agree with Rabbi Gilbert's assessment. Yes, Orthodox Jews think that 'conversations on matters of faith are futile' but, no, they do not think that they 'will be disadvantaged in such encounters', unless by this he means that were they to tell the truth about their own perception of Catholic faith they fear the offence that they would cause.

I think that I understand the Orthodox refusal because I shared in it. I was raised in a practising Orthodox Jewish home in Philadelphia, PA. Both my father and maternal grandfather were Talmudic scholars born in Jerusalem. Both had emigrated to the USA so as not to be dependent for their living on charitable donations from Diaspora Jewry. My grandfather became the head of two *Yeshivot*. My father was a *Shochet*, who killed chickens according to the rules of *Kashrut*. Our home was filled with the spirituality that comes from the love of Jewish scholarship. During Sabbath meals, especially when my grandfather was our guest, the conversation revolved around new insights into the biblical texts, the commentaries on the texts and even into the commentaries on the commentaries. As for Jesus, he was never mentioned. It was as though the pronunciation of his name would be an act of betrayal. Paul was not even known. My grandfather once told me that, as a child, he had come upon a Hebrew grammar. His father caught him paging through it on the front step of his house. So angry was he over the fact that my grandfather was studying *Lashon Kodesh* – the holy language – as though it were like any other language, that not only did he strike him across the face but also threw the grammar into the well in the square. If a Hebrew grammar was forbidden, you can be certain neither he nor anyone else in my family had ever read or even seen the New Testament.

On the basis of their total ignorance of Christian thought, they rejected Jesus for the identical reasons that their ancestors had, and for even greater reasons. Jesus' 'non-believing' Jewish contemporaries rejected him because a messiah had to restore Jewish sovereignty, and Jesus had not done so. They did not accept on the basis of hearsay that Jesus had been the first to enjoy the fulfilment of the Pharisaic belief in the resurrection of the dead. My grandfather and father had even more reason to reject the faith in Jesus than their ancestors because Jesus' contemporaries were not called upon to believe in his virgin and divine birth or that he was part of the divine Trinity, Christian revelations which emerged after his crucifixion. The transformation of the hoped-for Jewish Messiah into God, the rejection of circumcision and the Torah and casting the Jews into the role of Satan and the Anti-Christ made Jews reject Christianity with the same ferocity as Christians had rejected Judaism.

What made me change? As an adolescent I no longer believed in certain key tenets of Orthodox Judaism, for example, I could not accept that the Torah was dictated by God to Moses. Also, I decided to bridge the gap between my Jewishness and the Western world. That meant learning about Christianity. So I read the Gospels. While I was horrified by the abuse hurled upon the Jews for their rejection and involvement in the death of Jesus – knowing full well how many millions of Jewish lives were ultimately to be destroyed by such statements – I still warmed to the teachings of Jesus, who in certain respects reminded me more of the saintly Rabbi Akiva than did those modern, bigoted rabbis who believe that they are fighting the battle for God.

What had the greatest impact upon me, however, was the radical rethinking by the papacy towards Judaism and the Jewish people. The three major pronouncements which influenced me were:

1. Catholicism accepts the validity of the Jewish Covenant.
2. Catholicism, therefore, wishes the continuity of the Jewish people.
3. Jews can achieve spiritual salvation through participation in their own Covenant.

The papal acceptance of the special Covenant between God and the Jews poses a challenge to the Jews which has not yet been addressed, except perhaps by the Orthodox, who in their refusal to participate in theological discussions are closing the door to any reciprocity in the 'theological' reconciliation of the two faiths.

My subject is, I appreciate, not the Jewish and Christian Covenants, but it is the appreciation of the differing nature of these two divine Covenants which reveal the special values and insights which Jews and Catholics can contribute to the partnership to achieve *Tikkun olam*, translated by Dr Fisher as 'A partnership for the glory of God, the good of humanity and the future of the planet'. By accepting the Jewish origins of Christianity, and the value of Jews maintaining their historical covenant with God, the Pope has, in my view, challenged the Jewish community to reciprocate. I know that many Jewish leaders will feel that the Catholic Church still needs to do more to achieve forgiveness for their sins against the Jewish people before the onus of responsibility for the improvement in relationships shifts from them to us.

I disagree. The sources of Christian anti-Semitism were theologically based, even if they were motivated by political considerations, for example, moving the blame from Pontius Pilate to the Jews for the crucifixion in order to appease the Roman Empire. Therefore, if there is to be theological reconciliation, Jews need to consider accepting the validity of the Christian Covenant just as Catholics have accepted the validity of the Jewish Covenant. Orthodox Jews will not be able to do this because of the belief in their own exclusive partnership with God. Even Progressive Jews will find it difficult, if only because the Christian faith experience is so foreign to their own. But it is only by understanding and recognizing the 'otherness' that reconciliation and cooperation will become possible.

What does the Christian Covenant offer the spiritually thirsty? What strata of the human psyche does Christian imagery touch that Judaism does not and why has the Jewish Covenant been able to hold on to the loyalty of a people who have suffered ceaselessly for the sanctification of a God who was not able to deliver them – his obligation under the Covenant – from persecutors even though they faithfully kept his laws.

The Covenant between Abraham and God reveals both the strengths and weaknesses of the Jewish faith. Its strength is that the responsibility of Abraham's descendants is to keep God's commandments for which God will reward them with deliverance both physical and spiritual. Law is the essence of Judaism. Law is social. Law is collective. Salvation is collective. The individual can only find fulfilment – the secular equivalent to salvation – in an orderly and harmonious society which will enable him to pursue his own objectives and dreams. Faith in God, while the foundation of the Covenant, is secondary to obedience to God's laws, granted for the improvement of human society. The rabbis affirmed that all righteous gentiles have a place in the world to come, and God is attributed as saying, 'Had my people only forsaken me yet kept my laws!' Of course, the objective of a law-abiding society is the opportunity it gives each man and woman to come closer to the source of their creation and creative capacity – to become a co-creator with God of all things good and beautiful. The prophetic ideal is that nations shall not wage war anymore so that 'Every man will sit under his grapevine or fig tree and no one will disturb him' (Micah 4.4). This can only be achieved when the words of Micah are obeyed:

It has been told you, O man, what is good
And what the LORD requires of you
Only to do justice, to love goodness
And to walk humbly with your God. (6.8)

Collective salvation is the basis of the Jewish Covenant. 'No man is an island' could be its logo just as well as the rabbinic statement, 'All of Israel are responsible, one for the other'. The Jewish people, in the fulfilment of its Covenant with God, becomes a model for other nations of the world, but without any belief in theological exclusivity: 'For all the peoples go forward, each in the name of its god; but we will go forward in the name of the LORD, our God for ever and evermore' (4.7).

The weakness embedded in the concept of collective Covenant between God and the people of Israel is that the individual Jew is like a tree in the forest, who cannot escape victimization along with his fellow-trees in the event of a hurricane or forest fire. While there are promises of rewards for the individual in the life to come, this was a later development in Judaism and was not a condition of the Covenant. The collective Covenant also left single women or bachelors as an oddity in Jewish life. Also, its greatest failing is revealed when obedience to their part of the Covenant did not lead to divine reciprocity, physical protection and deliverance. This led rabbis and *tsadikim* over the span of the millennia to protect God's reputation for not keeping his part of the bargain by accepting responsibility for their suffering. It became a matter of course for Jews to say in their liturgy, 'It is because of our sins that we are exiled from our land.' As my teacher, Henry Slonimsky said, 'Israel saved God's face. It was a "gesture of generosity to God" to accept that their persecution was divine punishment for their sins.'

Whatever the weaknesses of the Jewish Covenant, it survives intact – so much so that it survives even when most Jews, overwhelmed with doubt, turn to agnosticism regarding the existence of God. Jews, however, value their identity as part of the Jewish people. They still feel that being a Jew involves a moral responsibility to change the world for the better. Even Jews who departed from or rejected their Judaism became beacons of light in search of social justice and the equality of opportunity for men and women of all social classes. There is a question whether Karl Marx's father converted before or after Karl's birth. But this was irrelevant to Henry Slonimsky who used to answer his own rhetorical question while lecturing on the Jewish prophetic vision of creating the moral superman – 'was Karl Marx

Jewish?' – 'Jewish? He was a *minyan* (quorum of ten)!' The call for social justice first expressed by Amos rings through the soul of every good Jew and has become the genetic inheritance of even those who left its religious borders. 'Let justice roll down like waters and righteousness like a mighty stream' (Amos 5.24).

It is out of an understanding of the weaknesses of the Jewish Covenant that we can appreciate the Christian Covenant of God through his anointed one – Jesus. The logic and the psychological basis of the New Covenant must be understood, especially by Jews and other 'non-believers' if they are to appreciate its significance even if they do not participate in it. By explaining what the New Covenant means to me, I hope I am not being arrogant to my Christian colleagues for whom the Covenant is the source of their being, comfort, wisdom and hope. I am seeking to find the means where I can transmit its message to fellow-Jews in a way that can command their respect.

If the New Testament is due to two men born as Jews, then we must accept that it grew out of Jewish roots and it behoves us to understand how this came about. What were the weaknesses of the Jewish Testament for which Christianity sought to compensate? The disciples of Jesus, even his apostles, could not understand Jesus' words when he told them that he had to die and be resurrected after three days. They, like their fellow-Jews, expected a physical saviour. When Jesus returns to them and instructs them for forty days, what most concerns them is when he will return to restore the sovereignty of Israel.

From the dispassionate point of view, the crucifixion of God's Messiah and the need to keep faith with and in Jesus, led to him becoming a biblical synthesis of the Messiah and the Suffering Servant who was resurrected from the dead in accordance with the belief of the Pharisees. The belief in physical resurrection is still prevalent, an essential part of Orthodox Judaism, to be fulfilled at the coming of the Messiah or at the End of Days. When other rebels against Rome, when other messiahs – 'King(s) of the Jews' – met a bitter end, they were forgotten. Not Jesus! His message lived on! More important, his crucifixion was not deemed to be a defeat but a victory! Even more significant than the justification of the Messiah's death was the new belief that redemption came not through the Law but the person of Jesus. As Paul sought to prove: the Law did not save. If by that he meant that keeping the laws did not bring human salvation, the evidence was on his side. From Paul's point of view, it was far better to believe in redemption through the risen Jesus who had a message for the whole world than in a code of laws which were a burden for the gentile world and prevented their conversion to a redeeming faith.

While Jews tenaciously held on to the hope of a human messiah who would actually wrest control from the Romans, as Judas Maccabaeus had from the Syrian-Greeks, allowing Jews to keep their faith and their laws, Paul forsook Jerusalem for Rome. In the face of Jewish disaster he turned his attention to the greater prize – the winning over of the gentile world to faith in a man-God who could give to those with such a faith a portion of the divine Spirit, thus enabling each individual to be saved even if the rest of society remained aloof and sceptical. The focus of the New Covenant moved away from collective Israel to the individual, from one people to all the nations of the earth.

Judaism had sown the seeds of monotheistic universalism and ethical monotheism. In every synagogue that Paul spread the word, there were 'Fearers of the Lord' – those who believed in the Jewish God but who had not converted. These were the gentiles whom Paul, and even Peter, won over to Jesus by accepting them as Christians even though they remained uncircumcised, so long as they kept the Noachide laws. The hope they gave to the individual in his quest for salvation was found by millions to be irresistible – the mystical faith that by believing in Jesus, the Anointed One, they could become at one with him and achieve salvation in his life and blessed eternity in the life to come. It was a comforting hope for individuals living in a world racked with pain. The knowledge that Jesus himself suffered and that suffering itself was a sign of nobility and not of weakness, also gave comfort to the poor and humble.

This for me is the significance of the Christian Covenant and why I can respect it without it being my covenant. I do not believe in Jesus but I understand his power to inspire the faith of others. When the rule of law lets the individual down, when justice remains a dream rather than a reality, there is a place for the individual sufferer to rest his soul. Christianity has transformed undeserved suffering into a virtue, which is to be born with pride and patience. I am not suggesting that it is less a Christian goal than a Jewish one to improve the world and to end suffering, but only suggest how I, a Jew, can appreciate the religious need met by the Christian Covenant for the individual living in a world suffused with the tears of the righteous and the oppressed. Ironically as in Christianity, just as Jesus has become the symbol for suffering humanity as well as Christ victorious, the Jewish people have become a symbol of the persecuted and Suffering Servant not only for Jews but for others as well. Why? Because whatever emphasis our different covenants have, we are all part of one humanity with similar needs and goals.

The contribution therefore that Christianity gives to humanity is a way of coping with individual suffering in a world yet unredeemed from human greed and self-worship. The frustration felt by Jews when our earthly hopes for redemption faded led to the rise of mystical sects and literature. Equally, human suffering in this world has led to a Christian liberation movement in which action is wedded to prayer. Throughout the millennia both religions have insisted on the primacy of justice and charity. But painted with a broad-brush Judaism's goal has been *Tikkun olam* through the acceptance of God's law of justice tempered with compassion. Christianity has sought *Tikkun olam* by a godlike conversion of the human spirit. But as each human being is a many splendid creation – both objectives may motivate us at different times in our lives. We all vary between reconciliation to 'being' and to an ambition for a 'becoming', to use the terms of Erich Fromm. And could we not say that Paul was influenced by Moses who reminded the Israelites that the law is neither in heaven nor across the sea but 'No, the thing is very close to you, in your mouth and in your heart to observe it' (Deut. 30.11–14) and by Jeremiah:

> But such is the covenant I will make with the house of Israel after these days. I will put my Torah in their inmost being and inscribe it upon their hearts. Then I will be their God, and they shall be my people. No longer will they need to teach one another and say to one another 'obey the LORD', for all of them from the least to the greatest, shall obey me. (Jer. 31.33–34)

The Catholic message cries out to the individual. The Jewish one cries out to the community.

Catholics will have to be patient with Jews when it comes to a partnership in theology. Judaism in its original expression had no theology of faith. Seeking an understanding of the nature of God is discouraged in Judaism, if not forbidden. Do not ask what God is, only ask what God wants. Jewish theology is Jewish ethics. Since the Holocaust and under the influence of Christian thought, Jews too have begun to wrestle, not so much with the nature of God's existence but more so with the problem of God's absence. Theology, however, is the basis of Christianity. The understanding of the nature of the Trinity has been argued with a passion that has led to heresies and the death of heretics. In our theological discussions, Jews will not wish to involve themselves in Christian theological debates. What we need to do is to appreciate how Christianity grew out of the human soul – and to recognize that the soul had a Jewish dimension.

What can we achieve through our partnership in theology? How can we together feed a world starved of the human values of purpose and selfless fellowship? We need to learn from each other. We Jews need to appreciate why Christianity has been the source of such divine art in music, painting and architecture. We need unashamedly to tap these sources. We need to read the New Testament for the truths it reveals about human nature and its quest for God. Might I say here that it would be helpful if the Vatican were to consider in future publications of their Bible to footnote offensive anti-Jewish passages and put them into a proper perspective? It would make it far easier for us to recommend its readings were this done. As a quid pro quo, we Jews should footnote those passages in the Hebrew Bible which smack of the barbarism of a tribal age.

Catholics should study Jewish sources to see the treasures of wisdom about human nature, the unequalled understanding that the rabbinic sages and philosophers had of the conflict between the human libido and super-ego, and their attempt to find a way for structuring a human society based on ethical norms in all areas of life – from sex and family life to business and charitable institutions.

Dr Fisher has referred in his paper to the joint publication from the pens of Jews and Christians of proposals for the resolution of social issues based on their own traditions. We will need more of them, but we will need even more than this. We need to explore with each other why people of two faiths who both believe in God and in the sanctity of life, in the equality of the sexes and the value of family life can differ so profoundly on matters of birth control, homosexuality, feminism and other such issues which make atheists feel morally superior to us. We have to explain together how religions based on divine authority can reconcile themselves to the democratic process which may legislate in opposition to our own traditional beliefs and practices. How can we jointly counter the secular attack on religion as being reactionary and authoritarian? And how can we in love show that the materialism of the consumer society is destroying the quality of human relationships? Catholicism and Progressive Judaism can challenge and learn from each other. If Catholicism, which is more inclined towards authority and faith, and Progressive Judaism, which is more inclined towards the autonomy of the collective conscience and law, can engage in constructive dialogue with respect for each other's sincerity, we can provide a model for others whose differences have led to bitter division. Indeed it may be the most positive example for those within our own religious ranks who are engaged in internecine hostility.

I know that my presentation has been full of generalizations. All of the points I have made, I am sure, could be picked to pieces. I hope that this will not prevent my conclusion from receiving a measure of sympathy: meaningful theological dialogue needs to be based on the understanding and respect for each other's covenantal relationship to God on which basis we can create a synergy of human creativity where each, according to our own divine mandate, can contribute to *Tikkun olam*, the fulfilment of God's goals for us when he created us to be his partners as his stewards of the world he has created.

Discussant

– John D'Arcy May

Rabbi Brichto deferentially suggests that all his points 'could be picked to pieces', but this is not my inclination after reading his very generous paper – quite the contrary. I was moved by his evocation of a 'home filled with the spirituality that comes from the love of Jewish scholarship' and struck by the practicality of his proposal that mutually repugnant biblical texts should be footnoted to minimize offence. The most significant thing in his paper, however, is his suggestion that the Covenant – the cornerstone of Jewish existence – has both strengths and weaknesses, which he proceeds to state plainly. With remarkable candour he proposes that recent 'papal acceptance of the special Covenant between God and the Jews poses a challenge to the Jews which has not yet been addressed . . . By accepting the Jewish origins of Christianity, and the value of the Jews maintaining their historical covenant with God, the Pope has, in my view, challenged the Jewish community to reciprocate' (p. 220). It is in the framework of this bold proposal that I wish to discuss some of the issues raised by Rabbi Brichto for my faith as a Roman Catholic.

In conversation with Rabbi Norman Solomon I once implied that the effort to remain faithful to the particularities of Orthodox practice must have imposed a great burden on the Jewish inmates of the Nazi death camps. With that hint of a smile which his friends know so well, Norman replied: 'We survived because of our observance.' Catholic equivalents such as abstaining from meat on Fridays – once the badge of fidelity in a hostile Protestant world – are a distant memory now, but this particularity of practice is relevant to certain things Rabbi Brichto said about historical particularity and narrative continuity. What has always struck me about Judaism is the way it exists in history. History is its urtext, not just the setting but the substance of God's relationship with the people to whose destiny God binds Godself in the covenant. Alongside this immediacy, the Catholic view of the world, although of course it too is the product of entanglements with many peoples' histories, can seem strangely abstract: principle comes before context, doctrine anticipates contingency.

But on one issue I would wish to question Rabbi Brichto further. I believe he overdraws the distinction between Jewish collectivity and Christian individualism, at least as far as the Roman Catholic tradition is concerned. I would prefer to say that, although the individualism endemic in Western culture has seeped into Catholicism – with liberalizing effects which are undoubtedly desirable – the 'catholicity' which defines that tradition is still an essentially communal affair, an awareness of belonging to a collectivity which always refers back to the eucharistic community and to the (in principle, if not in fact) worldwide communion of such communities. My memory of growing up in a small country town in Australia is very much one of belonging to a tightly-knit, self-supporting community. It compensated for its awareness of being an alien Irish Catholic minority in a society in which Protestantism was privileged by self-consciously pointing to Rome as its source of legitimacy, thereby transcending all local pettiness.

In contrast, while appreciating the role of the family, beautifully brought out in Tony Bayfield's paper, as the primary setting of Jewish liturgical practice, I see this family-based tradition as the nursery of individual talent and personal security in an often hostile environment. Just as medieval Catholicism gave birth to the Reformation, so pre-modern Judaism gave birth to Reform, both of which stress the responsibility of the individual and emancipation from human authority posing as divine. One could make the case that while Progressive Judaism has considerable elements of individualism, at least compared to the Orthodox, Roman Catholicism might be regarded as collectivistic in Protestant eyes. Rabbi Brichto is undoubtedly right when he says: 'The focus of the New Covenant moved away from collective Israel to the individual, from one people to all the nations of the earth' (p. 224). But his emphasis on Christianity giving 'a place for the individual sufferer to rest his soul', 'a way of coping with individual suffering', needs the complement of 'realized catholicity' as a structured universalism, manifested anew in each local context and in this setting providing the resources for individual solace. Indeed, as Rabbi Brichto well says, 'both objectives [the acceptance of God's law of justice . . . a godlike conversion of the human spirit] may motivate us at different times in our lives' (p. 225). If 'Christianity' in the abstract has fostered individualism in Western culture, Roman Catholicism is anything but individualistic and still has great trouble acknowledging individual liberties and cultural peculiarities.

This somewhat overdrawn distinction between collective and individual interferes with Rabbi Brichto's thought-provoking critique of the Jewish Covenant. 'Law is the essence of Judaism. Law is social. Law is collective. Salvation is collective' (p. 221) – only the first and last of these terse characterizations mark a clear boundary between the Jewish and the Catholic experience. The terms of the Covenant are such that the near-destruction of the Jewish people can only be seen as infidelity on God's part. Obedience to the Law should have warded off physical harm; the opposite was the case, just as it has been from biblical times. This admission leads Rabbi Brichto to a new appreciation of physical resurrection as an expression of hope which found its place in the tradition of the Pharisees and of the church, just as it compels him to repudiate the response of rabbis who, as his teacher put it, 'saved God's face' by 'accepting responsibility for their suffering'. If 'the Law did not save . . . it was far better to believe in redemption through the risen Jesus who had a message for the whole world, than in a code of laws which were a burden for the gentile world and prevented their conversion to a redeeming faith' (p. 223). Rabbi Brichto's question thus becomes extraordinarily stimulating:

> What strata of the human psyche does Christian imagery touch that Judaism does not and why has the Jewish Covenant been able to hold on to the loyalty of a people who have suffered ceaselessly for the sanctification of a God, who was not able to deliver them . . .'? (p. 221).

Catholics should ponder both parts of the question.

Closely bound up with this is another matter raised by Rabbi Brichto, the all-important question of ethics. 'Judaism had sown the seeds of monotheistic universalism and ethical monotheism', yet, as Eugene Fisher points out, Jews and Catholics, though they are virtually at one on some ethical issues, are publicly at loggerheads on others. The source of the problem could not be stated more succinctly: 'Jewish theology is Jewish ethics . . . Theology, however, is the basis of Christianity' (p. 225). As a product of the Roman Catholic 'system' I would add: more's the pity! The more I learn about religions other than either of our traditions, the more convinced I become that Christianity relies far too much on theology. My colleagues would defend it by saying that it is our indispensable means of engaging with the Western intellectual tradition, but I would reply that most academic theology is more apt to convince theologians than secular outsiders and that it simply bewilders all but the most determined enquirers from other faith traditions. The lasting legacy of the liberation theologians has been to restore the primacy of praxis as the basis of the church's credibility. I am convinced we have much to learn from the Jewish way of patiently examining all available sources and precedents in order to answer the only question that ultimately matters, the practical question: 'What should we do?' Christianity's love affair with doctrine, philosophy, theory goes hand in hand with the universalism implicit in 'catholicity', but it needs the complement of searching out God's will for the community in the given situation, which is so characteristic of Jewish 'theology'. Perhaps even more fundamental than our disagreements on 'matters of birth control, homosexuality, feminism and other such issues', despite the sources of morality we share in common, is the question of 'how religions based on divine authority can reconcile themselves to the democratic process' (p. 226). The juxtaposition of Catholic 'authority and faith' and Progressive Judaism's 'autonomy of the collective conscience and law' suggests that the respective roles of consensus formation and authority structures need to be further clarified in each case. But I certainly agree that this is an area in which we can 'challenge and learn from each other'.

'Where are the values?' is our leading question, but I wonder whether it is the right question. The search for values is undoubtedly complicated by the different emphases analysed in Rabbi Brichto's paper. Perhaps we should also ask, in conclusion, whether our common problem is all or even mainly about 'values'? A value is a subjective estimate of something's worth. This language only came into ethics midway through the twentieth century under the influence of phenomenologists such as Max Scheler. It needs further elaboration in order to be able to identify specifically moral values (this work was carried out by the Catholic philosopher Dietrich von Hildebrand, whose thought was certainly a welcome refreshment as I laboured though dry scholastic treatises on moral theology). But do our traditions actually offer 'values', and, even if they do, is this their main contribution to ethical discussion? Should we not rather be raising the question of morality's embeddedness in the nurturing matrix of religious traditions such as ours? Is not our joint challenge to the rapidly globalizing society of a postmodern world precisely the particularity and continuity of our worship and the faith and hope to which it gives testimony? These are not merely 'values' to which we 'choose' to adhere in a 'pluralist' context. They are our heritage, the vision of transcendence which ultimately gives morality its meaning.

In the light of this, the full significance of Rabbi Brichto's challenging paper becomes apparent. Our dialogue must indeed 'be based on the understanding and respect for each other's covenantal relationship to God on which basis we can create a synergy of human creativity' (p. 227). I can see this creativity extending to the ethical, the cognitive, the aesthetic and the spiritual spheres as Jews and Christians make progress in reconciling their ancient enmity.

The Values We Bring to the Partnership

– Eugene Fisher

In welcoming Pope John Paul II to the United States on the occasion of his meeting in Miami on 11 September 1987 with representatives of the world's largest Jewish community (after a summer of very strained relations), Rabbi Mordecai Waxman stated:

> A basic belief of our Jewish faith is the need 'to mend the world under the sovereignty of God' (*l'takken olam b'malkut Shaddai*). To mend the world means to do God's work in the world. It is in this spirit that Catholics and Jews should continue to address the social, moral, economic and political problems of the world . . . But before we can mend the world, we must first mend ourselves. A meeting such as this is part of the healing process that is now visibly under way between our two communities.[1]

In putting it just this way, Rabbi Waxman evoked not only the then-fractious instance of the Pope's meeting with Kurt Waldheim, the ex-Nazi president of Austria, but also the larger issue of the *Shoah* itself, with all its profoundly painful implications for the attempt at Jewish–Catholic reconciliation which is arguably for both of our ancient communities the most urgent task facing us at the dawn of the third millennium of our relationship. And Rabbi Waxman offered the hope that efforts that had taken place up to that time would continue to bear fruit, not just for Jews and Catholics, but also, as the assigned (anything but modest) title of this presentation indicates, for God's glory and for the betterment of humanity and the planet we inhabit.

The Pope's address, not coincidentally, affirmed the same themes. He affirmed the effort to develop 'a Catholic document on the *Shoah*',[2] 'common educational programs' on the *Shoah* and other matters of mutual concern. And he offered this vision:

> It is my sincere hope that, as partners in dialogue, as fellow

believers in the God who revealed himself, as children of Abraham, we will strive to render a common service to humanity, which is so much needed in this our day. We are called to collaborate in service and to unite in a common cause wherever a brother or sister is unattended, forgotten, neglected, or suffering in any way; wherever human rights are endangered or human dignity offended; wherever the rights of God are violated or ignored.[3]

Common educational programming and joint witness to God and service to humanity. These are themes that go back to the Second Vatican Council's declaration of the 'great spiritual patrimony' shared by Judaism and Christianity, and emphasized in subsequent implementing documents of the Holy See.[4] In his address to the Jewish community in the Great Synagogue of Rome in 1986, Pope John Paul II, after stressing the 'fundamental difference' between Judaism and Christianity with respect to 'the attachment of us Catholics to the person and teaching of Jesus of Nazareth', drew out the implications of our common biblical and spiritual patrimonies with regard to 'morality, the great field of individual and social ethics':

The ways opened for our collaboration, in the light of our common heritage drawn from the Law and the Prophets, are various and important . . . a collaboration in favour of man, his life from conception until natural death, his dignity, his freedom, his rights, his self-development in a society which is not hostile but friendly and favourable, where justice reigns and where . . . it is peace that rules, the *shalom* hoped for by the lawmakers, prophets and sages of Israel . . . In a society which is often lost in agnosticism and individualism and which is suffering the bitter consequences of selfishness and violence, Jews and Christians are the trustees and witnesses of an ethic marked by the Ten Commandments, in the observance of which humanity finds its truth and freedom. To promote a common reflection and collaboration on this point is one of the great duties of the hour.[5]

The topic you have assigned me is thus at once one of the great themes of the Council, of the present pontiff, and of both sides of the Jewish–Catholic dialogue today. It is not a new theme, but one on which there has been almost four decades of formal dialogue and even longer, at least in my country, 'dialogue of life'. Perhaps I can contribute best to the current endeavour by sketching at least a little of what has been done in these areas on the local and national levels in the United States, and common statements on the international level, with a comment or two along the way. I must note at the outset that, given the faith-filled nature of the deeply good Catholics and Jews involved, all that has been accomplished on the local and national levels in the United States has, ultimately, been done as a partnership, as we Catholics would say, *ad Maiorem Dei Gloriam,* for 'the greater glory of God.'

Historical Context of American Dialogue

First, the 'prequel'. Jews and Catholics both hit the shores of the United States as emigrants from Europe, together filling up the urban ghettoes of New York, Boston, Baltimore, Chicago, Detroit and ultimately points west (the Southern story is akin, but yet, distinct). Together, Jews and Catholics in America's great cities were kept out of the 'best' neighbourhoods, social clubs, schools, universities and professions. The phrase 'discriminating clientele' and its many cognates meant, to us, 'don't try to join', we will not let you in. You are unwashed, dangerous, exotic and have 'dual loyalties' – so we cannot trust you to be good Americans, you followers of the 'whore of Babylon' (the Pope) and Zion (e.g. the *Protocols*). We got the schlock-jobs. One of the earliest photographs in the history of the American labour movement, therefore, had demonstrators in New York carrying protest signs in two languages. Neither was English. One was Yiddish, the other Italian. And so the American labour movement, so crucial in world history (it ultimately led to the defeat of communism, certainly in the United States and arguably internationally – can you spell 'Solidarity'? – as well as to the founding of Israel, and American support for the fledgling state) was born, with 'foreign' names like 'Gompers' and 'Meany' leading the way.

This is different. Nothing like it, I would argue, had happened in Europe, though the creative synergy of the Irish Catholic Emancipation cause (lead by my one illustrious ancestor, Daniel O'Connell) in nineteenth-century Britain did raise the hopes and possibilities for the United Kingdom's put-upon Jewish population. In the North in the United States, there was the labour movement and 'local' politics, with the 'outs', Jews and Catholics, trying, together or in parallel fashion, to get 'in'. In the South, the tiny Jewish and Catholic minorities, lost in a sea of 'born again' Christians, most often clung together for comfort and support. But nowhere in the hemispheric-wide country of ours did Catholics exercise the type of 'Christian' secular power, as Catholics, that was typical of so many 'Old World' countries for far too long.

I do not mean here to put down the latter or, certainly, our gracious British hosts. Not only did Catholics in America not have the power their aristocratic religious confrères had in Europe but also they could not even imagine having it. Had they been doing all that well in Europe, of course, they would have stayed to enjoy it. So American Catholics have never, ever, politically oppressed American Jews, and have not really been in a position to discriminate socially or economically either, being with the Jews on the outside of the American 'establishment'. That is virtually a first, at least since Constantine in the fourth century.

The result was a pattern of cooperation between Jews and Catholics on a wide variety of common concerns. The Knights of Columbus and B'nai B'rith in Detroit got together, for example, during World War II for joint fund-raising dinners to provide funds for building the bombers that defeated Hitler and Japan. They continued after the war to work together. Many Catholic colleges welcomed those Jewish students who wished to attend. I do not think that there is a Catholic college or university campus in America (I exaggerate only slightly) that does not have a building or a programme named after a Jewish donor. If one recalls that over half of the Catholic colleges in the world are in the United States, one begins to understand the significance of the American Jewish contribution to the fulfilment of the Catholic Church's overall educational mandate.

The civil rights and peace movements brought Christian and Jewish leadership together in unprecedented public displays of solidarity in support of a common cause. Cooperation on the parish/synagogue level also came to be taken almost as a matter of course. When a synagogue in Florida some two decades ago was vandalized, the neighbouring parish not only participated in the cleanup but offered its church for Jewish services. When the parish in which I live was being built almost three decades ago, a Reform synagogue was planned for the neighbouring property. For several years while the latter was being built, the Jewish community regularly conducted its Sabbath services in the church, the crucifix being reverently taken down each Friday night and replaced at sundown on Saturday. Today, because of overflow, my daughter's religious education classes are given in one of the classrooms of the temple. There is no need to take down the Jewish religious symbols and sayings that cover the walls.

The Emergence of Formal Dialogue: Paired and Parallel Papers

The emergence of the theological dialogues between Catholics and Jews in the 1960s, made possible by the Second Vatican Council's mandate for opening the windows of the Church, took place in the context of two communities which had long maintained a cooperative attitude toward each other in a variety of areas of common social concern. The agenda for a four-day 'theological colloquy' which took place at St Vincent's Archabbey in Latrobe, Pennsylvania, in January of 1965 (almost nine months before *Nostra Aetate* was promulgated by the Council!) reveals much about the awareness of each other's concerns that had already developed by that early time in the dialogue. Indeed, it could still form a serviceable outline for our dialogues today. The scholars were paired, rabbi and priest, on the topics:

1. Evaluating the Past in Christian–Jewish Relations (Solomon Grayzel, John Sheerin)
2. The Bond of Worship, Our Debt to Each Other (Solomon Freehof, Aidan Kavanagh)
3. Biblical Scholarship: Bond or Barrier? (Samuel Sandmel, Roland Murphy)
4. Freedom of Conscience/Religious Liberty (Robert Gordis, Bishop John Wright)
5. Religion and the Public Order: Church, Synagogue and Social Action (Marc Tanenbaum, John F. Cronin)
6. Israel (*Am* and *Medinat*) as Idea and Reality (Jacob Agus, Gerard Sloyan)[6]

Even in this early endeavour at systematic theological dialogue, however, a problem that has continued to bedevil the full-scale, no-holds barred exchange between our two ancient traditions was noted by Rabbi Arthur Gilbert in his summary remarks:

I regret that only one Orthodox rabbi accepted our invitation. It is the conviction of the Orthodox rabbinate, based on theological grounds but motivated, I believe, much more by an understandable defensiveness and fear, that conversations on matters of faith are futile and that the Jews must, of necessity, be disadvantaged in such encounters. Instead, the Orthodox are ready to engage in any conversation designed to apply religious insight to a mutually significant problem in the social order . . . If only those fearful had been able to witness the graciousness, the honesty, and the concern for human dignity that embraced every exchange, then they would have realized how important and valuable such a colloquy can be! I regret their failure to be present because in honesty we needed their viewpoint as a corrective and as an enrichment to those views so well articulated in the four days of study and conversation.[7]

There may be those here today, three and a half decades later, who would echo Rabbi Gilbert's remarks! In the United States, Reform and Conservative Jewish institutions have carried the torch of dialogue for the whole Jewish community always explaining as objectively as possible, as Rabbi Gilbert did in this pioneering dialogue, the 'official' Orthodox position, though remaining unpersuaded by it, as he was. As, quite frankly, I am personally.

In any event, after the Council (whose declaration on Catholic–Jewish Relations, *Nostra Aetate*, No. 4 was greeted with much the same chorus of negative criticism from Jewish leaders as was the most recent statement of the Holy See, *We Remember*, on the *Shoah*),[8] dialogues in the United States proliferated almost immediately in amazing numbers on the local, diocesan level. These were validated but not, if truth be told, generated by the publication in January 1967 of the first *Guidelines for Catholic–Jewish Relations* ever issued in the history of the Church.[9] Already by 1972, for example, a 'living room dialogue' in Dayton, Ohio, on its own came up with the idea of a public conference on Catholic–Jewish relations that ultimately blossomed into the National Workshop on Christian–Jewish Relations (NWCJR). In the twenty years between the Third NWCJR in 1977 in Detroit and the late 1980s, when the Synagogue Council of America (SCA) bowed out of sponsorships of the Workshop, the SCA – which included the Orthodox rabbinical and congregational organizations – was very active in planning and implementing the Workshop, all according to what might be called a 'scrupulous but lenient' interpretation of the Soloveichik dictum.

Also following the faithful yet flexible model of interpreting Soloveitchik were the scholarly colloquia co-sponsored by the National Council of Synagogues and the National Conference of Catholic Bishops (USA) at the University of Notre Dame from the late 1970s to mid-1980s. The two volumes that came out of these colloquia were entitled, *Formation of Social Policy in the Catholic and Jewish Traditions* and *Liturgical Foundations of Social Policy in the Catholic and Jewish Traditions*.[10] As with the Latrobe dialogue, each topic was addressed by a Jewish and a Catholic scholar. Again, the listing of topics and scholars can give a glimpse of what is possible in the dialogue:

1. Social Policy Making Structures of our Religious Communities (Balfour Brickner and Francis J. Lally)
2. Religion and Family Policy (Seymour Siegel and (now) HE Cardinal J. Francis Stafford)
3. Religion and National Economic Policy (Ben Zion Bokser and George G. Higgins)
4. Religion and International Human Rights (J. Bryan Hehir and Michael Wyschogrod)
5. Methodology and Social Policy (Sol Roth and John Pawlikowski)
6. Liturgical Sources for Social Commitment (Lawrence Hoffman and John Gurrieri)
7. Health Care and Healing in Liturgical Expression (Kraus Walter Wurzburger and Dennis Kraus)
8. Spirituality and the Quest for Justice and Peace (John Pawlikowski and Jules Harlow)
9. Religious Sources for Conservation Ethics (Edward Kilmartin and Jonathan Helfand)
10. Liturgical Bases for Social Policy (Lawrence Hoffinan and Gerard Sloyan)

One of the most interesting observations made by Rabbi Daniel Polish in his introduction to the first volume was that, while our two traditions, founded on a common biblical mandate, very often come up with remarkably similar conclusions on the level of moral policy with regard to a given issue, the way we get there, interfacing ancient wisdom and contemporary sensibilities, can, on the level of 'the broad patterns of methodology' be quite different:

One factor seems clear to us. Two distinct forms of argument are represented in the papers. Jews and Catholics manifest different styles of formulating their thoughts about social issues. Each has its obvious strengths, and it is not suggested that one is superior to the other. The difference is inescapably and clearly exemplified in this collection. The Catholic papers involve an explication of theological underpinnings, a clear discussion of the development of the theological structure which frames consideration of the moral decisions that are made. There is rich ratiocination and rigorous logic reflected in them. The Jewish papers are, in the main, less theologically explicated. They are formulated less analytically. Instead, they express an emotional intensity, a passion to take the prophetic statement and make it live in the immediate situation . . . [But both] hold up the norm of faithful expression of the tradition as the ideal to be aspired to in religious response to social issues, even in the face of the complex factors which make this difficult.[11]

In our reflection on the second volume of papers (nos. 6–10, above), we asked a question that is fundamental as well to the task and vision of this present, international conference. Again, I shall quote at some length, not having found better words over the years to present these thoughts for your consideration here today:

Why, it might be asked, is the liturgy – of all subjects – dealt with in this dialogical fashion? Jews and Catholics share certain things – the Hebrew Scriptures; a painful, often conflictive, history of inter-action; even the historical background of Jesus' teaching. But liturgy clearly we do not share. Here we are very much separate and distinct from one another. Here we clearly go each our own way. That is precisely what motivated our selection of liturgy as the focus of this volume . . . to help each community gain a deeper understanding of the realities of the other . . . to come to know something of the prayer world and core values of our neighbours at the very point where we are most removed from and least known to one another. There is yet another reason. As each of our two faith communities turns inward for prayer, it takes its own practices and perceptions almost for granted. It loses sight of the fact that its patterns participate in a phenomenological morphology. Each of us can see ourselves more clearly as we are reflected in the encounter with the other. In their forms and actions, we may see aspects and elements of our own that we had not previously appreciated. In gaining insight into the reality of the other, we come to comprehend ourselves more fully.[12]

Finally, in this category, I would mention a work I co-authored with Annette Daum (of blessed memory) published in 1985 by the Union of American Hebrew Congregations. This was *The Challenge of Shalom for Catholics and Jews: A Dialogical Discussion Guide to the Catholic Bishops' 1983 Pastoral on Peace and War*.[13] Here, in addition to paired papers on 'developing attitudes toward peace and war', and on history, prayer for peace and non-violence, Annette and I prepared a joint survey of 'areas of agreement and divergence'. We found the former in issues such as the cost of nuclear arms and economic justice,

capital punishment, and care for the dying. We found the latter when
it came to the issues of pacifism and abortion (though there are some
on the Jewish left who would be close to Catholic pacifism, and some,
especially among the Orthodox, whose stance on abortion is likewise
similar to the Catholic attitude). Here, rather than simply setting our
traditions and contemporary understandings side by side, there was
a very real attempt to articulate our understandings together. That is
the model, working toward the ability to make joint statements
addressing the wider community, that Catholics and Jews first on the
local and then on the national level in the United States began to take
up increasingly in the 1980s and internationally in the 1990s.

Joint Reflections on Areas of Mutual Social and Theological Concern: The Los Angeles Model

In 1973, the Southern California Board of Rabbis and the Archdiocese
of Los Angleles began what has become one of the best ongoing
'priest/rabbi' dialogues in America.[14] In 1975, the Archdiocese of Los
Angeles, the Board of Rabbis of Southern California, and the
American Jewish Committee held a conference to celebrate the tenth
anniversary of *Nostra Aetate* and to identify current concerns. Ultimately, two ongoing dialogue groups emerged, one of which explored
'Respect for Life' issues and the other of which, the 'Priest/Rabbi
Committee', explored more directly theological concerns. Both are
distinguished by their willingness to submit their conversations to the
challenges and rigour demanded by producing a joint statement at
the end of their process of consideration.[15] As with the above efforts,
of course, the two ongoing committees normally began with
exchanges of papers on the topics to be pursued.

The Respect for Life committee took on first a potentially most con-
tentious issue, abortion. The format developed in their 1977 statement
to handle the topic proved useful to both it and to the priest/rabbi
team with other topics as well. First, there are joint reflections on the
foundational values both traditions share with regard to the sanctity
of life, drawing suitably on the Hebrew scriptures, and rabbinic and
Christian sources over the ages. Then, the Catholic and Jewish groups
each articulate authentically to their own traditions, but in a way
comprehensible to the other, the moral applications for our time.
Finally, and in a way that could still help many a community today,
they join together again to express five common and practical
'goals' that the two groups can pursue even taking into account
what divides them. Subsequently, the Respect for Life Committee has

taken on and made significant contributions to discussion of 'Caring for the Dying Person', 'The Nuclear Reality', 'A Covenant of Care' (with respect, for example, to the allocation of medical resources) and the Holocaust itself. These statements come as well with study guides, bibliographies, discussion questions, etc., making them quite user-friendly to other groups interested in pursuing such matters jointly.

Similarly, the Priest/Rabbi group has produced illuminating joint statements going to the heart of the theological dialogue between our two communities: 'Covenant or Covenants?', 'The Kingdom', 'Salvation/Redemption', 'Forgiveness/Reconciliation' and 'The Lord's Day and the Sabbath'. Any dialogue group on any level seeking to tackle these or related immensely complex and profoundly enriching topics, in my opinion, should have the Los Angeles materials at hand. They are excellent as a starting point and as a resource.

Joint Statements on the National (United States) and International Levels.

In June of 1990 the National Conference of Catholic Bishops' Committee for Ecumenical and Interreligious Affairs (BCEIA) and the Synagogue Council of America (SCA) issued its first joint statement, 'A Lesson of Value: A Joint Statement on Moral Education in the Public Schools'.[16] This has been followed by statements condemning pornography (1993) and Holocaust revisionism (1994), 'Reflections on the Millennium' (1998), and 'To End the Death Penalty' (1999). These statements, in the main, limit themselves to what can be said together – often resoundingly – on the issues of joint social and religious concern which they have taken up. They are the result of twice-yearly meetings between Catholic bishops, chaired by HE Cardinal William Keeler, and Jewish leaders representing rabbinical and congregational associations. The last two statements, in 1998 and 1999, it should be noted, were issued by the BCEIA and the National Council of Synagogues, the SCA having dissolved over internal Jewish issues.

The National Council of Synagogues (NCS) represents Reform and Conservative Judaism in the United States and Canada, approximately 90 per cent of religiously affiliated Jews in North America. The BCEIA does maintain an ongoing consultation with Orthodox Judaism which is co-chaired by HE Cardinal John O'Connor and Rabbi Fabian Schonfeld and also meets twice annually. The latter, of course, would feel itself bound by the above-discussed Soloveitchik principle, but not the former. Both dialogues, in the eyes of the Catholic Church, are infinitely precious.

With the exception of the reflection on the millennium, these statements have focused on concerns the two communities wish, as religious bodies, to raise to the attention of the wider, pluralistic society of the American body politic. It is the feeling, bolstered by experience, that Jews and Catholics, speaking together, will have a greater chance of being ' heard' in the community as a whole if they speak together than if they speak on their own, risking being brushed off by the secular media as representing only 'sectarian' interests. Though statements denouncing the death penalty were issued by the Jewish groups represented in the NCS as far back as the 1970s, and by the Catholic Bishops (albeit more tentatively then than now) in the 1980s, the fact that these two groups are so strongly opposed to capital punishment as to urge its abolition appeared to surprise many reporters in the media.

The twice-yearly meetings out of which the statements come likewise serve the perhaps deeper purpose of keeping the leadership of our two communities closely in touch with each other's concerns and needs. Nothing, really, is barred from the table of a full dialogue. We have discussed Israel and the plight of Christians in the Middle East, the Holocaust and the role of the Church, ancient history and modern history, the way we present each other in our textbooks and the way we should present each other in our classrooms and pulpits. Certain topics emerge as suitable for joint statement. But the ongoing forum, even when no statement emerges, has enabled our bishops' conference to keep in touch with Jewish concerns, and also provided us with the opportunity to express our Catholic concerns directly to Jewish religious leadership.

The joint 'Reflection on the Millennium' is a case in point. Jews were very concerned that things could get out of hand when Christians began celebrating, as they had at the turn of the last millennium. Catholic memory of history, however, is no less clear in helping us discern how to avoid at least repeating the mistakes of the past. And since Pope John Paul II had declared this year to be a Jubilee year, the opportunity to learn from Jewish tradition its understanding of what jubilee means in the Hebrew scriptures was one for which to be grateful. A number of dioceses and local Jewish communities, we know, have used the basic outline provided in the joint statement to frame their own efforts at making the turn of the millennium a time to reflect on the betterment of all in our society.

Finally, the two statements of the 1990s by the International

Catholic–Jewish Liaison Committee (ILC) need to be mentioned. In one sense these are modest. While they compare quite favourably with the American statements in terms of substance, they take on deceptively simple topics, the sacredness of marriage and the family (Jerusalem, 1994), on the one hand, and care for the environment as a religious act (Vatican City, 1998), on the other. Both, interestingly, rely heavily on the early chapters of the book of Genesis for their essential moral reference. Both needed, as well, extensive discussion not just between, but especially within, the two 'teams' which had come together to make them. So the issues that had to be resolved (or in a couple of cases simply not addressed) between and within the communities represented were in fact much wider and deeper than the finely-wrought prose of the two statements might first make apparent. That, of course, was by design of the drafters and the ILC as a whole which re-drafted both in plenary sessions.

In this, they are a microcosm of the relationship as a whole between the Catholic Church and the Jewish People, at once hope-filled and hesitant, trusting in God, but being very careful not to go too far too quickly, always concerned not to get too far ahead of the larger communities they represent. This is as it should be. One could say, in summing up this retrospective of dialogues on all levels between Catholics and Jews on the topic assigned to me, that the 'higher' the level the higher the stakes, and the more cautious the representatives are and need to be. Still, the rewards, for those involved, as I have been blessed to be, and, we fervently hope, for our respective communities, are prodigious.

Never before in the two-millennia-long history we share has anything like this series of joint statements between the Catholic Church and the Jewish People ever even been attempted, much less pulled off with such skill and delicate sensitivity to the underlying concerns and hesitations of the other religious community. We who are privileged to be involved are at times overwhelmed with our own sense of smallness, of inadequacy to the great opportunity that having lived in this particular generation has given us. We can change the course of centuries of mistrust between our two ancient peoples. More, we can turn the tragedies of the past into opportunities for the future, a future which will be better not just for our two communities, but perhaps for all of humanity. For if the deep enmity that has existed between Jews and Christians (caused, to be honest, in the main by Christian sins against Jews) can be overcome because our generation is overcome by the call of God and the needs of our fellow-human beings, virtually any human enmity can be overcome. If Jews and Catholics can move ever more surely toward reconciliation despite past wrongs, perhaps, just perhaps, the *Tikkun olam*, the 'healing of the world', which both of our faiths teach us is the ultimate goal of creation, is not a romantic vision but graspable possibility. Let us, together, reach for it.

Notes

1. Cited in E. Fisher and L. Klenicki (eds), *Spiritual Pilgrimage: Pope John Paul II on Jews and Judaism 1979–1995*, New York: Crossroad, 1995, p. 111.

2. This was issued by the Holy See's Commission for Religious Relations with the Jews in March of 1998 as *We Remember: A Reflection on the Shoah*, which has been published together with the remarkable series of statements of repentance for the *Shoah* issued by Bishops' Conferences in Europe and the United States by the US Catholic Conference under the title, *Catholics Remember the Holocaust*, Washington, DC: USCC Publications, 1998.

3. Fisher and Klenicki, *Spiritual Pilgrimage*, p. 109.

4. These can be found, along with *We Remember* in *Catholic–Jewish Relations: Documents from the Holy See* (London: Catholic Truth Society, 1999), which includes the texts of the Second Vatican Council's declaration, *Nostra Aetate* (1965), and the two previous universal teaching documents of the Holy See's Commission for Religious Relations with the Jews: *Guidelines for Implementing Nostra Aetate* (1974) and *Notes on the Correct Way to Present Jews and Judaism in Catholic Teaching* (1985).

5. Fisher and Klenicki, *Spiritual Pilgrimage*, p. 65.

6. Philip Scharper, ed., *Torah and Gospel: Jewish and Catholic Theology in Dialogue*, NY: Sheed & Ward, 1966.

7. Ibid., p. 296. Rabbi Joseph Soloveitchik's classic articulation of these concerns, 'Confrontations', had only recently, in 1964, been published in the Orthodox journal *Tradition* 6.2, Spring/Summer, pp. 5–29. Soloveitchik himself acknowledged in a footnote that Jewish tradition does not distinguish between religious issues of a social order and 'theology' as such. I have known several of the great rabbi's students over the years, since the *Tradition* article did provide them, as its author undoubtedly intended, with a formula enabling them to become involved in dialogue with the Church, even if in a carefully delimited way. These students of the Rav, interestingly, have been among those arguing for a broader rather than more restrictive interpretation of the rubric. In my own mind I have come to believe that what Rabbi Soloveitchik meant by 'theology' was not what we Christians mean by the term at all. Rather, what he had in mind is what we would call 'doctrine' and that in only certain specific aspects which involve the major dividing lines between our religious traditions, such as the doctrines of the Incarnation and the Trinity. Otherwise what he said would make little sense. In Catholic tradition, moral theology is no less theology than is, say, eschatology.

8. Cardinal Cassidy of the Holy See's Commission for Religious Relations with the Jews responded to Jewish concerns regarding *We Remember* in an address in May of 1998 given at a plenary session of the American Jewish Committee's annual meeting in Washington. This address clarifies and resolves a number of

the issues raised about the proper interpretation of the text. It is included in full in the USCC's *Catholics Remember the Holocaust* (pp. 61–76). I attempted to explain to my fellow-Catholics something about why the Jewish community tends to take a 'lachrymose' and critical view of well-meant official Catholic statements (and to Jews why Catholics often feel confused rather than enlightened by the criticisms) in, 'Catholics and Jews Confront the Holocaust and Each Other' (*America*, 11 September 1999), originally given as the annual John Courtney Murray Lecture at Fordham University.

9. My generation of the dialogue, which is not that of the pioneers, such as those who were present at St Vincent's Archabbey in 1965, but those who were young then and were given the awesome task of implementing institutionally the great vision of their elders, has seen numerous 'firsts' in the dialogue. It only shows, frankly, how terribly bad things had become over the centuries that Pope John Paul II's prayerful visit to the Great Synagogue of Rome in 1986 was the first time a Bishop of Rome had visited the synagogue since the pontificate of St Peter, who seems to have been a regular attendee. While still unusual in Europe and much of the world when the Pope did it in 1986, however, it should be noted that such visits by Catholic bishops to synagogues in the United States, while not quite commonplace, were by 1986 too common to be particularly newsworthy except in the local community itself.

10. The volumes were published in 1980 and 1983, respectively, by the University of Notre Dame Press and co-edited by myself and Rabbi Daniel J. Polish.

11. *Formation of Social Policy*, pp. xiii–xiv.

12. *Liturgical Foundations of Social Policy*, pp. xii–xiii.

13. Revd John T. Pawlikowski, OSM, and Rabbi Stephen Fuchs also contributed essays.

14. Other such ongoing dialogue efforts of note involving the leadership of the Jewish and Catholic communities of a given city or region include (but are by no means limited to!) Chicago, Albany, New York City, Philadelphia, Boston, Washington DC, and Baltimore. Differing areas enjoy differing models as appropriate. In some places, for example, there has emerged involvement of synagogues (and, increasingly, mosques) in local 'Councils of Churches'. In other places, institutes of Jewish–Christian studies, either independent or connected to a Catholic college or university, have emerged as the focal point of ongoing dialogue. A listing of these is given on the Jewish–Christian website: www.jcrelations.com maintained by Fritz Voll of Calgary, Alberta, Canada. The site contains a wealth of information and documentation in German as well as English.

15. See Alfred Wolf and Royale Vadakin, eds., *Journey of Discovery: A Resource Manual for Jewish–Catholic Dialogue* (Valencia, CA: Tabor Publishing, 1989), for the joint statements up to that time.

16. Published in *Origins* 20/9, 19 July 1990, pp. 132–6.

Discussant

– Ron Kronish

I would like to extract certain key themes from Eugene Fisher's paper and highlight them.

Tikkun olam – mending the world

This particular Hebrew phrase has been repeated many times and clearly has important resonances for both faiths. Repairing the world is something we should certainly do together, working on whatever specific issues we can agree upon. A clear example would be ecology. A statement was adopted at the International Catholic–Jewish Liaison Committee at the Vatican in March 1998. Now we need to develop an educational agenda and activist programme based on this statement. In general, we have relied too much on statements and not enough on common action after these statements.

Common educational programs on matters of mutual concern

This is also a good idea! We began to discuss it at the ILC meeting in the Vatican in March 1998 but the document on the Holocaust, which took up much of our attention, derailed us. Here and there one can find some common educational programmes but we need to develop a systematic, operational plan to re-educate the next generation – in schools, universities, seminaries, etc. – for the decades ahead.

In Israel, we are planning new educational initiatives now, as a result of the successful visit of the Pope, which was a great educational experience in itself.

Collaboration in favour of humanity

Israel's Chief Rabbi Lau said to Cardinal Cassidy, in Lau's office in Jerusalem in 1997 (before the Interreligious Coordinating Council in

Israel's conference on 'The Future of Jewish–Catholic Relations') that we need to march together hand in hand wherever there is human suffering – in Rwanda, in Bosnia, in other places in the world. But then nothing happened.

Catholic leaders and Jewish leaders should indeed march together for the sake of humanity. And should stand shoulder to shoulder in places of crisis in the world as they did in the Interreligious Council of Bosnia and at our dialogue with the Dalai Lama on 'Religion in Conflicts: Problem or Solution?' in 1999 in Tiberius.

Dialogue that leads to action is the best kind of collaboration. We have some past examples of collaboration to build upon, for instance, in the Civil Rights Movement in the United States.

Let us revitalize collaboration for peace. What could be more important than this, more meaningful, more urgent. Here I am referring to peace in Israel and the Middle East and also peace in other troubled parts of the world such as Ireland and Bosnia.

Let me emphasize the importance of the Pope's recent visit to Israel. It was a clarion call for the need for peace and reconciliation. We need to revive the work initiated by Eugene Fisher in 1983 with his *The Challenge of Shalom for Catholic and Jews – a Dialogical Discussion Guide to the Catholic Bishops 1983 Pastoral on Peace and War.*

Let me emphasize once again the need to move beyond theory, beyond simply understanding one another's similarities and differences, to common action.

In conclusion

I couldn't agree more with Dr Fisher's closing paragraph. The great opportunity facing us is not only to engage in honest and genuine theological dialogue but the opportunity 'to turn the tragedies of the past into opportunities for the future'. Not just for our two communities, but perhaps for all humanity. Therefore the need is, let me repeat again, for common action. Not just talking but also doing. Which is more important? *Talmud Torah* (Study of Torah) or *Ma'asim Tovim* (Good deeds, righteous action)? The answer, our tradition gives, is the Study of Torah because it leads (or ought to lead) to the doing of good deeds, to improving the world. We need more dialogue on a theological level but we also need shared programmes of education and action.

Discussion recorder

– Mary Kelly

I have tried to record a lively and wide ranging discussion according to subject matter.

Dialogue

There was considerable recognition of the need for the Jewish community to take up the challenge to reciprocate the recent efforts of the Churches in learning more about Christianity and its self-understanding. Rabbi Michael Hilton made the point that an awareness of history had been missing from our discussions. This dialogue had, in fact, existed for 2,000 years, not 50! He argued that, in fact, Jewish doctrine has been kept alive and developed by debate. Christians commonly held that in the first century the Jewish people were waiting for the Messiah. But it was not like that. Jewish messianism was a response to the dialogue – it was kept alive by it. Jews need to make an effort not only to understand Christianity but also to understand the profound Christian effect upon Judaism. Rabbi Sidney Brichto wondered whether, for the most part, historic contact and disputation had really been dialogue.

Rabbi Dr Jonathan Romain pointed out that, in contemporary society, Jews and Christians also share common experiences. Mixed-faith marriages are on the increase. Thirty-five per cent of those in Britain are between Jews and Catholics. This reflects a partnership 'on the street'.

Dr Joann Spillman expressed a worry about the conference. There has been so much place for Catholic input through recent documents and interest! A Protestant observer might think that this dialogue between Catholics and Jews accentuates the differences between Catholics and Protestants and suggests that the Jewish–Protestant dialogue is different. Roman Catholics in mid-West USA are not much interested in Church documents and are less rooted in the higher reaches of the Church.

Disagreement was voiced at this comment. There are differences between Catholics and Protestants but distinctive dialogues are important, both theologically and ethically.

Dr Janet Martin Soskice challenged some points made by Rabbi Dr Brichto. She said that Christianity is more than a way to salvation. Judaism was not the first to bring monotheism to the world. Aristotle was a monotheist. What is distinctive is the radical idea of God in history. Christ was the chosen of Israel for a purpose and Jesus is the Christian way into this.

Rabbi Brichto responded by insisting that it was ethical monotheism that Jews brought to the world.

Rabbi Dr Mark Winer said that there is a long history that is specific to Jews and Catholics and there are special shared elements within that dialogue. Interestingly, Protestant dialogue is often with former Jews. The uniqueness of a Catholic, like Eugene Fisher, is that though he has no trace of Jewish background he is so immersed in Judaism that he is able to dialogue with Jews as Jews.

Education

Rabbi Ron Kronish's insistence on the importance of education was reiterated and the need for vigorous analysis was put forward, for example, what is it that makes the *Shoah* educational? A plea for us to talk together about this was made. We have a richness between us that sets our dialogue in a different context from the usual context in secular Britain; a lot of experience and thinking about boundaries and differences can be beneficial. Both education about and education for need to be thought through much more.

Election

Rabbi Dr Michael Hilton referred back to previous discussions about chosenness and election and said that he did not think there was yet agreement about whether or not these concepts have any value today. Dr Eugene Fisher pointed out that election does not necessarily imply non-election or only one covenant. Rabbi Dr Brichto affirmed that chosenness is a good thing and is not arrogant because chosenness is for a particular task.

Theology and ethics

Both speakers and their discussants had stressed the importance of common action for the sake of humanity and pointed to statements by Christian and Jewish leaders calling for this. Yet according to Rabbi

Ron Kronish nothing had happened (or not enough). A good part of the discussion then focused on the dichotomy between theology and ethics and the relative importance of one or the other.

Theology and praxis are related. Theology matters greatly since the issue of covenant is directly related to imperialism and imperialism still traps. For as long as Jews experience Catholics as imperialistic and as denying Jews their space and the respect one sibling demands of another, joint action is hampered by anger, frustration and suspicion. Our view of the other determines our ability to work together.

Rabbi Mark Solomon referred to Rabbi Dr Sidney Brichto's paper and pointed out that though theological interchange was currently discouraged by Jewish Orthodoxy, it had not always been and was not forbidden. Moreover nineteenth-century ethics rather than theology had proved harmful. As Judith Plaskow said the right question is theological. Right ideas are fundamental. It is sometimes necessary to pit God against Torah. Christian theological debate is different and Jews do not want to get involved in it. But a caution – Christologies and soteriologies can be abusive to Jews, therefore it is necessary for Jews to educate themselves and vice versa.

Responding to Rabbi Kronish's reference to a Christian parallel to *Tikkun olam*, Dr Robert Murray cited a poem by the fourth-century Father of the Church, Prudentius, written for the funeral of his mother. It speaks of mother earth keeping the ashes warm. 'I entrust this dead to you.' Does that enable the 'repairing of life'?

Attention was drawn by Dr Edward Ondrako to Pope John Paul II's *Fides et Ratio* which refers to Mary as 'the table at which faith sits with God'.

Rabbi Ron Kronish proposed recommending a study of *Fides et Ratio* in Israel.

Dr John Pawlikowski pointed out that there have been theological deviations in Christianity. For example, Vatican II restored the true context of the Eucharist and Vatican II included critiques of the liberal tradition including capitalism. He cautioned using Mary in the dialogue since the image of Mary as virgin has been used for the exploitation of women.

In their summing-up both speakers commented on this discussion. Dr Eugene Fisher said that in his experience the conflict between theology and ethics was not a real one. It is not not either/or but both. Referring to John May's earlier caution about values, Rabbi Dr Brichto stressed the priority of behaviour – doing God's will. Jewish theology is basically Midrash. Jews must look at the place of women (cf. references to Mary).

6

Clarifying the Partnership and Setting Its Agenda

Sybil Sheridan

When Sir Sigmund Sternberg invited me to join a group of rabbis to go to the Vatican last year, I little thought it would have such an impact on me. I made a profound discovery: Catholics are serious about their dialogue with Jews.

It seems absurd to say this. So much has been published since the Second Vatican Council, so many of the current Pope's pronouncements have been on this theme, yet it was only when I could see for myself the sincerity of the individuals involved that I realized just how far the Catholic Church has come – changing its very theology in order to meet Jews – and at the same time came the realization that Jews have not moved one step in reciprocation.

Up to now, the overriding theme of the encounter has been overshadowed by the *Shoah* and the need for apology for past misdemeanours. This conference is a first in moving beyond that concentration on the past to a vision of a future where Jew and Catholic work together in a theology of partnership. A laudable vision, but I do feel that we Jews have a great deal to do in adjusting our own theology and learning more about Christianity if this relationship is to develop into a real partnership.

Rabbi Tony Bayfield opened the conference proceedings with the announcement that our discussions would be published in a book – the possible title of which would refer to the text from the Hebrew Bible 'And he fell on his neck and he kissed him and they wept'.[1] The theme which surrounds this statement – one of sibling rivalry, rejection and reconciliation – became the overriding metaphor for his paper on covenant. Yet there are problems with this passage, coming as it does from the story of Jacob and Esau which may, or may not help in furthering our dialogue. In the Hebrew text, the ancient scribes added a series of points over the word 'and he kissed him'. No one knows exactly why they are there, but they have alerted Jewish scholars for centuries to the suggestion that the word is not what it appears; that the kiss by Esau was effectively a bite and that they both wept from the pain inflicted by it.[2] It is not easy simply to remove the dots and take at face value the kiss – no more easy than it is to encounter one another today openly and equally with the shadow of 2,000 years of pain preceding us.

My own vision of Esau is coloured by Midrash – homiletic expositions of the biblical text in which pages and pages are devoted to vituperative comments elucidating his wickedness. Esau becomes Edom becomes Rome . . . it is not possible overnight to reinvent him as the fine upstanding man he probably was. Moreover, the kiss that is not what it appears makes a comeback in the New Testament in the kiss of Judas. Have we travelled so far down the path of dialogue that we can regard that particular incident with equanimity? I think not.

Personally, in terms of sibling rivalry, I prefer the image given us by Rabbi Alexandra Wright – of Rachel who wrestled with God some time before Jacob did, and who afterwards is truly reconciled with her sister.[3] Their relationship contains the same elements of rivalry, of trickery and of supplanting but without the threat of violence that accompanies the brothers' story. As Carol Gilligan suggests[4] boy's games/men's actions are dominated by laws and principles which must be adhered to at all costs. Girl's games/women's actions are determined by relationships which become much more important than rules. In dialogue we are talking relationships, not rules. If we stood by our religious principles we would not – could not – be talking together, therefore a female model presents a better picture of what we wish to achieve.

Indeed, the Midrash gives us two examples of how this could be a useful metaphor for our situation. In one, the question is asked why the matriarchs are barren and the answer is given, because God wishes to hear voices in supplication. In the cases of Sarah and Rebeccah, it is their husbands who pray to God. In the case of Rachel all four wives of Jacob come together in prayer for her to be blessed with a child.[5] The image of four women, from different backgrounds, of different faiths, all praying together for what just one of them needs – that is a powerful image of partnership.

But there is another Midrash in which the destruction of the Temple and Jerusalem by the Babylonians is considered.[6] The People Israel has lost its Temple and is in exile as punishment for the sin of idolatry. God is about to depart from the people when the ministering angels intervene and ask God to reconsider. God agrees to summon up Abraham, Isaac, Jacob and Moses to plead for the people, but remains unmoved by them. Then Rachel, unbidden, breaks through the ranks and before God says,

> Sovereign of the Universe, it is revealed before Thee that Thy servant Jacob loved me exceedingly and toiled for my father on my behalf seven years. When those seven years were completed and the time arrived for my marriage with my husband, my father planned to substitute another for me to wed for the sake of my sister. It was very hard for me, because the plot was known to me and I disclosed it to my husband; and I gave him a sign whereby he could distinguish between me and my sister, so that my father should not be able to make the substitution. After that I relented, suppressed my desire, and had pity upon my sister that she should not be exposed to shame. In the evening they substituted my sister for me with my husband, and I delivered over to my sister all the signs which I had arranged with my husband so that he should think that she was Rachel. More than that, I went beneath the bed upon which he lay with my sister; and when he spoke to her she remained silent and I made all the replies in order that he should not recognise my sister's voice. I did her a kindness, was not jealous of her, and did not expose her to shame. And if I, a creature of flesh and blood, formed of dust and ashes, was not envious of my rival and did not expose her to shame and contempt, why shouldest Thou, a King Who liveth eternally and art merciful, be jealous of idolatry in which there is no reality.[7]

God on hearing these words relents and does not cast off the people forever.

In the Midrash it is the fact that Rachel was able to overcome her envy in such an impossible situation that ensures God's continuing presence in the world; how much more so in this secular age is the overcoming of our tensions and differences vital to ensure God's continuing presence in this postmodern secular, materialistic and confused world.

This same proem contains the phrase that Rabbi Brichto quoted to us in the discussion about modernity and postmodernity; the words 'Woe to the King who succeeded in youth, but failed in old age.'[8]

The king here is God – a daring, if not alarming, picture. But it need not present, as Rabbi Brichto suggested, the possibility of the death of God. In the context of the *Shoah* and the seeming absence of God from the world at that period, it could be a testament to the powerlessness of the divine in the face of human savagery. We have not a dying God but a changing God.

This calls to mind the conversation in Torah that Moses has with God after the people have erected the golden calf.[9] God initially decides to destroy the people but Moses points out that God's reputation in the world depends on the survival of the nation.

Why should the Egyptians say 'with evil intent did he bring them forth to slay them in the mountains and to consume them from the face of the earth'?[10]

So God 'repents' the intention.

We have now looked at two incidents where God threatened to leave Israel: after the incident with the golden calf, and after the idolatry that led to the destruction of the Temple. In both cases it is human beings that persuaded the divine presence to remain with the people. Today, after the grossest form of idolatry that was Nazi ideology, it is easy to say – as so many do – that God is no longer with us.

It is up to us, we the religious, to reaffirm God's presence, to restore God's reputation among the unbelieving of the world, and this time we must do it together. In a changing world, with a changing God we must promote a changing religious outlook if we – and therefore God – are to survive.

Setting the Agenda

I propose, before meeting together again, we Jews meet and prepare ourselves for future encounter.

We should consider the following emerging from the themes of this conference:

1. Partnership in Covenant. This is less significant for Jews today, but in the light of the importance Catholics place on this we have a duty to look carefully at our covenantal relationship with God and examine what place Catholics and others have in this.

2. Understanding election. Many references were made to the election of all. What does this really mean? Should we be changing our liturgy from 'who has chosen us from all peoples' to 'chosen us with all peoples'?

3. Reading our sacred texts. Today it is time we Jews read the New Testament and studied it with Christian teachers in order to gain a Christian understanding. Only then will we be able to

understand how Catholics use our Bible, and only then can a true dialogue over texts begin.

4. The challenge of modernism and postmodernism. Here issues of individuality versus communality raised its head. Progressive Jews think and are educated as individuals, yet our faith still reflects a communality – we are all Israel. But is this helpful in understanding the other?

5. Religion, government and society. We must look closely at the role religion plays today in the world. We are now a leisure activity rather than the core of a person's being. How does that change our faith? For the first time, in Israel, Jews are in a position of power rather than powerlessness. Can we learn from the Catholic Church how to use and not abuse that power?

6. What are the values we bring to partnership? *Tikkun olam* – the reparation of the world was reiterated several times as the common goal, but can we 'do theology together'? Can Jews involve themselves in Christology and soteriology? We need to learn and understand more before we can tackle these issues.

A future conference is a must. We have started something tremendous here and we have only scratched the surface of fundamental issues. My hope is that such a conference to be held in eighteen months or two years will develop these themes, while small working parties meet and exchange views, learn and develop their understandings in the meantime.

Notes

1. Gen. 33.4.
2. *Midrash Rabbah Genesis* 78.9.
3. Gen. 30.8.
4. Carol Gilligan, *In a Different Voice: Psychological Theory and Women's Development*, Cambridge, MA, and London: Harvard University Press, 1982.
5. *Midrash Rabbah Song of Songs* 2.41.
6. *Midrash Rabbah Lamentations Proem* 24.
7. Ibid., Soncino edition, London 1977, p. 48.
8. Ibid., p. 43.
9. Ex. 32.7–14 .
10. Ex. 32.12.

Kieran Heskin

Someone said to me early on in the conference, when they discovered the stage at which I was to enter the proceedings, 'all you need say when your time to speak comes is: "there is one person who has not been mentioned so far in this conference and that is God!" ' I cannot, however, make that assertion. God has been to the fore in our thoughts and proceedings. We began and ended our daily deliberations with acts of worship. The first half of the conference, which dealt with Covenant, election and sacred texts constantly pointed us in the direction of the source of our being.

The first point, however, that I would like to make is that those of us who are Catholics have perhaps something to learn from our inter-church dialogue that may be of benefit for our inter-faith dialogue. As we look back over the past fifty or so years of dialogue between our Church and other churches, we can see the tremendous change that has resulted from a change of focus. For centuries we concentrated on visible structures and on visible differences rather than on our relationship with God and on what we shared in common. We were great advocates of 'Perfect Society' theology. In our thinking the Catholic Church and the state were two perfect societies because they had within them all the means that they required to achieve their ends. Membership of the Church was in the words of Robert Bellarmine 'as tangible as membership of the State of Venice'. Those were members who were baptized, accepted papal authority and all the means instituted by Christ for salvation, for example, the seven sacraments. In accordance with this kind of thinking there was no accommodation for Protestant, Jew or Muslim.

The Second Vatican Council, as mentioned by Dr Ondrako, produced a major breakthrough in our dealings with other churches and with other faiths. When the Bishops in Council looked beyond the visible structures of our Church and how it differed visibly from other churches, they discovered that all Christians claimed a special relationship with Jesus, there were great similarities in their manner of worship, for example, in their celebration of Baptism and the Lord's Supper and in their use of the Bible . . . Likewise, when they looked at other faiths, for example, the Jewish Faith, they discovered communities who worshiped the one true God, who were guided by the revealed word of God . . . They accordingly developed a theology in *Lumen Gentium* that accommodated in a respectful and positive manner the faith and cultic activity of other churches and faiths.

In view of the above, if we are to make progress in our dialogue with each other we would be wise:

- to keep God at the centre of our deliberations
- to see what unites us at least as clearly as we see what divides us
- to develop an understanding and appreciation of each other's cultic practices.

The second point that I would like to make is that although much has been written and a great deal of progress has been made in Catholic–Jewish relations over the past thirty-five years, one wonders how much consciousness there is of this at 'grass-roots' level among either Catholics or Jews. I wrote an article for *The Tablet* in March 1996 in which I said, 'what happened in Christ's passion cannot be blamed on all the Jews then living, without distinction, nor upon any of the Jews of today'. This is a point that has been made in three Vatican documents over the previous thirty years. As soon as the article appeared, the Religious Correspondent of *The Times* (London) was on the 'phone saying, 'Your 'phone must be very busy today in view of your provocative article.' My comments were carried by *The Times* the next day. I discovered some weeks later that it was also reported as the second item on radio news in Jerusalem that weekend. Thirty-one years after the publication of *Nostra Aetate*, one of its central statements was considered a groundbreaking statement in the United Kingdom and Israel. This made me aware of the difference between putting the right statements in place and diffusing their contents.

As summarizers we have been asked to make some suggestions as to where we might move from here. As I look to the future, I would like to see a Jewish statement on Jewish–Catholic relations, perhaps in the form of a response to the Vatican documents on Catholic–Jewish relations. For me one of the most striking statements of the conference occurred in Rabbi Tony Bayfield's paper where he said that he acknowledges the New Testament as a book of revelation for Christians, as a document describing what he would characterize as a covenantal experience. This is a comment that could perhaps be fleshed out by the World Union for Progressive Judaism. This is something that you could do very much on your own between this and whatever meeting may ensue from this. This city could then be remembered in circles such as ours not only for the Balfour Declaration – a declaration that had such a profound effect on Jewish and world history – but also for the 'Bayfield Declaration'.

My second hope for the future would be that we would

increasingly support and affirm each other in a world that is full of challenge to both our faiths. There was a lovely example of such support during the Pope's recent visit to Israel. Rabbi David Rosen, who has been here with us, was asked on television: 'Will the Pope apologize on behalf of the Church for Anti-Judaism?' Rabbi Rosen said, 'He will apologize for the sins of individuals in this regard.' The question was asked again: 'But will he apologize on behalf of the Church?' Rabbi Rosen replied: 'The Pope cannot apologize on behalf of the Church because in Catholic theology the Church is regarded as the mystical body of Christ. It is therefore not possible for the Pope to apologize on behalf of the Church, his apology will be in relation to members of the Church.' It was very moving to see a Rabbi explaining the Pope's difficulties in terms of Catholic theology. That is the kind of understanding, sensitivity and co-operation to which all of us who are engaged in Jewish–Christian dialogue should aspire.

Finally, the point has been made by Rabbi Professor Magonet that Christians have much to learn from sources such as rabbinic Midrash and the medieval Jewish commentators. I agree but I must also add that I have a very vivid memory of Robert Gordis emphasizing in conversation that the reverse is also true: ideas that occur in seminal form in the Hebrew scriptures often appear in more fully grown and developed form in patristic, medieval and modern Christian thought. The light of revelation has shone on both our traditions and as a consequence we are each capable of enriching the other. In the years ahead, under the guiding hand of the one, true God, may we do just that.

Mark Winer

This conference arose out of the interreligious endeavour to make the Millennium a turning point in the relationships among religions. We hope to use the energy of Millennial Madness to get religions to put aside their past mutual demonization. Interreligious dialogue and action has already begun to change the world. One of the central themes in the papacy of Pope John Paul II has been repentance for the history of Christian anti-Semitism. He has termed the century which we are now concluding 'the Century of the *Shoah*' – the Century of the Holocaust, the century which gave the world the most extreme example of human evil. Imagine, the twentieth century, the century in which we were born and lived our lives, the twentieth century may be remembered most for the worst horror ever perpetrated by human beings. Indeed, more people died during the twentieth century because of religious intolerance than in all of history combined. The twentieth century has not only been the century of the *Shoah*. It has also been the century of Bosnia, of Northern Ireland, of India and Pakistan, of Rwanda, of Kosovo. We used to think that we were more civilized than people who lived a thousand or two thousand years ago.

Precisely because the past century has been so destructive, we should concentrate on making the future better. For me the central message of the late Rabbi Hugo Gryn's teaching was that our experience of the *Shoah* must redouble effort to construct a world which would not permit a Holocaust to be visited upon any people on the face of the earth. He rejected the use of Jewish suffering for any kind of Jewish moral triumphalism. Hugo Gryn insisted that we work for *Tikkun olam*, building alliances with others to 'repair the world'. And more and more of the others, particularly in the Christian world, really have become our partners.

The Talmud relates a story of a rabbi who asks where the Messiah is. Told that the Messiah sits at the gates of Rome, he goes there and asks him, 'When are you coming?' The Messiah responds, *'HaYom – im b'kolo tishma'oo'*, 'Today, if you would hearken to God's voice'. (Ps. 95.7). The coming of the Messiah depends upon us, if we would only hearken unto God's commandments.

For a long time, Judaism has concentrated its focus on bringing about the messianic kingdom through action. The *mitzvah* (religious obligation) system and righteous action, prayer and *Tikkun olam* – that is the Jewish way. As in many other aspects of the Jewish tradition, Jewish messianism is dialectical. As the twentieth-century Jewish theologian Emil Fackenheim puts it, we Jews work to bring about the coming of the Messiah by performing righteous deeds as if all depends upon human action. And we pray as if all depends upon God.

A vignette illustrates the Jewish idea of the coming of the Messiah. A rabbi was visiting Jerusalem. Shopping for a book, he stopped in a local bookstore. After selling him the book, the bookseller said to him, 'The Messiah is coming. Get ready.' The rabbi thanked him very much for the tip, and laughed all the way home. But then, he got to thinking, just in case he ought to get ready. He went to the Western Wall, and prayed all night, waiting for the Messiah.

Just as he had expected, the Messiah didn't come. He went to the bookstore to complain to the bookseller. 'I stayed up all night at the Wall, waiting for the Messiah, but the Messiah never came.' 'Oh', said the bookseller, 'You were waiting for the Messiah? While you were waiting for the Messiah, the Messiah was waiting for you.'

Post-millennialists realize that whatever change is possible in the order of the world comes through careful planning, discipline, hard work and continual focus. A life which combines religious practice and social action advances the cause of making the world a better place. Rituals and traditions keep us focused and disciplined, as we inevitably encounter frustrations, disappointments, opposition and rejection. Those who know ultimate truth, those who claim they never sin, those who demonize others who disagree with them – they are the enemies of the real Messiah.

Interreligious dialogue is a relatively new concept, a product of the modern world's uneasy embrace of pluralism. From a pluralistic perspective, those loyal to their own commitments affirm the legitimacy and authenticity of the distinctively different commitments of others. As Diana Eck emphasizes, pluralism is the opposite of the relativism or universalism of 'we are really all the same'. Pluralism celebrates diversity and mutual respect for the differences among people.

The stake in pluralism and in its religious manifestation is crucial. Every modern religion has a major fault line between its fundamentalists and pluralists. Unless our world learns to live in pluralism, human beings will sooner or later destroy civilization through modern technology. As Hans Küng has written, 'No peace between nations, without peace between the religions. No peace between the religions without dialogue between the religions.'

The idea of ongoing, positive interfaith relationships – at least among mainstream religious bodies – is firmly entrenched in the modern world. Ministers, priests and rabbis exchange pulpits, host each other's congregations, and dialogue on a wide variety of religious, social and political issues. They often serve together on commissions to promote social harmony and avert conflict. Nationally, cooperation is the norm among major denominations on a panoply of humanitarian and political issues. The commitment of British society and the modern world to diversity should not be taken for granted. Democracy is a fragile commodity. It is preserved only by diligent labour, by the utmost vigilance, and by cautious, principled alliance-building among society's constituent groups. It is to that labour, to that vigilance, and to that alliance-building that we must become dedicated.

For the vast majority of human beings, and particularly for those who regard religion as the vessel for instilling loving and progressive values, the tempest of religious intolerance has elicited defensive reaction and retreat. As the British-Jewish community turns increasingly inward to address questions of continuity, it is in danger of losing sight of the need for building community and common values in the larger society and throughout the world. Similarly, many non-fundamentalist Christians and other moderate human beings have withdrawn from global concerns in the wake of fundamentalist religious polarization.

The modern world's epidemic of interreligious bigotry can be healed. To do so we must assert the values of pluralism, social responsibility and education as a part of the effort to bring people of opposing views together and to contain extremism. We Progressive Jews challenge others of all religious orientations to respond to their traditional roots in generating compelling visions of the positive possibilities for human interaction. We urge them to respond to these visions by constructing coalitions of common concern for nurturing our dysfunctional human family toward greater health.

Words alone are insufficient. The work of interreligious reconciliation requires a core of lay and clergy activists knowledgeable across the spectrum of religious experience and trained in the skills of community organization and conflict resolution. While many express religious beliefs, along with political and other views, intervention into the intense values-laden issues that shape the interreligious arena demands thoroughly trained volunteers and credentialed professionals. Thus, the first objective for interreligious dialogue and action should be to develop the discipline of interreligious studies and activities through advanced degree programmes, seminars and workshops.

We must facilitate cooperative relations among the existing interreligious bodies. We should build upon our existing relationships with the full range of national and international Catholic, Protestant, Evangelical, Orthodox Christian, Muslim and other non-Christian world religious central bodies, striving to stimulate and support joint bilateral and multilateral activities. While much has been accomplished in the realm of interreligious understanding since the end of the Second World War – most notably, the work of the Second Vatican Council as embodied in *Nostra Aetate* – serious interreligious tensions and antagonism persist throughout the world. The last quarter of the twentieth century has witnessed the intensification of some of these antagonisms into chronic states of religious and political warfare, giving rise to unprecedented acts of violence and terrorism.

Less dramatically, but no less importantly, this same period has also been characterized by an increasing sense of moral malaise. Traditional values and behaviours have been abandoned or transformed, witness the stunning increases worldwide of family dissolution through divorce and abandonment, and children born out of wedlock. The 'cultural wars' around life-style issues have broadened into political battles, in Iran and in many other Islamic countries, most notably, but also in Israel, in India, and in Japan. In some instances, religious fundamentalists have become political extremists.

The role of religion in political activity has never been more hotly debated. Almost everywhere, fundamentalist and conservative religious groups have dominated the debate over family and social values, calling for unforgiving remedies that negate traditional religious values of social compassion. Christian and Jewish moderates have not taken leadership in addressing the issues of social conflict and decay. This reflects the failure of religious liberals and moderates to set the terms of debate and the parameters of politically acceptable solutions. Thus, for the most part, the traditional religious values of social compassion have disappeared from the public debate on the most compelling issues of the day.

This is not to say that those espousing cultural pluralism have been entirely overshadowed in the current debate. Still, the proponents of diversity have been unsuccessful in articulating the value base underlying their world-view of mutual respect. The traditionally broad-minded values of fairness and support for the disadvantaged have been overwhelmed in the current debate.

Tikkun olam – repairing the world – is not easy work. In a passage attributed to the second-century Rabbi Tarfon, *Mishnaic* Tractate *Pirke Abot* reassures us in our multi-millennial messianic labour to repair the world.

'Hayom katzeir v'hamlachah m'rubah v'hapoalim atzelim v'hasachar harbay uvaal habayit dochek. Lo alecha hamlacha ligmor, v'lo ata ben chorin l'hibatel mimenna'. 'The day is short, the labour is enormous, and the workers are lazy. The pay-off is also enormous and the Master urges us on. It is not incumbent upon us to complete the task, but neither are we free to desist from it.'

7

Concluding the Encounter
– Sidney Brichto

The feelings of warmth between the Catholic and Jewish conferees was almost palpable. Indeed, I could go so far as to say that the spirit of understanding which had developed between the two polarities of the Abrahamic faiths was stronger than those between the Jewish participants. Perhaps, this is because on the Jewish side the differences regarding our faith and practice impinge on our daily lives as we seek to persuade each other towards our own view. No doubt on the Catholic side there is also tension as it too confronts the demands of the modern world for change. There must be 'modernists' and traditionalists within the Catholic hierarchy as there are within the ranks of Progressive rabbis. As we work to bring people into the Kingdom of God, our differences create that very disharmony which we are seeking to remove from human life. Did not St Paul call St Peter a hypocrite and did not the patriarch Gamaliel compel the great Elisha ben Abuyah to appear before him with his staff and money purse on the day that the most revered sage argued, in opposition to the patriarch, was the Day of Atonement, the holiest day of the Jewish year?

It is a cause for concern within the Jewish community that the Chief Rabbi of the United Hebrew Congregations of Great Britain and the Commonwealth can accept the pluralism that allows him to recognize and come so close to the leaders of other faiths, but is not able to do so with those of his own community. This has led the patron of this conference, Sir Sigmund Sternberg, to suggest that it may now be more important to have a Council of Jews and Jews than a Council of Christians and Jews. The same applies within many Christian denominations and within the Muslim world. Too often, religious leaders, partly because they are convinced that they are God's representatives, and partly because they suffer in the imperfection of their humanity, lack that humility which is the basis of true understanding and sympathy.

The humility and understanding that I experienced in dialogue with representatives of the Catholic Church convinced me that these colloquia must continue, not only to move forward towards a greater appreciation of each other's faith but also to teach us to be more understanding and more charitable in spirit to those within our own communities, where differences can have an even greater impact on the lives of our members.

Rabbi Bayfield's image of the reconciliation between Esau and Jacob (p. 1) for the partnership being forged between Catholic and Jew was challenged by Rabbi Sheridan, who preferred the image of the conflict between Rachel and Leah (p. 253). Both are appropriate for the reasons they offer. I would suggest a compromise. 'Esau–Jacob' is more appropriate to the reconciliation of Christian and Jew because while they came from the same source, they struggled with each other in their youth and their enmity forced them to live at a distance from each other. 'Rachel–Leah' is appropriate to reconciliations within intra-faith relationships as both sisters not only came from the same stock but were always bound to each other by their marriage to Jacob. The analogy is apposite because the tension between two competitive sisters living together must be greater than that of Esau and Jacob, whom even after their reconciliation never met again until their father's funeral.

But Catholics and Jews must do better than did our ancestors. Jacob made a promise to Esau which he broke. Fearing that the reconciliation between Esau and himself might dissipate, he declines his suggestion that they journey together. He makes an excuse and tells him that they will meet again in Seir, when he has no intention of doing so (Gen. 33.12–14). While Jews and Catholics have struggled and wept together, they must now unlike Jacob and Esau never part company. We must journey together! The reconciliation is the foundation, not the pinnacle of our joint ambition to bring the whole world into God's Kingdom.

This was Cardinal Edward Cassidy's conclusion in the final words of our conference: 'Unless I know how you differ from me, I cannot really understand you.' This is the call for mutual respect of each other's beliefs and ideals. But these words were followed by the affirmation of our unity and the challenge to carry on our work together for the benefit of the world:

Election is a gift we have received from God so that we can be a gift to others – to bring hope in their lives. I feel we have achieved a deeper understanding of each other and I welcome future dialogues to help us meet the challenges of a democratic and pluralistic world in the twenty-first century.

These words imply that the task before us requires more than mutual understanding and respect. That is the foundation of the building, which is to fulfil the mission that God gave to Abraham: 'To be a blessing unto the nations'. Our 'Partnership in Theology' has a greater objective. It is to build together. Isaiah said to our ancestors: 'It is too small a task for you to serve me only to preserve the tribes of Jacob and to restore the survivors of Israel – I will make you a light to the nations, so that my salvation may reach to the ends of the earth.' This was the mission that the prophets accepted on behalf of Israel and the apostles accepted as the core of their own Christian faith. This is the meaning of election as Cardinal Cassidy so movingly said – to bring hope into the lives of others.

What is to be the nature of future dialogues 'to meet the challenges of a democratic and pluralistic world in the twenty-first century'? I welcome the suggestions made by the last three contributors to this volume, but would like to add my own. At the next colloquium we should define the terminology of our faiths. The relationship of Covenant and Election will need to be explored. Does membership of a covenanted people make an individual 'elected', or does it require individual commitment or a constant affirmation of faith? The Christian concept of 'Grace' will need to be understood by Jews as the vehicle for God's help in achieving personal salvation. Is the *Z'hut Avot* – the merit of the ancestors – the Jewish equivalent, by which Jews, regardless of their personal behaviour, remain part of an *Am segulah*, God's missionary people, which enables them to accept the privilege and responsibility of 'chosenness'. Of course, 'chosenness' will need to be fully debated. In a pluralist world, 'chosenness' appears as politically incorrect. It was significant that at our conference, the Jewish delegates had a greater problem in coming to terms with the concept than did their Catholic counterparts.

The revolutionary acceptance by the Vatican of the validity of the Jewish Covenant will also require further clarification. Does this new 'openness' towards the possibilities for salvation also apply to Islam? And what of those agnostics who lead a life of selfless commitment to the mission of *Tikkun olam*? How do we, not only Catholics but Jews and members of other religious faiths, work with them, and how do they fit into the picture of our vision for the fulfilment of the Messianic age? This could have been one of the challenges to which Cardinal Cassidy was alluding: taking note of the reality that there are many 'godless' people who are walking in his ways while men who subscribe to faith in Him have been guilty of defacing the humanity created in his image.

Another challenge of the pluralist democratic world will be the conflict between authority and autonomy. What are the religious foundations of our faith which we cannot surrender to the democratic vote? How can Catholicism and Judaism deal with situations where deep differences may arise between them and democratic governments, for example, over abortion, the death penalty, the banning of *shehitah* or circumcision. The attempt, often successful, to change the images of our faith to comply with non-sexist attitudes should also be explored with respect and courtesy. While these are problems internal to each of the faiths, it may very well be that dialogues on these issues will be considered with greater understanding in a larger forum when we are already committed to respect and even learn from the deep differences which we recognize divide us.

The modern challenges to both our faiths are enormous, but both Catholic Christianity and Judaism has shown the resilience to meet similar ones over the millennia. No doubt, we will with God's inspiration meet them in the future as we have in the past. The question is whether our dialogues can help us together to meet the challenges, and even to rise above them to fulfil the destiny promised to the ancestors of our faiths – as the Cardinal said so simply but so profoundly: 'to be a gift to others – to bring hope into their lives'. The Cardinal and the participants in the Millennium Conference left with the belief that our newly formed partnership could help achieve this. So let us now take the next step which is to arrange to meet again soon.

The Contributors and Participants

Bayfield, Rabbi Tony Professional head of the Reform Jewish Movement in Britain. A graduate of Leo Baeck College and former congregational rabbi, he has been involved in interfaith dialogue for many years. Currently convenes a Jewish–Christian–Muslim dialogue group. With Marcus Braybrooke published *Dialogue with a Difference*, the fruits of a nine-year long Christian–Jewish Dialogue Group.

Ben-Chorin, Rabbi Tovia Serves Congregation JLG Or Chadasch Zurich. Born and grew up in Jerusalem. 1961, BA Hebrew University. 1964, ordination Hebrew Union College, Cincinnati. Served congregations in Israel and Manchester (1974–7). Active in interfaith (Israel/Europe) for two decades.

Block, Rabbi Richard A. July 1999 became Chief Executive of the World Union for Progressive Judaism in Jerusalem. Prior to rabbinical studies graduated with honours from Yale Law School. 1982, ordination, Hebrew Union College, Cincinnati. 1987–99, Senior Rabbi of Congregation Beth Am Los Altos Hills, California. Active in all aspects of communal life and author of many publications.

Boys, Professor Mary C. SNJM Skinner and McAlpin Professor of Practical Theology at Union Theological Seminary in New York City. Among her books are *Jewish–Christian Dialogue: One Woman's Experience* (1997) and *Has God only One Blessing? Judaism as a Source of Christian Self-Understanding* (2000) (both from Paulist Press).

Brichto, Rabbi Dr Sidney Executive Vice-President and Director of the Union of Liberal and Progressive Synagogues (1964–89). Chairman of Council of Reform and Liberal Rabbis (1974–6). Co-founder of the Israel Diaspora Trust (1982–). Director of the Joseph Levy Charitable Foundation (1989–99). Writer and Bible translator.

Cassidy, Edward Idris Cardinal Australian-born former Apostolic Pro-Nuncio to China and Bangladesh and Apostolic Delegate to Southern Africa. President, Pontifical Council for Promoting Christian Unity, and Commission for Religious Relations with the Jews 1989–2001.

Cullen, Fr Peter Catholic Chaplain at the University of Sheffield. Co-Chair of the Sheffield Branch of the Council of Christians and Jews (CCJ) and Vice-Chair of their Dialogue Committee. Involved with the work of CCJ since 1990.

Dorff, Professor Elliot N. Ordained 1970 a Conservative rabbi by Jewish Theological Seminary of America. 1971 earned Ph.D. in Philosophy, Columbia University. He has, since then, directed the rabbinical and masters programmes at the University of Judaism, where he is currently Rector and Professor of Philosophy. He teaches a course on Jewish Law at the University of California, Los Angeles.

Fisher, Dr Eugene J. Since 1977 staff person in charge of Catholic–Jewish Relations for the National Conference of Catholic Bishops (USA). Since 1980 Consulter to the Holy See's Commission for Religious Relations with Jews and a member of the International Catholic–Jewish Liaison Committee (ILC). Currently also serving as Catholic Co-ordinator for the ILC's International Historical Commission studying the twelve volumes of published material from the Vatican archives.

Goldberg, Rabbi Dr David J. Senior Rabbi, The Liberal Jewish Synagogue. 1999, awarded Gold Medallion of International Council of Christians and Jews for Interfaith work. Winner of 1999 *Premio Iglesias* for *Verso la Terra Promessa* (translation of his book *To the Promised Land: A History of Zionist Thought*).

Goldstein, Rabbi Dr Andrew Senior, Rabbi Northwood and Pinner Liberal Synagogue which he has served for over thirty years. Co-editor of the new Union of Liberal and Progressive Synagogues *High Holy Day Prayer Book* and is on the Theology Committee of the International Council of Christians and Jews.

Henderson, Right Reverend Charles J. Bishop of Tricala and Area Bishop of Southwark. Chairman, The Committee for Catholic Jewish Relations. Vice-Chairman, Council of Christians and Jews.

Heschel, Professor Susannah Eli Black Professor of Jewish Studies at Dartmouth College where she chairs the Jewish Studies Programme. Author of several books on Jewish–Christian relations and on feminism and religion including *Abraham Geiger and the Jewish Jesus* and *Feminist Readings of Classical Jewish Texts*.

Heskin, Revd Dr Kieran Vicar General in the Diocese of Leeds, Moderator of the Curia and a Parish Priest. He is a member of the Committee for Catholic–Jewish Relations of the Catholic Bishop's Conference of England and Wales and Joint Chairman of Leeds Council of Christians and Jews.

Hilton, Rabbi Dr Michael Serves Kol Chai – Hatch End Jewish Community in North West London. He is the author of *The Gospels and Rabbinic Judaism* and *The Christian Effect on Jewish Life*.

Jardine, Sr Clare nds Co-Director of the Study Centre for Christian–Jewish Relations in London having completed studies at Heythrop College, University of London, and Leo Baeck College, London. Currently teaching a course on Christian–Jewish Relations at Heythrop College.

Keenan, Peter W. Adviser to the Department for Mission and Unity of the Catholic Bishop's Conference of England and Wales, in which capacity he acts as Secretary to the Committee for Catholic–Jewish Relations. He is also a member of the Board of the CCJ. Head of the Religious Studies Department of St Dominic's Sixth Form College, Harrow, Middlesex.

Kelly, Sr Mary nds Mary Kelly is a sister of Sion. Co–Director of the Study Centre for Christian–Jewish Relations in London. 1987–97 she edited the SIDIC journal which is published in Rome.

Kronish, Rabbi Dr Ron Director of the Interreligious Coordinating Council in Israel (ICCI). Rabbi, educator, author, lecturer and speaker. Over the past nineteen years in Jerusalem has served as Director, Israel Office of the American Jewish Committee (1988–92), Co-Director the Melitz Centres for Jewish Zionist Education (1979–88) and as a lecturer in education at Tel Aviv University and Hebrew University, Jerusalem.

McDade, Revd John SJ Principal of Heythrop College, University of London. He teaches Systematic Theology and Christian–Jewish Relations.

McGarry, Fr Michael   Paulist priest originally from Los Angeles, worked on his graduate theology at St Michael's College in the University of Toronto and later at the Hebrew University in Jerusalem. Author of *Christology after Auschwitz*; he has been involved for many years in Jewish–Christian relations and *Shoah* education. Currently Rector of the Tantur Ecumenical Institute in Jerusalem.

Magonet, Rabbi Professor Jonathan   Principal, Leo Baeck College where he also lectures in Hebrew Bible. For over thirty years he has co-organized the annual Jewish–Christian Bible Week and for twenty-seven years the Jewish–Christian–Muslim Student Conference at Bendorf. He is a Vice-President of the World Union of Progressive Judaism.

May, Dr John D'Arcy   Postgraduate study in ecumenical theology at the Catholic Ecumenical Institute, University of Munster, where he taught for eight years after receiving his doctorate in 1975. 1983 Doctorate in History of Religions from the University of Frankfurt. 1983–7, ecumenical work, Papua New Guinea. 1987–90, Director of the Irish School of Ecumenics in Dublin, where he is currently Associate Professor of Interfaith Dialogue and Ethics.

Middleburgh, Rabbi Dr Charles H.   Executive Director of the Union of Liberal and Progressive Synagogues. He has a BA Hons in Ancient and Medieval Hebrew and Aramaic and a Ph.D. in Targumic Studies. He lectures at Leo Baeck College in rabbinic practice.

Murray, Dr Robert   Jesuit priest. Lecturer in Biblical Studies, Heythrop College (University of London). Sometime teacher of Aramaic at Leo Baeck College, London. Experienced participant in Jewish–Christian shared Bible study, Bendorf and elsewhere.

Ondrako, Revd Dr Edward J. OFM Conv   Conventual Franciscan Friar. Graduate of the Humanities Doctoral programme at Syracuse University where he wrote about the controversy between W. E. Gladstone and J. H. Newman and its relation to Vatican II. He has been a Newman Chaplain for twenty years, and is Theologian in Residence at Cornell University where he teaches religious studies.

Parsons, Revd Richard   Priest of the Diocese of Westminster. Teaches at St Dominic's College, Harrow, the Diocesan Seminary, Allen Hall, and the Mill Hill Missionary Institute. Has a particular interest in Ecumenical Theology. Currently studying with the Catholic University of Louvain in Belgium.

Pawlikowski, John T. OSM Ph.D.   Priest of the Servite Order. Professor of Social Ethics, Catholic Theological Union, Chicago. Since 1980, member of US Catholic Bishops Advisory Committee on Catholic Jewish Relations and by Presidential appointment on Executive Committee of US Holocaust Memorial Council and chairs its Church Relations Committee. Written and edited more than 20 books.

Romain, Rabbi Dr Jonathan   Minister of Maidenhead Synagogue in Berkshire. He is also well known as a writer and broadcaster both on Reform Judaism and mixed-faith marriages. He is currently finishing a book on religious conversions in modern Britain.

Rosen, Rabbi David   Former Chief Rabbi of Ireland. Currently Director of the Israel Office of the Anti-Defamation League and the ADL's Co-Liaison to the Vatican. President of the International Council of Christians and Jews and the World Conference on Religion and Peace. Key Israeli negotiator involved in the establishment of full relations between the Vatican and Israel.

Sarah, Rabbi Elizabeth Tikva   Rabbi of Brighton Progressive Jewish Congregation. Co-Rabbi of the Jewish Lesbian and Gay Group. Lecturer at Leo Baeck College where she chairs the Rabbinic In-Service Training Team. She has edited three books and contributed some three dozen articles to various journals and is currently writing a book, *Teaching Texts and Telling Tales: A Jewish Feminist Exploration of Torah*.

Scholefield, Dr Lynne   Lecturer in Religious Studies at St Mary's College, Strawberry Hill. Her doctorate used dialogue as a way of approaching a study of the culture of a Jewish and Catholic secondary school. She is both researching and participating in women's Jewish–Christian dialogue.

Shepherd, Sr Margaret nds   Sister of Sion. Director, The Council of Christians and Jews. MTh; Dip Jewish Studies; BA; Dip Ed.

Publications: *Dialogue with a Difference* (1992); *Splashes of God-light* (1997); *The Holocaust and the Christian World* (2000).

Sheridan, Rabbi Sybil   Studied Theology and Religious Studies at Cambridge University before training for the Rabbinate. Rabbi of Thames Valley Progressive Jewish Community. Lecturer at Leo Baeck College. She is the Jewish representative on the Bishops' Conference Committee for Catholic–Jewish Relations and active in many inter-faith groups.

Solomon, Rabbi Mark BA (Hons) MA   Born in Australia. Ordained at Jews College, London. Lecturer in Talmud at Leo Baeck College. Rabbi at the Liberal Jewish Synagogue, London. He is deeply involved in interfaith dialogue.

Soskice, Dr Janet Martin   University Lecturer in Theology and Fellow of Jesus College, Cambridge. Past President of the Catholic Theological Association of Great Britain. 1997, McCarthy Visiting Professor at the Gregorian University, Rome. Author of *Metaphor and Religious Language* (1984).

Spillman, Dr Joann   Associate Professor and Chair of the Dept of Theology and Religious Studies, Rockhurst University, Kansas City, US. She received her Ph.D. from Temple University. She is active in the Christian Scholars' Group of the Institute for Christian and Jewish Studies. Publications include 'The Image of Covenant in Christian Understandings of Judaism' in the *JES*, Winter 1998.

Sternberg, Sir Sigmund   Hungarian-born businessman and leading figure in international interfaith affairs. Awarded Papal Knighthood in 1985. Templeton Prize for Progress in Religion, 1998. President, Reform Synagogues of Great Britain.

Stroumsa, Professor Guy   Born in France. Martin Buber Professor of Comparative Religion and Director, Centre for the Study of Christianity, at Hebrew University, Jerusalem. Most recently published *Barbarian Philosophy: The Religious Revolution of Early Christianity* (1999) and *La formazion dell' identita Cristiana* (1999).

Tabick, Rabbi Jacqueline   Rabbi of North West Surrey Synagogue in Weybridge; Chair of the World Congress of Faiths; member of the Inter-Faith Network Executive and Westminster Diocesan Committee for Refugees. Vice-President, Reform Synagogues of Great Britain.

Thoma, Prof Dr Clemens SVD Dean of Institute for Jewish–Christian Research at University College, Luzern, since 1981. Professor for biblical studies and Judaism at the Theological Faculty, Luzern, since 1971. First editor of 'Freiberger Rundbrief' and since 1976 consultant for issues of the Church's relations to Judaism at the Vatican Secretariat for Christian Unity.

Van Luyn, Mgr Adrian H. SDB Member of the Society of St François de Sales. Appointed Bishop of Rotterdam in 1993. President of the Episcopal Commission for Judeo-Christian Relations. Vice-Chancellor of the Theologische Faculteit of the Katholieke Universiteit, Nijmegen. President Pax Christi, Nederland, and member of the Pontifical Council for Culture since 1998.

Winer, Rabbi Dr Mark Senior Rabbi, West London Synagogue; Chairman, Interreligious Affairs, World Union for Progressive Judaism; President, National Council of Synagogues of the USA, 1995–8.

Wright, Rabbi Alexandra Rabbi at Radlett and Bushey Reform Synagogue. Former Co-Chair, Assembly of Rabbis, Reform Synagogues of Great Britain; Co-ordinator of rabbinic student supervisors, Leo Baeck College. Contributor to Women in Religion series: *Hear Our Voice*, ed. Sybil Sheridan, and *Taking up the Timbrel*.